Democracy and Conflict

Democracy and Conflict

Kenneth Arrow's Impossibility Theorem and John Dewey's Pragmatism

Frederic R. Kellogg

LEXINGTON BOOKS
Lanham • Boulder • New York • London

Published by Lexington Books
An imprint of The Rowman & Littlefield Publishing Group, Inc.
4501 Forbes Boulevard, Suite 200, Lanham, Maryland 20706
www.rowman.com

86-90 Paul Street, London EC2A 4NE

British Library Cataloguing in Publication Information Available

Library of Congress Cataloging-in-Publication Data

Names: Kellogg, Frederic Rogers, author.
Title: Democracy and conflict : Kenneth Arrow's impossibility theorem and John Dewey's pragmatism / Frederic R. Kellogg.
Description: Lanham, Maryland : Lexington Books, [2024] | Includes bibliographical references and index.
Identifiers: LCCN 2023046297 (print) | LCCN 2023046298 (ebook) | ISBN 9781793654281 (cloth) | ISBN 9781793654298 (epub)
Subjects: LCSH: Democracy—Philosophy. | Conflict (Psychology) | Pragmatism. | Arrow, Kenneth J. (Kenneth Joseph), 1921-2017—Political and social views. | Dewey, John, 1859-1952—Political and social views. | Social choice.
Classification: LCC JC423 .K366 2024 (print) | LCC JC423 (ebook) | DDC 321.801—dc23/eng/20231113
LC record available at https://lccn.loc.gov/2023046297
LC ebook record available at https://lccn.loc.gov/2023046298

Contents

Foreword viii

Introduction xiii

1 Kenneth Arrow's General Possibility Theorem 1

2 Dewey's Agonistic Pragmatism 13

3 Problematic Conflict and Transformation 29

4 Dewey's Naturalized Utilitarianism 43

5 Agonistic Deliberation 57

6 Uncertainty and Legal Theory 71

7 Legal Principles 83

8 Empirical Naturalism in Law 99

9 Naturalizing Objectivity 117

10 Dewey's Democracy and Conflict 127

Bibliography 139

Index 155

About the Author 165

Foreword

Brian E. Butler, The University of North Carolina, Asheville; Author of *The Democratic Constitution: Experimentalism and Interpretation* (2017)

Urgent and strident claims of voter fraud. Blatant and discriminatory gerrymandering. Attempts to pack the Supreme Court. Attacks on local election officials. All these actions could be just manifestations of power politics and everyday strategic action. But they might exemplify a more general skepticism toward democratic processes.

What if it is not all politics as usual but a moment where influential yet flawed theories about democratic process are at least partially animating these actions? In *Democracy and Conflict: Kenneth Arrow's Impossibility Theorem and John Dewey's Pragmatism,* Frederic R. Kellogg offers a vigorous and convincing defense of democratic practice. He does this by constructing a critique of what he thinks is a highly influential but flawed conception in Kenneth J. Arrow's General Possibility Theorem. He contrasts this with a new and important reading of John Dewey's democratic thought.

It is extraordinary that Kenneth J. Arrow's insistence on the inevitability of authoritarianism in democratic process has not, until now, been compared to the vastly different assumptions and conclusions that follow from John Dewey's organic theory of democracy. In *Democracy and Conflict*, Kellogg explains that the underlying culprit is utilitarianism—specifically, its ingrained immediate and universal viewpoint, which Henry Sidgwick in 1874 called "the point of view of the universe," which Arrow uses but Dewey finds conceptually impoverished.

Arrow's General Possibility Theorem is a formal proof that, if you assume that all utilities (or individual preferences) are discrete and identifiable at one moment (the immediate and universal viewpoint), there is no possibility of a "rational order." Slightly more directly, Arrow's theorem purports to offer a formal proof of the proposition that, given an assumed set of relatively simple conditions as well as some generally accepted standard economic assumptions of rationality, no domain of diverse individual preferences can be ordered except by the imposition of an external fiat or dictatorship.

This proof has been very influential and has cast a long shadow over democratic theory, despite the clear fact that, as Amartya Sen and Bernard Williams concluded in 1982, "utilitarianism can't be lived." From Arrow's argument, it is thought inevitable that agenda-setters in democratic processes will have non-trivial control of outcomes, and democratic processes will not suffice for a full ordering of discrete preferences of any complexity. There will need to be outside decision-makers to intervene, and, in turn, those sources will determine rankings. Therefore, democracy is fundamentally and irretrievably flawed. The power of agenda setting becomes the central issue.

This formalist analysis has been found convincing enough that it has been utilized to undermine the hope for a democracy that is neutral between preferences and to create numerous influential formalist and narrow academic and political agendas. Many of these dominate political thought today. It is difficult to overestimate the influence Arrow's proof has had on contemporary democratic thought.

As Kellogg notes, one influential response has been to advocate for something generally described as "deliberative democracy." This concept seems to move properly in the direction of process and inquiry. Instead of passive preferences being formally aggregated, democracy does seem to require, indeed encourage, deliberation over which preferences should count, resulting in values changing. This helps explain the standard emphasis on free speech and public discussion in democratic process that Arrow's conception of democracy renders inexplicable. But how exactly does deliberation help the democratic process in the face of real-world disputes? And how does deliberation encourage careful inquiry into the problems democratic processes have to solve? In a society characterized by strong polarization over entrenched and passionately held political beliefs, many of which treat opposing beliefs as enemy threats, how does deliberation alone help bring about acceptable solutions?

Kellogg draws on Dewey to offer an alternative view that Dewey called organic democracy. It not only turns Arrow's assumptions on their head but also offers a solution to some of the most pressing contemporary issues in democratic theory and practice. Contrary to Arrow's analytical assumptions and his conception of democracy, Kellogg shows that Dewey's greatest insight was that solving shared problems, from the small to the large, is the central stuff of democracy, and their resolution involves, indeed requires, extended conflict for the constant *transformation* of preferences. Thus, Arrow's theorem and the assumptions it is based upon, still dominant in welfare economics, are utterly flawed. There is no catalog of preferences (which Arrow marks with letters like *a, b, c,* etc.) for the universal eye to visualize.

Preferences are in continuous formation, in continuous reconstruction, as shared social habits are incrementally worked out.

Kellogg argues convincingly that Arrow's ability to postulate fixed preferences is drawn from unexamined assumptions of economic equilibrium theory. He shows, additionally, that Dewey's analysis also shakes utilitarian theory to the core by "naturalizing" it. In so doing, it undermines contemporary intergroup conflict theory too, seen here as narrow and irreducibly partial.

In passages that have been largely ignored until *Democracy and Conflict* foregrounds them, Dewey is shown to offer an agonistic yet constructive form of democratic deliberation. What Kellogg describes as "naturalized utilitarianism" in Dewey addresses how, in normal problematic conflict, older habits and utilities can be democratically hammered into new and stable knowledge. In the multiple anvils of particular problems, from village referenda to social discrimination, democratic inquiry reconstructs preferences through democratic inquiry, broadly understood. Dewey's "naturalized utilitarianism" pictures a constant context of multiple problems in various stages of discovery, definition, and potential resolution.

This is a quite different conception of democracy from the one that occupies a central and yet tenuous place in current dialogue. Ostensible democratic processes are generally followed for the required minimal political legitimacy, while the very processes are under constant threat, both empirical and theoretical. At best, from this one gets a picture of democracy as a necessary evil.

Dewey's conception of democracy, as developed by Kellogg, sees democracy as central to political and social progress. In the *actual* world of specific struggles, Dewey's extended problematic inquiry applies a naturalized utilitarian balancing of opposing values, in particular cases, toward stable ends. Freedom claims and utility claims are placed in perspective along with multiple other local claims. Dewey's logic of conjoint inquiry, or "social intelligence," is a continuing process that transforms as it responds. It builds on Charles Peirce's 1877 description of naturalized philosophy as the fraught human progress from doubt to belief. Peirce emphasized that reasoning starts in a position of doubt and is resolved when the specific doubt is removed. And while Peirce emphasized the social aspect of scientific inquiry, Dewey advances beyond Peirce with the insight that solving specific problems is the essential task of a polity or "public," and that the task of identifying, defining, and resolving them is one of constant dispute, in which deliberation and dialogue is inherently agonistic. Kellogg writes:

> Conversation alone is inadequate for resolution of conflicts in a democracy. Conflict is accompanied by discourse, but preferences are grounded in habits.

> Social habits, and shared patterns of conduct, aggregate in opposition to each other and resist adjustment in response to discourse alone. Yet habits and preferences demonstrably adjust in the process of conflict resolution, potentially resolving Arrow's impossibility problem.

Those "habits" include ways of acting, believing, and articulating truths through language.

Importantly, two habitually separate fields of welfare economics and pragmatist philosophy are brought together here, as well as legal theory. Kellogg's analysis finds empirical support in the works of legal theorists Edward Levi, Karl Llewellyn, Alexander Bickel, and Oliver Wendell Holmes Jr. His alternate view of democracy effectively solves some of the more difficult conceptual issues in contemporary democratic theory and practice. As opposed to Arrow's main assumption that democracy is about the aggregation of sets of discreetly identifiable preferences, all these theorists see society as "diachronic" or changing. This, in turn, allows for a quite different conception of democratic process—one that includes law. Indeed, Kellogg illustrates the contested and often extended problematic situations in democracy with examples of gradual change in the law.

Of paramount interest for law and these other areas is Kellogg's effort to explain an elusive phrase that Dewey used in applying scientific practices to social issues: "empirical naturalism." Kellogg emphasizes, in a way that greatly strengthens and informs *Democracy and Conflict,* that Dewey and Holmes were mutual admirers, both skeptics of *a priori* values and ideological reasoning. Where urgent shared problems have seemed to invite or require value reasoning, they actually require further experience to move toward inclusive resolution. This grounds a strong critique of judicial recourse to "moral principle," which Ronald Dworkin maintained in his refutation of H. L. A. Hart's legal positivism.

As Kellogg argues, Dewey emphasized that early stages of problematic situations are characterized by confusion and uncertainty. Where problems multiply and resistance prevents the adjustment of habits, the lack of progress toward resolution presents opportunities for exploitation. Kellogg takes considerable pain to illustrate the practical effect of Dewey's idea of a "scientific" approach to social problems, which he often referred to as "empirical naturalism":

> Political polarization is most evident when inclusive paths and sources of problem resolution have become least effective. When the most controversial problems are locked in a state that Dewey describes as confusion and uncertainty, the voting and representative process alone is least likely to bring any of them to a successful resolution. Beneath general and salient divisions lie more

> specific and indistinct ones, driven by embedded habits and beliefs that resist easy convergence. Dewey's meliorist response is a salutary experimental remediation driven by extended dispute. The most effective response to polarization lies in dedicated and persistent remediation of the specific underlying conflicts.

Ultimately, Kellogg shows how Dewey's insights extend with revolutionary impact into contemporary economics, democratic theory, conflict theory, pragmatism, utilitarianism, public choice, logic, ethics, and natural science. He builds a broad critique of contemporary thought from an unrecognized flaw in economic theory's understanding of democracy—its unexamined preference stability—and a similarly ignored strength in pragmatism, the transformative continuum of inquiry.

The argument in *Democracy and Conflict* is a significant challenge to classical utilitarianism and its dependence on a synchronic, omniscient viewpoint. Kellogg's original analysis overturns synchronic legal theory and challenges its effect on judicial policy. It turns finally to the synchronic "oscillation" between objectivism and relativism in philosophy and ends with Dewey's challenge to libertarianism. Dewey is revealed as a far broader innovator and radical reformer of the Western canon than has previously been recognized. Kellogg offers a vigorous and convincing defense of democratic practice through a new and important reading of John Dewey's democratic thought, a reading that properly undercuts some of the current skepticism toward democratic process.

Introduction

The economist Kenneth J. Arrow, in *Social Choice and Individual Values* (1951), famously showed how a society of diverse preferences can only be governed by fiat. Given that individual preferences are distinct and given certain reasonable conditions, no nondictatorial ordering is feasible through voting, or indeed any "rational system" of social choice. One grave but plausible conclusion is that electoral democracy cannot govern.

The American philosopher John Dewey died in 1952, too soon to respond to Arrow's extraordinary demonstration. He had produced *The Public and its Problems* in 1927, with the theme that voting and electoral mechanisms do not, as Arrow states as an axiom, define democracy and democratic self-government.[1] In many writings over several decades, Dewey had offered an account of society in which the crucial social response to shared problems was through continuing inquiry, including dispute and conflict.[2] For Dewey, this could, and indeed must, be capable of coordinating aggregated preferences in a transformative process. In this context, Dewey redefined the very concept of "rational."

If democratic social ordering is not possible through voting, what then? Since the 1980s, political scientists have focused on decisions through

[1] Arrow opens "In a capitalist democracy there are essentially two methods by which social choices can be made: voting, typically used to make political decisions, and the market mechanism, typically used to make economic decisions." Kenneth Arrow, *Social Choice and Individual Values* (New Haven: Yale University Press, 1951), 1. Dewey's theme in *The Public and Its Problems* (New York: Henry Holt & Co., 1927) is "There is no sanctity in universal suffrage, frequent elections, majority rule, congressional and cabinet government. . . . They are not the whole of the democratic idea, but they express it in its political phase. . . . Regarded as an idea, democracy is not an alternative to other principles of associated life. It is the idea of community life itself," 144–48.

[2] Dewey's inclusive use of the term "conflict" is compared to other viewpoints in chapter 10.

representative "deliberation." Philip Kitcher, in *Moral Progress*,[3] recently emphasized the importance for moral progress of sympathetic understanding of others through "ideal conversation."[4] Conversation alone is inadequate for the resolution of conflicts in a democracy. Conflict is accompanied by discourse, but preferences are grounded in habits. Social habits and shared patterns of conduct aggregate in opposition to each other and resist adjustment in response to discourse alone. Yet habits and preferences demonstrably adjust in the process of conflict resolution, potentially resolving Arrow's impossibility problem.

A pragmatic theory of preference conflict is distinct from the Marxist model of power-oriented class or group conflict. Pragmatic conflict is not strictly constituted of group power struggles but of aggregating preferences, a more common, indeed endemic, formation and interaction of opposing opinions and beliefs in response to multiple shared problems. Preference conflict theory illuminates the boundary between inquiry and violence in the polarization of aggregated opposing interests. Conflict is subject to manipulation for money and political influence, but it is also open to a fluid Deweyan "transformation," in what he called the *continuum of inquiry*, through which specific problems can be democratically recognized, defined, and resolved by incremental group preference adjustment as discrete problems are identified and remedial practices are adopted through stakeholder input, enforceable by law.

Pragmatism draws from radical naturalism, connecting reasoning and philosophy to natural life, as Charles S. Peirce articulated in his 1877 essay "The Fixation of Belief." All knowledge is driven by the "irritant" of doubt, leading to inquiry and belief.[5] This was extended by Dewey to recognition of an agonistic aspect of inquiry: an empiricism grounded in extended dispute and conflict and a *social* inductivism, a logical inference grounded in conjoint human activity, rather than J. S. Mill's model of inference from immediate comparison of particulars. Dewey's progression from doubt to belief is constantly driven by various sources of individual and social inquiry, including specific conflicts and their need for stable resolution. Conflict drives the acquisition of information and the adjustment of habits and beliefs. Where resolution is adequately representative of all relevant interests, pragmatic conflict serves as a democratic motivator and a precarious but unavoidable avenue toward justified order.

---

3 Philip Kitcher, *Moral Progress*, The Munich Lectures in Ethics, with comments by Amia Srinivasan, Susan Nieman, and Rahel Jaeggi (Oxford: Oxford University Press, 2021).

4 John Rawls, Juergen Habermas, and Richard Rorty have notably also offered versions of a deliberative model for democratic choice.

5 Charles S. Peirce, "The Fixation of Belief," in *Collected Papers of Charles Sanders Peirce*, ed. Charles Hartshorne and Paul Weiss (Cambridge, MA: Belknap Press, 1978), 3:242.

Pragmatic conflict can then be distinguished from the violence-prone Marxist model as a *discovery* process and an *adjustment* process. How this works is developed below in a comparison of the utilitarian roots of Arrow's theorem and its fundamental reliance on the concept of *social states*, grounded in economic theory dating from the earlier work of Lionel Robbins, Abram Bergson, Paul Samuelson, and the extensive contributions of Amartya Sen. Against this is Dewey's advanced alternative focus on *problematic situations,* to which unfortunately little attention has been given by economists.

The concept in social welfare economics of a "social state" privileges a present, immediate assessment of the nature and condition of society through present preferences, whereas the Deweyan "situation" is concerned with an ongoing process of recognizing, defining, and addressing shared problems, large and small: from a village upgrading a street to a nation's attitude toward the status of women or racial minorities. Broad attitudinal conflicts are pervasive, involving social equity as well as the existential problem of climate change. Problems are enmeshed from the outset in conflicts, and battles over causation, definition, and remediation. While the analysis of a social state is static, that of a problem must recognize distinct stages. When these are understood, as Dewey sought to make them, democracy itself can be better understood.

The fundamental elements of a social state (which Arrow demarcated with the letters x, y, z, and so on representing distinct preferences) are conceptually unique, while those of an actual problem are fluid and subject to adjustment, what Dewey insistently called "transformation." Dewey's analysis is of an extended process, or "continuum," a diachronic rather than synchronic conception of social inference, and of possible resolution through democratic inquiry. Dewey shared with Arrow the overall purpose of framing a rational conception for the assessment and improvement of social welfare. The purpose of the following chapters is to better understand the dynamic element of democratic inquiry that Dewey conceives but Arrow ignores.[6]

Kenneth Arrow's object was to determine whether it is formally possible to construct a formula for social decision by an immediate aggregation of known individual preferences. The actual contested patterns of aggregation reflect factors that he failed to recognize. While Dewey's agonistic

---

[6] Arrow's fixed preferences follow the theory of competitive equilibrium, assuming convex preferences, perfect competition, and demand independence. Preferences are assumed stable through equilibrium; but Arrow's general possibility theorem extends beyond consumption preferences to all "individual values." In Dewey's agonistic social inquiry, the assumption of demand independence does not apply, as individual preference aggregations are not independent of cultural and political values. Deweyan inquiry is thus a study not of equilibrium but rather of disequilibrium caused by demand *dependence*. See chapter 1 *infra*; Kenneth J. Arrow and Gerard Debreu, "Existence of an Equilibrium for a Competitive Economy," *Econometrica,* vol. 22, no. 3 (July 1954), 265–290.

pragmatism has many diverse aspects from one conflict to the next, it is the purpose here to explicate its distinctness from the utilitarian tradition underlying Arrow's conception. The notion of unremitting conflict may be unsettling, but it is an inadequately recognized aspect of democratic life.

Dewey introduced a new social and interactive logic, often referred to as "social intelligence," which has yet to be fully recognized and elucidated.[7] Deduction in normative reasoning is dependent on conjoint action. Notably, it applies to the work of our law courts. Social intelligence provides a valuable critique of the tendency of powerful judges to exercise plenary power by unilateral deduction from sweeping political or ideological views rather than deferring to careful, successive, and piecemeal assessments in specific instances or stages of a given controversial issue: the precarious continuum of inquiry into all urgent ongoing problems.

Justification of a rule by democratic institutions is less a matter of mathematical calculation than public perception, agreement, and conjoint conduct. Failed justification in our society might be called a spectrum disorder; it is never total, even as justification itself is never complete. We may be destined forever to be a society of some form of conflict, and improvement is always possible as evaluations and preferences are adjusted by contact with opposing interests.

The argument in chapter 1 addresses Kenneth Arrow's General Possibility Theorem and comments of Amartya Sen to illustrate the synchronic "social state" model of social preferences. Chapter 2 presents and compares John Dewey's account of diachronic preference formation and aggregation in "problematic situations," which will be called "agonistic pragmatism." Chapter 3 illustrates that comparison with an account of the stages of transformation through successive judgments of a shared problem in the continuum of inquiry, in which particular disputes (denoted by a small cap q) define and address an emergent broader conflict (denoted by a large cap Q). Chapter 4 examines how shared normativity emerges from successive judgments, comparing the classical utilitarian account of rule formation with the pragmatist account, which I describe below as Dewey's "naturalized utilitarianism."

In chapter 5 I turn to evidence of an agonistic pragmatism in the legal process; chapter 5 is an illustration of agonistic deliberation drawn from accounts of extended legal problems and the complexity of the struggle for definition and resolution. Chapter 6 elucidates the radical nature of uncertainty at an early stage of a shared problematic experience, given that resolution will require adjustments of prior habit, belief, and language, the nature of which

[7] See James Gouinlock, "Dewey's Theory of Moral Deliberation," *Ethics*, vol. 88, no. 3 (April 1978), 218–228.

cannot be known in advance. Chapter 7 attributes failure to recognize a continuum of legal inquiry to the history of legal theory, including the problem of premature deduction from general propositions rather than specific considerations that have particular relevance before a larger problem has been fully explored by successive judgments. Chapter 8 examines the proper function of legal principles in particular judgments as an exemplification of Dewey's empirical naturalism and provides a case study of its application.

Chapter 9 explores Dewey's logic of social induction and his radical naturalization of objectivism and compares it with the accounts of objectivism and relativism by the pragmatist philosophers Richard Rorty and Hilary Putnam. Chapter 10 addresses the distinctness of Dewey's problematic approach to conflict and democracy from other leading approaches and compares it to the classical liberal tradition associated with Friedrich Hayek.

Chapter 1

Kenneth Arrow's General Possibility Theorem

Kenneth J. Arrow's seminal work, *Social Choice and Individual Values,* begins: "In a capitalist democracy there are essentially two methods by which social choices can be made: voting, typically used to make political decisions, and the market mechanism, typically used to make economic decisions." Arrow goes on to mention two other methods, dictatorship and convention, but these relate to forms of society that he distinguishes from ours, even while demonstrating that electoral mechanisms cannot work.

Arrow deploys a view of *social states* drawn from economics, relating to individual preferences for commodities and economic roles. His "General Possibility Theorem" is actually a general *impossibility* theorem. Widely, if not uniformly, accepted by welfare economists, his theorem extends to the impossibility of ordering any social domain with assumed distinct preferences, however extensive, not just by voting but by any method except dictatorship. Professor Allan Feldman of Brown University said of Arrow's theory that it

> provides an unambiguous answer to the question "is there a foolproof way to derive complete and transitive social preference relations?" The answer is No. This clearly negative result casts doubts on all assertions that there is a general will, a social contract, a social good, a will of the people, a peoples' government, a peoples' voice, a social benefit, and so on and so forth. That is, it casts doubt on all notions that . . . attribute preferences to society that are comparable to preferences for an individual. Therefore it casts doubts on vast areas of 20th century social thought.[1]

---

[1] Allan Feldman, *Welfare Economics and Social Choice Theory* (Boston: Martinus Nijhoff, 1980), 191.

But it does not necessarily cast doubt on John Dewey's pragmatism, which in one vital respect stands in contrast to the utilitarian roots of Arrow's thesis as well as much contemporary social thought. Arrow follows a utilitarian tradition assuming immediate and stable individual preferences and the assumption that every individual has their own distinct set of them.[2] In contrast, Dewey's pragmatic model emphasizes the critical importance of problem-solving in potentially transformative continuing inquiries. The very preferences assumed to be stable by Arrow are subject to case-by-case adjustment in the course of Deweyan inquiry.

Arrow delineates his universe of fixed preferences as lettered variables, like x, y, and z, representing distinct preferences. A simple demonstrable model takes three individuals, 1, 2, and 3, who have the divergent preferences x, y, and z. It is then a straightforward mathematical problem to investigate how they might vote on their preferences, or what rational method might exist for resolving disagreement. A simple mathematical exercise underlies Arrow's General Possibility Theorem for all systems:

> Assume a society composed of three voters, 1, 2 and 3. Assume also that they are presented with three mutually exclusive proposals, x, y and z. The voters must choose under majority rule between proposals x and y. Proposal x will win because both 1 and 2 prefer x to y, and will vote accordingly; 3, who prefers y, will be outvoted. If instead the electorate is presented with a choice between y and z, y will win because that is preferred by 1 and 2. If the voters are given the choice between x and z, z will win because voters 2 and 3 will vote for z.

The conclusion? The majority wants both x and not-x. Note that if this summary (by the author of this chapter, not by Arrow) were to say that 1, 2, and 3 "are deliberating," rather than "are presented with" the three proposals, it would add an element of time and the possibility of dynamic interaction. Yet Arrow himself considers neither such factors nor the possibility of preference transformation over time, because he does not consider the relation of particular preferences to specific shared problems.

There are four "natural conditions" that define Arrow's rationality: decisiveness, Pareto optimality, independence of irrelevant alternatives, and non-dictatorship.[3] They are grounded in an instantaneous view of any group of individuals, however large, and specify that each individual has a set of

---

[2] A leading authority for this view is George J. Stigler and Gary S. Becker, "De Gustibus Non Est Disputandum," *American Economic Review*, vol. 67, no. 2 (March 1977), 76–90.

[3] Sen presents the four conditions as follows:U (unrestricted domain): For any logically possible set of individual preferences, there is a social ordering R. (An ordering is a ranking that is reflexive, transitive and complete.)

"known individual tastes"—that is, a set of distinct and stable preferences. His conclusion is that the fourth condition cannot be met: there is no possible order for such a group other than by authoritarian fiat. Although the conditions have been described as reasonable and normal, they relate to an assessment to be made at one given moment in time; they relate to a definitive choice such as presented to a vote.

The clearest short exposition introducing Arrow's General Possibility Theorem is given by another Nobel Prize winner Amartya Sen:[4]

> Take three persons 1, 2 and 3 with the following preferences over three alternatives x, y, z. [Sen then posts a diagram of 3 columns, in which different preferences of 1, 2 and 3 are listed as x, y and z]
>
> 1 2 3
> x y z
> y z x
> z x y

Sen concludes:

> In majority decisions, x defeats y, which defeats z, which in turn defeats x. The [social ordering] R generated by majority rule violates transitivity and even weaker conditions of consistency than that (such as acyclicity). And since each alternative is defeated by another available alternative in the available set, there is no majority winner—no "choice set"—for the available set [x,y,z].

Arrow asserts:

> These alternatives are *mutually exclusive* [my emphasis]; they are denoted by the small letters x, y, z. . . . On any given occasion, the chooser has available to him a subset S of all possible alternatives and he is required to choose one out of this set. (1951:12)

I (Independence of irrelevant alternatives): The social ranking of any pair {x,y} will depend only on the individual rankings of x and y.

P (Pareto principle): If everyone prefers any x to any y, then x is socially preferred to y.

D (Non-dictatorship): There is no person 1 such that whenever this person prefers any x to any y, then socially x is preferred to y, no matter what others prefer. The General Possible Theorem: If there are at least three distinct social states and a finite number of individuals, then no social welfare function can satisfy U, I, D and P.

Eric Maskin, Amartya Sen, Kenneth J. Arrow, Partha Dasgupta, Prasanta K. Pattanaik, and Joseph E. Stiglitz, *The Arrow Impossibility Theorem* (New York: Columbia University Press, 2014), 35.

4 Eric Maskin, et al., *The Arrow Impossibility Theorem*, 29f.

If two individuals holding x and y are in active disagreement, might they resolve it over time? If so, can preferences x and y be properly considered "mutually exclusive" during that time? Arrow's thesis claims to address all preferences regarding individual values. If his theory of preferences applies to the political values polarizing contemporary western societies, democratic government is indeed in a desperate situation.

But if instead there is *interaction over time*, at what point in the inquiry are opposing preferences considered sufficiently rigid to be "mutually exclusive"? Throughout society, many individual preferences are arguably distinct at any given moment, but many others are tentatively held and are changing by degree through active engagement among preference-holders. Arrow at each instantaneous point would insist on dictatorship as the only choice option. His conception of dictatorship cuts off inquiry at a purely hypothetical point within the problematic continuum.[5]

There are circumstances in which Arrow's model appears applicable. In a small committee meeting where the participants come with firm and unyielding views on a proposition, the voting paradox and Arrow's thesis may prove accurate, in that the proposition fails to garner a clear majority. However, concrete choices that are ultimately put before a committee, or even a referendum, may have previously been subjected to particularized formative inquiry and thus have *already* been subject to Deweyan adjustment and transformation.[6] Yet the next step in Arrow's argument is to apply the same logic to society as a whole: multiple individuals holding multiple unyielding preferences, with no clear outcome from voting. Arrow (1951) makes the error of overextending the assumption of mutually exclusive preferences. His claim that no "rational" system of ordering other than dictatorship is possible in a vast society of diverse preferences assumes that everyone is like the unyielding committee members.[7]

---

[5] I am grateful to Brian Butler of University of North Carolina, Asheville, for articulating this point.

[6] Arrow's model is said to work for situations like a referendum. However, unlike the symbols x, y, and z, referendum alternatives are specifically framed. They are not undefined like letter symbols, as in "$1 million for schools, police, or roads." Referenda are generally particularized, like "$1 million for construction of a new elementary school building on the corner of Ash and Main Streets," versus "$1 million for hiring and training 25 new officers," and $1 million to repave Route 56." Alternative proposals are subject to particularized formative inquiry, including citizen input, and shaped through transformative conflict.

[7] "The aim of the present paper is to show that these difficulties are general. For *any* method of deriving social choice by aggregating individual preference patterns which satisfies certain natural conditions, it is possible to find individual preference patterns which give rise to a social choice pattern which is not a linear ordering. In particular, this is very likely to be the case if, as is frequently assumed, each individual's preferences among social states are derived purely from his personal consumption-leisure-saving situation in each." Kenneth J. Arrow, "A Difficulty in the Concept of Social Welfare," *Journal of Political Economy*, vol. 58, no. 4 (August 1950), 330, emphasis in original, footnote omitted.

If individuals 1, 2, and 3 *actively* disagreed over any comparison of x, y, and z regarding a specific shared problem, there would be a potential conflict that might be resolved. Arrow's proof applies the basic analysis to any group of any size, up to and including an entire country. His calculation reaches the impossibility conclusion for an unlimited domain of individual preferences, and it carries the same assumption into that vast domain, positing the unyielding nature of the entire body of preferences as well as the *instantaneous* comparison of them all. Can a *changing* preference, one that is by definition not fixed and discrete from all others, be represented by a ranking of fixed alternatives x, y, or z? If not, then Arrow's calculus is missing a key element of the social utility calculus: the positions marked as x and y are in transformation, such that an acceptable alternative course may be reached. Unlike the general utility maximization principle driving Arrow's inquiry,[8] actual inquiry involves particular problems seeking solutions.

Arrow's model is not accurate and comprehensive if preferences, economic and otherwise, are subject to continuous *adjustment* in the wake of interaction and internal conflict. If preference change *is* possible through problematic disputes and non-violent, resolution-oriented social conflict, the latter is a saving force in democratic society, breaking free from the tight grip of the impossibility theorem. If there is a dispute between individuals 1 and 2 over the nature of x, or of the difference between x and y, and the two individuals are given time to work it out, perhaps coming to a new version of x (call it "x prime"), or perhaps to a convergent revision of the predicated opposition between x and y, there would be no necessity of a dictator. This is a very different conclusion from that of Professor Feldman, that Arrow's "clearly negative result casts doubts on all assertions that there is a general will, a social contract, a social good, a will of the people, a peoples' government, a peoples' voice."

Arrow's model, which he describes as "formal" and based on "natural" conditions,[9] is a hypothetical model—a "flash camera" image picturing a society of immediate and determinate individual preferences—which is contested by Dewey's model of multiple problematic situations. It is distinct from, and oblivious to, a dynamic social environment, incorporating both settled problems that have created new preference accommodations and

8 Arrow, *Social Choice and Individual Values,* 3: "If we continue the traditional identification of rationality with maximization of some sort (to be discussed at greater length below), then the problem of achieving a social maximization derived from individual desires is precisely the problem which has been central to the field of welfare economics."

9 "It should be emphasized here that the present study is concerned with the *formal* aspects of the foregoing question. That is, we ask if it is formally possible to construct a procedure for passing from a set of known individual tastes to a pattern of social decision-making, the procedure in question being required to satisfy certain *natural* conditions [my emphasis]." Arrow, *Social Choice and Individual Values*, at 2.

unsettled problems where preferences are still at odds. Individual attitudes and preferences cannot accurately be described as a fixed image if they are in different stages of resolution in continuing inquiries. Arrow's theorem and the voting paradox ignore the genealogy of preference, the role of disagreement, and the extended continuum of inquiry. Arrow applies his model to any universe of preference-holding individuals, but it holds only if the entire universe of relevant preference-holders is *static within the (arbitrarily chosen) instant of inquiry and choice*. The model tacitly presumes instantaneous choice in an unchanging framework.

SOCIAL STATES

As Amartya Sen explains,

> In his classic study, Arrow (1951) takes orderings of the individuals over the set of alternative *social states* to be the basic constituent of collective choice. He is concerned with rules of collective choice which make the preference orderings of the society a function of individual preference orderings, so that if the latter set is specified, the former must be fully determined.

There follows a summary of the three characteristics that the ranking relation must satisfy to count as an ordering:

> First it must be "transitive," i. e., if *x* is at least as good as *y*, and *y* is at least as good as *z*, then *x* should be at least as good as *z* . . . Second, the relation must be "reflexive," i. e., every alternative *x* must be thought to be at least as good as itself. Third, the relation must be complete, i. e., for any pair of alternatives *x* and *y*, either *x* is at least as good as *y*, or *y* is at least as good as *x* (or possibly both). A man with a preference relation that is complete knows his mind in choices over every pair.[10]

Sen's last sentence is illuminating: a preference relationship in a social state is a matter of all individuals knowing their immediate mind. Arrow's theorem thus assumes that all preference relations are settled at the moment of analysis.[11]

Sen in 1970 analyzed a variety of possible meliorations of Arrow's impossibility result through relaxed conditions, in particular by modifying the assumptions of the independence of irrelevant alternatives. That condition

---

[10] Amartya K. Sen, *Collective Choice and Social Welfare* (San Francisco: Holden-Day Inc., 1970), 2–3.

[11] Arrow, "A Difficulty in the Concept of Social Welfare," 334–335.

requires a limiting comparison of two alternatives to determine whether any given individual prefers one alternative or the other, regardless of any third possibility. It can be relaxed in ways that allow for taking into account more information about individual well-being. Sen (1970) introduced interpersonal comparison to the choice functions and allowed information about utility levels or intensities to play a role in the comparison. Yet he noted that the impossibility theorem remains nevertheless intact as an analysis of social choice.

> One way of interpreting the various "impossibility" results is to say that there is no "ideal" system of collective choice that works well in every society and for every configuration of individual preferences (as proposed by the use of the condition of "unrestricted domain" employed in virtually all the impossibility theorems). . . . There is nothing outstandingly defeatist in this modest recognition.

Sen's rigorous 1970 exposition of Arrow ends with this assessment of Arrow's demonstration of the limits of collective choice theory, as a "pure" system:

> Finally, it is worth emphasizing that while "pure" systems of collective choice tend to be more appealing for theoretical studies of social decisions, they are not the most useful systems to study. With this in view, this book has been much concerned with "impurities" of one kind or another, e.g., *partial* interpersonal comparability, *partial* cardinality, *intransitive* social indifference, *incomplete* social preference, and so on. The pure procedures, which are more well known, seem to be the limiting cases of these systems with impurities [chapter references omitted].[12]

Sen offers an important but not fundamental critique of Arrow. However, Dewey's work shows that the rationality underlying Arrow's system is not the only, or even the best, approach to social choice in a democracy. It is not a *pure system* under Deweyan pragmatism, but rather an alternative hypothesis.

PREFERENCE FORMATION

What is the nature of preferences in Arrow's conception, and how are they formed? While the concept of a social welfare function originates in the analysis of consumer activity, the preferences of Arrow's theorem extend to broader values: "no sharp line can be drawn between tastes and values."[13]

---

[12] Sen, *Collective Choice and Social Welfare*, 200.

[13] Arrow, "A Difficulty in the Concept of Social Welfare," 336. Arrow later notes that consumption tastes can be modified by "general standards" such as "equity." Arrow, *Social Choice and Individual Values*, at 18, noted by Sen, *Collective Choice and Social Welfare*, at 6.

That would extend Arrow's theory to *political* preferences, which is why Alan Feldman reaches his dismal conclusions. The theorem would cover even preferences that have aggregated on either side of the recent political polarization among American citizens and those of other countries with a similar experience. If generalized preferences against federal spending on social programs, or in favor of decreasing medical insurance and social security, are subject to Arrow's thesis, there would be no room for adjustment.

There is an extensive literature on the manner in which preferences are *revealed* through observed behavior,[14] but the issue of content formation is ill developed in economics, which focuses on the process of stabilization through equilibrium.[15] Arrow's General Possibility Theorem extends beyond consumption preferences to all "individual values." Demand independence, one of the three conditions for preference equilibrium, cannot be assumed in Dewey's agonistic continuum, as aggregated individual preferences, especially in conditions of political polarization, are not independent of cultural and political values.[16]

Amartya Sen takes note of the issue of preference formation in his introduction to *Collective Choice and Social Welfare*. The brevity of his comment, as well as its equivocation, suggests that the formation of individual preferences is not an extensive concern:

> It is possible to argue that a theory of collective choice should be concerned merely with the derivation of social preference from a set of individual preferences, and need not go into the formation of individual preferences themselves. This view has attractions, not the least of which is its convenience in limiting the exercise. However, it is a somewhat narrow position to take, and the genesis

---

[14] See, e.g., Paul Samuelson, "Consumption Theory in Terms of Revealed Preference," *Economica*, vol. 15 (1948), 243–253. Stanley Wong and Philip Mirowski, *The Foundations of Paul Samuelson's Revealed Preference Theory: A Study by the Method of Rational Reconstruction* (London: Routledge, 2006).

[15] Formation in the sense of content should be distinguished from stabilization, which Arrow and Debreu have illuminated through the theory of equilibrium in a competitive economy. Arrow and Debreu, "Existence of an Equilibrium for a Competitive Economy," 265–290. Arrow's preferences are assumed stable according to the theory of competitive equilibrium, assuming convex preferences, perfect competition, and demand *independence*. Deweyan inquiry points toward a study not of stability through equilibrium, but rather of preference adjustment through disequilibrium, due to demand *dependence* on non-individual vectors in group preference conflict. This topic, engaging recent literature on *sequential* equilibria, extends well beyond the scope of the present analysis. See David M. Kreps and Robert Wilson, "Sequential Equilibria," *Econometrica*, vol. 50, no. 4 (July 1982), 863–894.

[16] See Thomas Frank, *What's the Matter With Kansas?* (New York: Macmillan Co., 2005). I am grateful to Hector Luisi for suggesting the connection between Arrow's preference stability and equilibrium theory.

> of individual preferences may indeed be relevant for postulating rules for collective choice.[17]

Sen's comment, that ignoring individual preference formation is a "somewhat narrow position," leads (in his following sentence) not to an examination of the problem but to a comment on their "configuration":

> We shall find that the effectiveness of different rules of collective choice depends much on the precise configuration of individual preference orderings, and these configurations will, in general, reflect the forces that determine individual preferences in a society. Just as social choice may be based on individual preferences, the latter in their turn will depend on the nature of the society. Thus, the appropriateness of alternative rules of collective choice will depend partly on the precise structure of the society.[18]

This is not a redirection of the analysis toward the question of content formation, but a turn toward the relation of preferences to the "precise structure of society." It is a circular argument for readers concerned with the actual phenomenon of emergent and shifting preference aggregation in a polarized environment, where aspects of the structure of society are themselves at issue. Sen leaves the issue of "precise structure of the society" as a matter of existing preferences, and there is little discussion of the "forces" that determine it.

In closing his introduction to the 2017 expanded edition of *Collective Choice and Social Welfare*, Sen writes, "The development of the study of preference relations in the standard literature has been largely motivated by consumption theory and demand analysis, which is not always helpful for problems of collective choice."[19] This would suggest that other preferences are derived in the manner of patterns or habits of consumption. Economic analysis has concerned itself with the relations between demand and supply for particular commodities. These are understandably less vulnerable to political and cultural value orientation and, hence, less likely to be affected by polarization. It would be helpful for Sen to illuminate why such orientation is "not always helpful." Nevertheless, Sen raises an issue: concern for the forces determinative of social values, which pragmatism can and must address.

---

17 Sen, *Collective Choice and Social Welfare,* at 5. David M. Kreps, in his 2021 Kenneth Arrow Lecture, "Not Every Couple Should Have a Prenup: How the Context and History of Exchange Affects Personal Preferences, and Why This Matters Both to Economic Theory and to Practical Human Resource Management," addressed how the history of exchange can change personal preferences in systematic ways.

18 Sen, *Collective Choice and Social Welfare,* at 5.

19 Sen, *Collective Choice and Social Welfare,* Expanded Edition (Cambridge, MA: Harvard University Press, 2017), 51.

RATIONALITY

In defining his approach to rationality in 1950, Arrow wrote:

> If we adopt the traditional identification of rationality with maximization of some sort, then the problem of achieving a social maximum derived from individual desires is precisely the problem which has been central to the field of welfare economics. However, the search for a clear definition of optimum social welfare has been plagued by the difficulties of interpersonal comparisons. The emphasis, as is well known, has shifted to a weaker definition of optimum, namely, the determination of all social states such that no individual can be made better off without making someone worse off.[20]

James Buchanan asked how Arrow could posit his conclusion of an overall *social* preference derived from individual preferences. Buchanan commented that society simply cannot have transitive preferences like an individual:

> The proper approach to social welfare functions appears to begin with the frank admission that such functions are social, not individual, and therefore are of a fundamentally different philosophical dimension from individual values or from individualistically oriented decision-making processes. It seems meaningless to attempt to test such choice processes for social rationality.

He contends that a social state analysis fails to capture the real nature of preferences.

> It is difficult to know exactly what is meant by "rational social choice" in the Arrow analysis. Social rationality appears to imply that the choice-making processes produce results which are indicated to be "rational" by the ordering relation, that is, the social welfare function. But why should this sort of social rationality be expected? Certainly not because it is required for the derivation of the function in the first place. The mere introduction of the idea of social rationality suggests the fundamental philosophical issues involved. Rationality or irrationality as an attribute of the social group implies the imputation to that group of an organic existence apart from that of its individual components. If the social group is so considered, questions may be raised relative to the wisdom or unwisdom of this organic being. But does not the very attempt to examine such rationality in terms of individual values introduce logical inconsistency at the outset? Can the rationality of the social organism be evaluated in accordance with any value ordering other than its own?[21]

---

20 Arrow, "A Difficulty in the Concept of Social Welfare," 329.

21 James M. Buchanan, "Social Choice, Democracy, and Free Markets," *Journal of Political Economy*, vol. 62, no. 2 (April 1954), 116

Buchanan asks whether the rationality of the "social organism" can be evaluated in accordance with any value ordering other than "its own," imputing an organic existence apart from that of its individual components. But Buchanan does not address what this might imply.[22] He raises a question that demands further inquiry into how individual preferences actually contribute to the "nature" and "structure" of society.

Arrow (as Buchanan notes) made a leap to generality that is not supported in his general impossibility claim, where he wrote:

> The aim of the present paper is to show that these difficulties are general. For any method of deriving social choices by aggregating individual preference patterns which satisfies certain natural conditions, it is possible to find individual preference patterns which give rise to a social choice pattern which is not a linear ordering.

This was followed by a revealing concession:

> In particular, this is very likely to be the case if, as is frequently assumed, each individual's preferences among social states are derived purely from his personal consumption-leisure-saving situation in each.[23]

Arrow's entire thesis is based on the assumption that all of the social preferences to be covered by the impossibility theorem are based on a non-conflictual model of "consumption-leisure-saving." Presumably, consumption and demand are less likely to be subject to social dispute and conflict; the choice of competing breakfast cereals does not often follow a model of

[22] "In a very real sense collective choice cannot be considered as being reached by voting until relatively unanimous agreement is achieved. In so far as the attainment of such consensus is impossible, it is preferable that the actual choice processes display possible inconsistency to guaranteed consistency. The molding and solidifying of individual values into fixed ordering relations sufficient to make ordinary majority voting fit the Arrow conditions for consistency would mean the replacement of accepted democratic process by something clearly less desirable . . . The market does not establish the optimum social state in the sense that individuals, if called upon to vote politically (act collectively) for or against the market-determined state in opposition to a series of alternatives, would consistently choose it. This may or may not be an important conclusion, depending on the value-judgment made concerning the appropriateness of majority approval as the criterion of optimum collective choice. But the essential point here is that the market does not call upon individuals to make a decision collectively at all. This being the case, market choice is just as consistent as, and no more consistent than, the individual choice of which it is composed. . . . The consistency of market choice is achieved without the overruling of minority values, as would be the case if ordinary political voting were made consistent. Therefore, in a very real sense, market decisions are comparable to political decisions only when unanimity is present. The question as to what extent this lends support to the utilization of the market as the decision-making process when it is a genuine alternative to voting opens up still broader areas of inquiry which cannot be developed here." Buchanan, "Social Choice, Democracy, and Free Markets," 121–123.

[23] Arrow, "A Difficulty in the Concept of Social Welfare," 330.

shared-preference dispute resolution. Such issues manifestly do not get to the law courts.

We will focus here instead on salient disputes (such as gender discrimination and medical assisted death) that involve shared interests based on patterns of conduct, which the courts have sought to resolve by finding similarities and laying down standards. The next chapter examines Dewey's vision and how it relates to deliberative democracy. Aggregate preference assessment is central to social choice theory, but to determine how such preferences actually aggregate and how social decisions can or should be made is not an easy task. Social choice theory is missing a most important element: analysis of conflict in the nature and disposition of social problems.[24]

[24] I am grateful to economist Ronald S. Warren for many instructive comments and suggestions on a draft of this chapter. Responsibility for misconceptions and omissions is mine.

Chapter 2

Dewey's Agonistic Pragmatism

I turn now to the salient differences between Arrow and Dewey. Dewey's principal book on government was *The Public and Its Problems* (1927), a thesis that democracy is more than electoral machinery and regulatory bureaucracy. It is rooted in community, where it lives or dies: "There is no sanctity in universal suffrage, frequent elections, majority rule, congressional and cabinet government." Democratic forms "are not the whole of the democratic idea, but they express it in its political phase" and "Regarded as an idea, democracy is not an alternative to other principles of associated life. It is the idea of community life itself." His remark that there is "no sanctity" in democratic mechanisms rings especially true today. We must look at specific problems and their empirical solutions.[1]

What precisely are "preferences" when seen in the context of actual *problems*? For Arrow, the social welfare calculus of any given group (or "domain" in Arrow's terminology), from the *family* to the *committee* to the *village* to the *nation*, is simply the immediate sum of what the component individuals would "prefer." But for *what*? Is the family deciding on a vacation, the committee on an expenditure, or the village on a baseball park? *Formation* is the key to understanding what preferences are and how they are defined. Preferences are formed in response to actual choices, that Dewey sees and describes as generically "problematic." By this, he simply means that choices involve more than one option, and there are (at least) two sides to the question of what to do.

Preferences in Dewey's model may represent a variety of distinct categories (like consumer brand, problem remedial, problem definitional, public policy, political, cultural value, religious, etc.). No two individuals will have

[1] Dewey, *The Public and Its Problems*, 144–145, 146, 148; LW 2:326-8.

the same response to an emergent shared problem. If preferences are formed in response to problems, how then do they *aggregate*? When the problem is an individual one, such as whether I should take the day off from work, that's personal. For the committee, the village, or the nation, preferences aggregate, first around proposed definitions of a problem and of possible causes and resolutions. They do not *actually* aggregate, as Arrow implies, in a contextless, abstract sense, to be designated by letter symbols like x, y, and z. Arrow's inference is that they are already complete at a given moment of inquiry.

Arrow's hypothetical model of immediate ordering of preferences as discrete entities has been described by Amartya Sen:

> A society consists of a group of people with a variety of preferences and priorities. To make fitting social decisions on behalf of the group as a whole, the society must take serious note of the people's (possibly diverse) views and interests. Aggregate assessment is central to social choice theory, but to determine how such aggregate social decisions should be made is not an easy task. There can be, as Horace pointed out long ago, "as many preferences as there are people." That is the task that social choice theory has to address.[2]

Preferences in this passage are both diverse and *sui generis*, existing in any group just because humans have their "(possibly diverse) views." For Dewey, the above statement would read

> a society consists of a group of people with a variety of *shared problems; these galvanize and define their shared* preferences and priorities. To make fitting social decisions on behalf of the group as a whole, the society must take serious note of the people's (possibly diverse) views and interests *and find ways for them to converge (or otherwise resolve) for the problems to be addressed.* [my italics]

Sen writes that society must take serious note of preferences, as they determine social choice; but their existence is no less serious for Dewey. Assuming preferences can be distinctly identified, how should they be taken into account in the assessment of "social welfare"? Arrow and Dewey share the same underlying goal of improving social welfare through democratic means, as described by Sen when he writes that the subject of social choice

> includes making difficult judgments on what is happening to a group such as a nation—or even to the world population as a whole. Is it better off or worse than it was earlier? Has social inequality in the group diminished or increased?

[2] Sen, *Collective Choice and Social Welfare,* expanded edition, x.

> Is there more poverty now than before? How extensive is it? Or, to go into institutional judgments, can the social decisions that emerge be seen as really democratic?[3]

The difficulty and complexity of such fundamental issues only underscores the unlikelihood that an immediate or "synchronic" voting perspective alone can illuminate how social welfare is "diminished or increased." For Dewey, welfare is not a matter of sorting immediate preferences or desires. There are many specific problems in American society, above which there is today the broader problem of extreme polarization. For Dewey, as James Gouinlock emphasized, problems arise "in conditions of associated life."[4] Those conditions include values and disagreement regarding them; Dewey asks how rigid individual values are and what the extended effects of disagreement are.

Comparison with Arrow elucidates recent debates over the precise nature of Dewey's democratic vision. Two issues in particular have led to confusion: whether Dewey was adequately "pluralist" in recognizing the contested nature of diverse visions in society, and whether he is properly described as a "deliberative democrat," as that concept has emerged since the 1980s. Insofar as Dewey was pluralist in recognizing value diversity, he was not committed to "deep pluralism," accepting opposition among values as inherently fixed and defined, like Arrow's preferences. Values become active and visible in the context of problematic disputes and are open to adjustment in a *transformative* continuum of inquiry. Insofar as Dewey privileged deliberation (his favored term was "communication"[5]), it includes the context of resolving problems through the process of extended communicative dispute. As I will explore in chapter 5, Dewey recognized an *agonistic* form of deliberation.[6]

---

[3] Sen, *Collective Choice and Social Welfare,* expanded edition, x–xi.

[4] "All persons strive in various ways to improve the quality of their existence. They are funded with an array of desires and aversions, and effective in their conduct is a diversity of moral commitments. Human beings function in complex, demanding, and perplexing circumstances, so the tasks of discerning and achieving intrinsically welcome forms of experience are typically difficult. These problems arise, Dewey held, in conditions of associated life, and it is in the same conditions where instruments for the effective prosecution of these tasks might be contrived." Gouinlock, "Dewey's Theory of Moral Deliberation," 219.

[5] Ralph Sleeper, *The Necessity of Pragmatism: John Dewey's Conception of Philosophy* (New Haven: Yale University Press, 1986).

[6] John Shook writes in "Pragmatism, Pluralism, and Public Democracy" that "Dewey applied diffuse multiculturalism to transcend cultural essentialism's paradoxes of power by taking the sociological stance that people most effectively organize over common current problems, not the past" and "For Dewey, public conflict resolution is typically improved as more citizens are involved in its deliberations." Shook, "Pragmatism, Pluralism, and Public Democracy," *Revue Francais D'Etudes,* vol. 124, no. 2 (2010), 20.

Dewey scholars have debated over the presence of a "deep pluralism" in his writing, in which values in society are "incommensurable."[7] Isaiah Berlin advanced the notion of the "incommensurability" of values as a generic aspect of contemporary human experience. Berlin's deep pluralism implied a skepticism drawn from a tradition doubtful of moral progress from the long experience of violent European conflict. As with Berlin, there is a tendency of pluralist theory to take specific experience as characteristic of a universal condition. For Dewey, this was the fallacy of selective emphasis; the appearance of incommensurability is drawn from initial resistance to practical commensuration in the early stages of multiple emergent problems, and it is aggravated by the phenomenon of political polarization.[8]

Values become active and visible in the context of problematic disputes and are open to adjustment in the transformative continuum. Insofar as Dewey privileges deliberation, it is in the context of resolving problems through the inevitable process of extended conflict, which requires the production of new information, leading to a new understanding and eventually to revised patterns of action and belief. For Dewey, the welfare of society depends upon the successful resolution of problems inclusively addressed and defined, not (as for Arrow) in response to a hypothetical overall aggregation of individual preferences.

Individual as well as social life is a flow of continuous challenges. The actual experience of preference satisfaction is derived from comparisons with alternative outcomes. Such comparisons do not take place in the abstract calculation of a hypothetical social state; they take place in the ongoing context of daily life and its constant flow of challenges and disappointments. Challenges are shared with other individuals and can be resolved through

---

7 See, e.g., Michael Eldridge, "Why a Pragmatist May Be a Pluralist," *Transactions of the Charles S. Peirce Society,* vol. XLI, no. 1 (2005), 119–122; Cheryl Misak, "Pragmatism and Pluralism," *Transactions of the Charles S. Peirce Society*, vol. 41, no. 1 (Winter 2005), 129–135; Scott Aikin and Robert Talisse, "Why Pragmatists Cannot Be Pluralists," *Transactions of the Charles S. Peirce Society*, vol. XVI, no. 1 (Winter 2005); Robert Talisse, *A Pragmatist Philosophy of Democracy* (New York: Routledge, 2007); Melvin Rogers, "Dewey, Pluralism, and Democracy: A Response to Robert Talisse," *Transactions of the Charles S. Peirce Society,* vol. 41, no. 1 (2009); Scott F. Aikin and Robert B. Talisse, "Pragmatism and Pluralism Revisited," *Political Studies Review*, vol. 14, no. 1 (February 12, 2016); Scott Aikin and Robert Talisse, *Pragmatism, Pluralism, and the Nature of Philosophy* (New York: Routledge, 2018).

8 Deep political pluralism drew from the prolific writing of Isaiah Berlin, who was forty-one at the time of Dewey's death in 1952. Berlin drew on the nineteenth century writing of Alexander Herzen, whose outlook was skeptical of grand post-Enlightenment theories comprehending perennial human problems; Berlin attacked the tradition of "monism," the doctrine that reality and knowledge form a rational, harmonious whole, that there is ultimate unity or harmony between human ends. Berlin's rejection of monism supported an insistence on the "diversity and incommensurability of genuine human goods" and its inherent connection to human freedom. I. Berlin, *Against the Current: Essays in The History of Ideas*, ed. Roger Hausheer (New York: Penguin Books, 1979 [1955]), xvi, 188f.

communal effort. Perhaps the most obvious example is the potential danger to the general welfare of climate change.

There is conflict in the ethical or moral aspect of choice:

> [U]ncertainty and conflict are inherent in morals; it is characteristic of any situation properly called moral that one is ignorant of the end and of good consequences, of the right and just approach, of the direction of virtuous conduct, and that one must search for them.[9]

Dewey's vision of the distribution of social preferences responds to an *uneven* universe of *ongoing* problems, some more defined and addressed than others. It is a *dynamic* and "plural" but fluid environment, unlike Arrow's static arrangement of letters and numbers subject to instant calculation. Society and social welfare do not present one univocal abstract problem and cannot be represented as such; all general problems are unfinished and grounded in specific ones. A Deweyan "social welfare function" is therefore resistant to graphic symbolization. As a visible scenario, it might be comparable to diverse and constantly changing weather patterns, with some areas of relative calm and others of turbulence.

Dewey's conception envisions constant incremental group preference adjustment, as discrete problems are identified and remedial practices are generated. Specific problems can be more or less democratically recognized, defined, and resolved. How inclusive and factually comprehensive resolution occurs will affect democratic ideals and institutions. The weather analogy is not exact but will serve a limited purpose in comparison to the static Arrovian vision. It is important to scc that, whilc morc complcx and in constant flux, it implies a better approximation of assessing the ongoing welfare interests of society. The crisis of today is better understood through the lens of Dewey's vision. His outlook permits assessment of the granular nature of problems and their formation, definition, and ultimate resolution through transformative action and transformed practices.

As described in 1932, Dewey's view of society includes constant active struggle:

> [T]here is no single thing denominated "society"; there are many societies, many forms of association. These different groups and classes struggle in many ways against one another and have very diverse values. Men associate in friendship and in antagonism; for recreation and for crime; they unite in clubs and fraternities, in cliques and sects, in churches and armies; to promote science and

9 Dewey, "Three Independent Factors in Morals," in *The Essential Dewey* (Bloomington: Indiana University Press, 1998), 316; LW 7:324.

> art and to prey upon others; they unite in business partnerships and corporations. Then these social units compete vigorously against one another.[10]

Within this ubiquitous competition are problems arising from opposing habits and beliefs, the prevalent "arrangements in social life":

> What do exist are conflicts between some individuals and some arrangements in social life; between groups and classes of individuals; between nations and races; between old traditions embedded in institutions and new ways of thinking and acting which spring from those few individuals who depart from and who attack what is socially accepted. There is also a genuine difference of convictions as to the way in which, at any given time, these conflicts should be met and managed.[11]

The existence of "different convictions as to the way in which conflicts should be met and managed" can be seen in today's polarization and suggests the prevalence of distinct and often opposing models of moral progress itself. Current attitudes toward sexual assault, affirmative action, climate change and remediation, policing, gun regulation, and teaching controversial subjects, all contribute to a palpable, although not easily definable, ideological line between liberal and conservative politics. The framing of that line by opposing agencies is a project designed to gain and consolidate political power. Power is thus a constant goal of preference definition and aggregation. It is not a situated force requiring brute overcoming, as envisioned by Karl Marx. While Dewey is reluctant to ontologize power, his view is perhaps closer to Michel Foucault's model of power as dispersed and pervasive rather than wielded by people or groups by way of "episodic" or "sovereign" acts of domination or coercion.[12]

As John Ryder has observed, Dewey based democracy on community and common interests. For Ryder, "we have not resolved the problem of the existence of conflicting interests, and a workable theory based on common interests would have to do so."[13] But Dewey does provide considerable insight into the overall problem of conflicting interests.[14] Unlike Arrow, he

---

[10] Dewey and James H. Tufts, *Ethics* (New York: Henry Holt & Co., 1932), 359; LW 7:324.

[11] Dewey and Tufts, *Ethics*, 358–359.

[12] "'Power is everywhere' and 'comes from everywhere' so in this sense is neither an agency nor a structure." Michel Foucault, *The History of Sexuality: The Will to Knowledge* (London: Penguin, 1998), 63. In *Ethics* Dewey and Tufts describe class dominance as a conflict of values. *Ethics*, 360–361. See also Colin Koopman, "The History and Critique of Modernity: Dewey with Foucault against Weber," *Philosophy and Social Criticism*, vol. 36, no. 5 (August 30, 2007). https://ssrn.com/abstract=1011514 or http://dx.doi.org/10.2139/ssrn.1011514.

[13] *Pragmatism Today*, vol. 12, no. 2 (Winter 2021), 11.

[14] See Christophe Point, "What's the Use of Conflict in Dewey? Toward a Pedagogy of Compromise," *Education and Culture*, vol. 34, no. 2 (2018).

saw attitudes as malleable and responsive. Dewey's 1938 *Logic: The Theory of Inquiry* emphasizes that all problems (social or scientific) are addressed in stages. A perceived problem is at first ill-defined: "Indeterminate situations are marked by confusion, obscurity and conflict. They require clarification. An unsettled situation needs clarification because as it stands it gives no lead or cue to the way in which it may be resolved."[15]

Dewey emphasizes the intimate connection between public distress and unresolved social conflicts. A crisis of confidence may accompany the unclarity of an "indeterminate situation." Contemporary life in America is a collection of specific indeterminate problems contributing to a massive unsettled situation, underlain by multiple unresolved social, economic, and educational issues, all of which are seen by Dewey as subject to transformative inquiry.

Such matters are not easily accessible to deliberation-as-conversation. Philip Kitcher, in *Moral Progress*, draws on Dewey to develop what he conceives as a "pragmatic naturalist" approach to moral and ethical philosophy, following his *The Ethical Project*.[16] He cites three historical examples of moral progress: the abolition of slavery, expanded opportunity for women, and acceptance of same-gender relationships, to develop a method of moral inquiry.

How might that method illuminate the striving, and fierce conflict, of the suffragist movement, the Stonewall riot, the American Civil War? Kitcher's commentators in *Moral Progress* raise this question, one writing

> The history of much moral progress . . . has not been fundamentally a history of conversation at all, but a history of power: the wielding of power by the dominant against the oppressed, and the eventual seizing of that power, or some small part of that power, by the dominated.

But this model of conflict, deriving from Karl Marx, does not neatly fit the multiple domestic conflicts of the past, or especially of the present.

Moral Progress follows Kitcher's sweeping genealogical history in *The Ethical Project,* which focused on the three historic examples. This chapter addresses the methodological issue—what lessons are implied by this history—and the recent problem of national and global polarization that Kitcher has yet to address. In the United States, that now includes the reversal in June 2022 of *Roe v. Wade*, a gathering of conservative antipathy toward same-gender relations, a failure adequately to respond to gun violence even against young children, negative attitudes toward underlying differences of

[15] Dewey, *Logic: The Theory of Inquiry* (New York: Henry Holt & Co., 1938), 185; LW 12:186.
[16] Kitcher, *The Ethical Project* (Cambridge: Harvard University Press, 2011).

race and national origin, and a turn toward authoritarianism in one of the two major political parties. Authority is Arrow's default position when elections fail; his thesis provides compelling reason for an account of progress that explains how a society of multiple diverse preferences can adjust to resolve urgent controversies.

Moral progress becomes harder to define in a struggle among radically opposing—and shifting—views. Kitcher (with Dewey) rightly rejects the "Discovery View" that it consists in the finding of mind-independent moral truths.[17] In his alternative account, individuals and societies make moral progress as they amend their practices to identify problematic situations. Ultimately, they overcome moral problems through conversation. In emphasizing the need for sympathetic understanding of others through "ideal" conversation, Kitcher echoes ideas developed by Rawls and Habermas, while insisting that his methodology, unlike ideal theory, is intended for use by real people in the real world.

It is unfortunate that this discussion has come to rely on just two opposing versions of "real-world" naturalism. One is the model of discourse and rational deliberation; the other is the model of raw power conflicts among opposing groups. The latter model, deriving from Marx (since modified by Mouffe, Laclau, and others), is unclear on how resolutions are effectively "seized" by the powerless. Neither model holds realistic prospects for resolving the multiple disputes and problems driving global polarization. Neither ideal conversation nor the eventual reallocation of power (nor Mouffe & Laclau's hegemony-centered "agonistic democracy"[18]) provide an explanatory avenue for the actual adjustment of resistant individual preferences.

Dewey's conflict theory recognizes the potential for a *transformation* of presumed firm preferences in the resolution of often extended conflicts. Conflict is accompanied by discourse, which Marxists tend to ignore, but preferences are grounded in habits, which discourse theory underestimates. Social habits, or shared patterns of conduct, resist adjustment in response to discourse alone. Yet habits and preferences *do* demonstrably adjust in the process of conflict resolution. The very definition of a problem is adaptable, and the terms of debate can and will change over time.

> Kitcher attributes enormous, indeed plenary, agency to ideal conversation. He sees progressive changes of the past as unnecessarily slow and unsteady—moral progress could have been faster and more thorough, had a methodology been

[17] Kitcher, *Moral Progress*, 20.

[18] Chantal Mouffe and Ernest Laclau, *Hegemony and Socialist Strategy: Towards a Radical Democratic Politics,* revised edition (London and New York: Verso, 2001); see ch. 10.

applied called "democratic contractualism," outlined in eleven steps.[19] When a situation is defined as morally problematic, moral inquiry proceeds in a manner designed to include all stakeholders to proceed toward inclusive resolution. Kitcher's methodology includes measures to seek a joint "justified acceptance of a situation as problematic." It includes periodic reviews of the status quo independent of actual complaints of or perceptions of a problem. Philosophers play a role in assuring that such questioning of the status quo is undertaken on a regular basis.

The aim of naturalism is toward the actual, not the ideal. The suffragists were not invited to "converse," but Kitcher counts that as a correctable error. Insofar as their path was an exchange of views, it was pushing relentlessly against opposing habits and beliefs. Some men argued women were too delicate for such a change: "It is unwise to risk the good we already have for the

---

[19] The 11 steps are:

1. A situation is prima facie morally problematic if there is some individual or group of individuals who resent the fact that the accepted moral framework permits it.
2. If a situation is prima facie problematic, and if its problematic status is urgent, it should initiate moral inquiry.
3. Properly pursued moral inquiry initiated by a prima facie problematic situation consists in an ideal conversation appropriate to that situation.
4. If a challenge is brought to members of a particular group, then it counts as urgent just in case a fully inclusive, optimally informed deliberation among representatives of the different perspectives within the group, committed to presumptive sympathy with the challengers, would endorse that challenge as one of the urgent candidates for moral inquiry.
5. A group's moral inquiries into challenges are justified just in case (i) each of the challenges investigated belongs to the set of urgent candidates, and (ii) there is no challenge selected for investigation such that some challenge not selected is unanimously ranked as more urgent by the deliberation through which the urgency of challenges is measured.
6. A situation is justifiably taken to be problematic just in case a properly pursued moral inquiry initiated by that situation would generate the conclusion that it is indeed problematic.
7. An ideal conversation appropriate to a prima facie problematic situation is a discussion in which the perspectives of all the stakeholders with respect to that situation are represented, in which proposals for responding to the situation are only considered if they, and the judgments put forward in their support, are consistent with the best information available in that situation, and in which the participants are mutually engaged.
8. A proposal is a justified resolution of a problematic situation just in case the transition from the problematic situation to that proposed would be endorsed in an ideal conversation in which the perspectives of stakeholders with respect to both situations were represented.
9. A change in moral practice is progressive just in case it would be retained in an indefinitely proceeding sequence of justified resolutions.
10. Even in the absence of challenges, societies should periodically assess whether restrictions on the appropriateness of ideals of the self for some subgroups can be justified. As in other cases of moral inquiry, urgency is measured through attempts to estimate the suffering and confinement caused if the orthodox assumptions about appropriateness of ideals turned out to be unwarranted.
11. Any moral inquiry in which claims about the proper restrictions on ideals of the self are employed to support the view that the perspectives of the challengers should not be targets of sympathetic engagement should generate a secondary inquiry into the aptness of those ideals for people who are currently viewed as unsuited to adopting them. Kitcher, *Moral Progress*, 34f.

evil which may occur." When Virginia Louise Minor's registration to vote in St. Louis in 1872 was rejected, she appealed to the Supreme Court. Nine male justices declined to interpret the 14th Amendment's "all persons" to include women. An ensuing harsh exchange of views was carved from experience: Jane Addams, in a speech before the Chicago Political Equality League in 1897, declared "I am not one of those who believe—broadly speaking—that women are better than men. We have not wrecked railroads, nor corrupted legislatures, nor done many unholy things that men have done; but then we must remember that we have not had the chance."

As the 1918 flu spread among soldiers toward the end of First World War, women surged into the U.S. workforce, undercutting arguments that they were too fragile or mentally unfit. Unequal pay and working conditions galvanized their cause, ultimately succeeding not as a seizure of power but as a convergence of national preferences. On August 18, 1920, the 19th Amendment, passed by Congress the previous June, was ratified by Tennessee, the final necessary state. National preferences had changed. Yet today, with *Roe* overturned, and as the MeToo movement and counter-reaction demonstrates, the struggle for women's full equality is ongoing. Rather than a conflict between discrete groups for a share of power, the ongoing struggle is better explained as a further opposition and continuing conflict of preferences, habits, and beliefs.

Contemporary conflicts reflect opposing preferences that arise from a clash of views of the future. That there is robust opposition over the very idea of progress is newly evident; we are again in a period of ubiquitous conflict, and a period also of potential transformation. Conflict among opposing preferences is evident in problems large and small, and conflict can lead to adjustment of those preferences. Response to conflicts can promote social transformation and operate as an ordering process outside of the formal public sphere.

Conflict can be a negative obstacle, but a potentially positive force where conversation fails to change preferences and habits. Take two quite different contemporary examples: the general polarization of domestic politics along party lines, and by way of contrast, the issue-specific dispute over medical assistance to a willing patient's death, or voluntary euthanasia. For many years, the euthanasia issue was acutely problematic and ill-defined, until Dr. Jack Kevorkian devised a program to challenge the status quo, using a device that only a patient could activate. Thereafter occurred a period of engagement and reassessment of the complex array of medical, legal, family, and other issues surrounding medically assisted death.[20]

In transformative inquiry, an initial binary standoff is replaced by the comparison of multiple considerations. At Dr. Kevorkian's trial, the principal

[20] See, e.g., Robert F. Weir, ed., *Physician Assisted Suicide* (Bloomington: Indiana University Press, 1997); Robert Young, *Medically Assisted Death* (Cambridge: Cambridge University Press, 2007).

opposing choices were whether a particular death was suicide or homicide—personal autonomy vs. the right to life. Opposing sides were galvanized by abstract ideological reasoning. Although the general issue is hardly settled for all opinions, compared to the struggle over medical assistance for abortion it has reached a stage of comparative stability. The public debate over assisted death continues, but has adapted to new criteria. This phenomenon of adjustment, what might be called "transformation of the reasons environment," requires more than ideal conversation. A critical question is how the process implicates democratic values.

Both of these examples are shared conflicts that have spanned years and have already effected transformations in American society; and both continue to do so. While political polarization does not appear anywhere near resolution, assisted death has visibly gone from a more problematic stage to one of increasing resolution, having been spurred by the conviction of Jack Kevorkian for homicide in 1999. It took Kevorkian's prison sentence to open up the topic to considerations beyond homicide versus suicide.

The very definition of a problem is adaptable, and the terms of debate can change over time. Some basic conditions of this process of adjustment are examined in the chapters that follow. Philosophy in the twenty-first century has its own transformational disputes. Dewey's pragmatic naturalism, widely ignored until Richard Rorty's *Philosophy and the Mirror of Nature* in 1979, has mounted a comeback, both with and against analytical models and ideal ethical theories. Kitcher's effort is a welcome contribution for American pragmatists, a growing community that kept Dewey's naturalism alive during years when the American Philosophical Association was dominated by analytic philosophers. Since Rorty, Dewey scholarship has given less emphasis to Dewey's concern for transformations that must occur in conflict resolution and in logic itself. Both Dewey and Kitcher follow Charles Peirce's pragmatic naturalism, the progress from doubt to belief, driven by conflict over shared problems. If "naturalism" refers to the actual world, pragmatism needs a revised theory of conflict and its resolution.

The controversial criminal prosecution of Jack Kevorkian in 1999 was part of the process through which information was introduced into the unsettled situation plaguing the desperation of suffering patients and their families. Thereafter, the situation gained clarity through continuing related events, each of which embodied what Dewey refers to in his logic as a "further inquiry": "There is continuity in inquiry. The conclusions reached in one inquiry become means, material and procedural, of carrying on further inquiries. In the latter, the results of earlier inquiries are taken and used without being re-subjected to examination."[21]

[21] Dewey, *Logic*, 140; LW 12:143.

In the inquiry into social problems, resolution requires what Dewey often characterized as transformation in reasoning, as in the following passage describing the progress, obviously difficult and complex, from the uncertainty of outright conflict to "modified" understanding:

> Since transformation of a problematic situation (a confused situation whose constituents conflict with one another) is effected by interaction of specially discriminated existential conditions, facts have to be determined in their dual function as obstacles and as resources; that is, with reference to operations of negation (elimination) and affirmation, the latter being determination of materials as positively agreeing with or reinforcing one another. No existing situation can be modified without counteracting obstructive and deflecting forces that render a given situation confused and conflicting.[22]

Dewey's reference to "negation," "affirmation," and the "determination of materials" signifies a transformation of the reasoning process, as opposing sides are engaged in a process that incorporates experience broader and deeper than an exchange of opinions in discourse. Adjustment within problematic situations is a critical factor in moving a dispute, such as medical euthanasia, to greater stability, even when not reaching a final resolution. It is an element of social interaction that transcends even the most ideal conversation. As Scott Aikin and Robert Talisse have characterized Dewey's approach (although disputing him), "The democratic process is one in which individual preferences, attitudes, and opinions are informed and transformed rather than simply aggregated."[23]

As with the criminal trial of Dr. Kevorkian, often at first there is an unyielding binary choice. As conflict drives further inquiry, there emerges a new model. The individuals in village V, holding opposing preferences regarding a dispute whether to supplant fossil fuels with wind or solar technology, might hold opposing preferences regarding an initial plan, based on multiple factors such as cost differential (*c*), land use (*l*), and aesthetic impact (*a*). After time T, a plan is found in which opposing preferences are reconciled by adjustments affecting *c, l,* and *a*, and a revised project (whether wind or solar) is agreed on. Information in a problematic continuum increases with input from alternative viewpoints. Resolution is not assured, but disagreement motivates further inquiry and adjustment of expectations.[24]

---

[22] Dewey, *Logic*, 499–500; LW 12:493.

[23] Dewey, *Logic*, 97; LW 12:99.

[24] A recent example of progress from polarized town opinion to experimental resolution over a dam removal in Camden Maine is reported in *The Free Press*, www.freepressonline.com, vol. 38, no. 3 (September 20, 2022), 1.

Dewey's precarious continuum of inquiry is not, strictly speaking, comparable to "deliberative democracy" in the sense advanced by contemporary writers.[25] While the continuum of inquiry involves discourse, it does not match Philip Kitcher's account of ideal conversation. The current literature on deliberative democracy arose from criticism of traditional democratic theory for excessive dependence on electoral machinery. Broadly defined, the concept of "deliberation" has served as a supplemental source of legitimacy for law. But an idealized model of deliberation does not overcome Arrow's impossibility problem. Kitcher's careful analysis of ideal deliberation can serve as a representative example of how current deliberative democracy is conceived by pragmatists.

Kitcher's deliberation by "ideal conversation" is initiated by perceived resistance or "resentment" of the *status quo* by "some individual or group of individuals." It then requires:

> discussion in which the perspectives of all the stakeholders with respect to that situation are represented, in which proposals for responding to the situation are only considered if they, and the judgments put forward in their support, are consistent with the best information available in that situation, and in which the participants are mutually engaged.[26]

The problem is that "the best information available" is not readily accessible until later stages of the experience and definition of a shared problem, and must be uncovered and sifted through toilsome experience. The role of an agonistic continuum of inquiry in obtaining relevant information, and expressing relevant attitudes and preferences, is an imperfect but essential aspect of a truly naturalistic pragmatic inquiry.

Certainly there is "deliberation" in extended conflict, but it is accompanied by continual discovery and redefinition. Dewey's reference above, to diverse groups that "compete vigorously against one another," suggests that agonistic interaction is analogous to ongoing competition, not for situated power or rhetorical victory, but for overall practical advantage. Friedrich Hayek, in his 1968 essay "Competition as a Discovery Procedure," called competition "a procedure for discovering facts which, if the procedure did not exist, would remain unknown or at least would not be used," whose "outcomes are

---

[25] Accounts of deliberative democracy differ on precisely who deliberates and how. There are both "elitist" and "populist" deliberative models. See, e.g., Ethan Leib, *Deliberative Democracy in America* (University Park: Penn State Press, 2009); James Fishkin, *When the People Speak* (Oxford: Oxford University Press, 2011); Dennis F. Thompson, "Deliberative Democratic Theory and Empirical Political Science," *Annual Review of Political Science,* vol. 11 (2008), 497–520. See also Shane Ralston, "Dewey's Model of Moral Deliberation Unfiltered," *Education and Culture, vol.* 26 (2010), 23–43.

[26] Kitcher, *Moral Progress,* 37.

unpredictable and on the whole different from those that anyone would have been able to consciously strive for; and that its salutary effects must manifest themselves by frustrating certain intentions and disappointing certain expectations."[27]

As Hayek wrote, "we do not know in advance the facts we wish to discover with the help of competition." Exploration follows motivation, which is galvanized by problematic urgency. Hayek also noted the effect of competition on behavior change: "competition represents a kind of impersonal coercion that will cause many individuals to change their behavior in a way that could not be brought about by any kind of instructions or commands."[28] The phrase "impersonal coercion" suggests reluctant but voluntary adjustment. Behavior change is thereby possible in a manner not directed by fiat, but by information crucial to the diverse purposes of multiple actors.

Economic competition is, in essence, an orderly form of natural social conflict.[29] Meanwhile, orchestrating outcomes through conversation in the real world is fraught with difficulty. Opponents in shared conflicts bring self-interest to the table. Opinions are supported by confirmation bias, group-think, false information, gaming, hidden assumptions, and overriding political motives. In September 2022, President Emmanuel Macron of France announced the creation of a National Council for Reconstruction, with members from all parts of political and civil society, to hold regular meetings across the country to find answers to the most pressing national problems. All opposition parties boycotted the first meeting for purely political reasons, as did many of the most powerful unions and the head of the country's Senate.

It is challenging to gather representative participants to discuss any particular problem, even more so to address all of a nation's "most pressing" ones. The global polarization of preferences into a sweeping ideological dualism has presented an even greater obstacle to the natural disputations that surround particular shared problems. Polarization has tended to block particular inquiries into specific issues. But this should not obscure the importance of Dewey's extended specific continua of inquiry and their potential for surmounting obstacles to orchestrated conversations, such as those proposed by Macron or envisioned by Kitcher. An extended agonistic continuum of inquiry can provide time and opportunity for correcting bias and false information. It is a potentially open forum for interested participants, driven by

27 Hayek, "Competition as a Discovery Procedure," *Quarterly Journal of Austrian Economics,* vol. 5, no. 3 (Fall 2002), 9–10; also in *New Studies in Philosophy Politics Economics and the History of Ideas* (Chicago: Chicago University Press, 1978), 179–190.

28 Hayek, "Competition as a Discovery Procedure," 10, 19.

29 Justice Oliver Wendell Holmes's dissent in *Abrams v. United States* compared the opposition of ideas to a "marketplace." See Vincent Blasi, "Holmes and the Marketplace of Ideas," *The Supreme Court Review,* vol. 2004 (2004), 1–46.

extended feedback from experience. Many obstacles must be overcome, and an agonistic pragmatism turns a focus of inquiry toward them.

Extended conflicts can create experiential feedback to refute false information, rhetorical and political gaming, and (not least) unanticipated and unintended consequences. The feedback loop, which refers to the opportunity for uncensored comment and active response in a free society, permits and supports radical experimental solutions. False information should be expected, but it is not fatal to the continuum. Sources of information are subject when exposed to the assignment of degrees of credibility and trust, like the five stars of products assigned by shoppers at Walmart. Fake news is a threat to democratic ordering, but it is not the end of democracy. Dispute and conflict are an imperfect source of information and reform. They call for an open and fair inquiry into the nature of agonistic inquiry and the resolution of shared problems. Such is the only alternative to fiat for the adjustment of individual preferences. As Kenneth Arrow demonstrated, dictatorship is a mathematical certainty in the absence of preference adjustment and change.

In embracing the ubiquity of conflict, Dewey's problem-based model occupies a logical space outside both contemporary deliberative democracy and recent theories of agonism advanced by Chantal Mouffe and Ernesto Laclau, that reject the possibility of reaching consensus purely through deliberation.[30] Dewey emphasizes the precarious nature of a democracy rife with conflicts at every level. The representation of diverse voices from those affected by outcomes, and inclusion of comprehensive relevant information, are never assured. Rather than a zero-sum model of power held, defended, or seized, political power is sought by shifting alliances and various means other than strict electoral mechanisms, including ideological and conspiratorial framing, soliciting diverse positions into a narrative designed for repetition in public media.

Dewey observed that attempts to theorize conflict as a uniform property are dubious: "No general theory about the individual and the social can settle conflicts or even point out the way in which they should be resolved."[31] His attitude is unsparingly naturalist, and forces attention to specific problems rather than abstract concepts. Conflicts drive the acquisition of information and the need for adjustment of habits and beliefs. Where resolution is adequately representative of all relevant interests, Dewey's pragmatism views conflict as

---

30 The agonistic democracy model of Mouffe and Laclau questions the empirical attainability of consensus in post-Cold War democracies. While space limits discussion here, their (2001) preface to the earlier text (1985) summarizes conflict as inevitably universalized into "hegemonies" and relying on creation of a "new hegemony," one that expands "discourse" to allow "a possible alternative to the present economic order" and "the possibility of different modes of regulation." Mouffe and Laclau, *Hegemony and Socialist Strategy*, xvi.

31 Dewey and Tufts, *Ethics*, 359; LW 7:324.

a dialogical motivator and a necessary pathway toward the ideal of a justified order. The nature of human conflict is itself subject to change, yet humanity may be naturally destined for some form of conflict and its resolution.

Pragmatic conflict is a form of public inquiry that goes on all the time, in between the more occasional elections and referenda. It cannot be broken down into component parts permitting mathematical assessment of welfare units. The two critical elements of Dewey's logic of inquiry missing from Kenneth Arrow's analysis are the occurrence of specific problems and their subjection to distinct stages in a social continuum of inquiry.[32] Arrow fails to address the conditions surrounding the persistence of aggregated preferences, their reinforcement in habits, their opposition in ubiquitous disputes and conflicts, and most importantly, their necessity for adjustment for social order or progress in resolving disputes. Opposing Arrow, Dewey's model of social rationality is not a detached calculation from a hypothetical fixity, a constructed "social state" that ignores vectors of information acquisition, action, and change.

For civil society to continue, persistent disputes must be resolved, whether or not they can be put before an electorate for a majoritarian vote. Conflicts influence preferences, while suffrage alone, though essential to democracy, does so indirectly, if at all. A new dynamic for democracy thus comes into view. It involves interactions among emergent disputes and their ongoing agonistic inquiry throughout American society, directly affecting the formal process of referenda and elections. Democratic inquiry does not begin and end with voting, an insight that was fundamental to Dewey's philosophy of democracy.

Preference conflict theory illuminates the boundary between inquiry and violence in the polarization of aggregated opposing interests. It clarifies the precarious path to a fluid Deweyan transformation in the continuum of inquiry, through which specific problems can be democratically recognized, defined, and resolved by incremental group preference adjustment, as discrete problems are identified and remedial practices are adopted through accessible stakeholder input, bypassing ideology in their enforcement through law.[33] It remains to elucidate the process that Dewey insisted can lead to "transformation" and "unification," in what he called "social intelligence."

---

[32] Christophe Point, in his 2018 article "What's the Use of Conflict in Dewey? Toward a Pedagogy of Compromise," writes that "conflict is indispensable for understanding the theory of inquiry and its validity in the search for knowledge." It is part of a "pedagogy of compromise" in Dewey's educational philosophy. "The risk is that if there is a disagreement between stakeholders due to the difference in the interests of each, then this can impede or even completely inhibit any special investigations. In this case, refusing to accept conflict as a dynamic political tool forces the public and critics to think of a democracy that is blind to strikes, blocked situations, and social confrontations, in short, of the violence of those who do not want compromise." *Education and Culture,* vol. 34, no. 2 (2018), 69–88. See also Dewey, *Democracy and Education* (New York: Macmillan Co., 1916), chs. 19–26.

[33] Incremental group preference adjustment and enforcement through law is addressed below and in Frederic R. Kellogg, *Pragmatism, Logic, and Law* (Lanham: Lexington Books, 2021), 27–77.

Chapter 3

Problematic Conflict and Transformation

As noted in the previous chapter, preferences for Dewey are formed in response to actual choices, which he saw and described as "problematic." Adopting Peirce's radical naturalism, ascribing human knowledge as driven from doubt to belief, Dewey begins with the question, What is doubt in the real world of experience, and where does it come from? The shared experience of problematic situations is an obvious source and motivator. The problem of a lost shoe this morning motivates me to look under the bed; I may recognize an individual problem immediately. Yet recognition of *shared* problems is rarely immediate and must come from exploratory and often doubtful communication, driving conjoint, if not always formalized, inquiry. As is evident in America today, it is not uncommon for the definition of a shared problem to be open to dispute.

There is more than one option in a new "problematic situation," and there are (at least) two sides to the question of how to respond. When questions arise, they must be sorted out in stages or phases of response, which can at first appear less like actual inquiry than rank uncertainty, even confusion. Preferences follow, reflecting prior habits of conduct and belief. Individual preferences emerge in diverse and distinct categories, before aggregating around specific positions or claims.[1]

---

[1] Karl Popper observed in 1962, with no reference to Dewey, that "every rational theory, no matter whether scientific or philosophical, is rational in so far as it tries to solve certain problems. A theory is comprehensible and reasonable only in its relation to a given problem-situation, and it can be rationally discussed only by discussing this relation" (Popper's italics), *Conjectures and Refutations: The Growth of Scientific Knowledge* (New York: Basic Books, 1962), 199; "The way in which knowledge progresses, and especially our scientific knowledge, is by unjustified (and unjustifiable) anticipations, by guesses, by tentative solutions to our problems, by *conjectures* . These conjectures are controlled by criticism; that is, by attempted *refutations* which include severely critical tests." *Conjecture and Refutations,* vii. For Dewey, "The starting point of any process of

A problem must be defined before remedies are proposed, engaging opinions and disputes over policy, technology, political paths, cultural, moral, and religious values. Thus the controversial term "situation" that Dewey used indicates the somewhat amorphous condition out of which inquiry emerges. It could hardly be more unlike formal logic, which posits an *a priori* universal process. Logical inference for Dewey is a conjoint, interactive, and often extended and messy process, that he referred to as "*social* intelligence."

Dewey's idea of the "situation" was puzzling to formal logicians, of whom the greatest living exponent was Bertrand Russell, who ventured that Dewey's term must refer to "no less than the whole universe."[2] That interpretation assumed a universalization of logical terms that Russell sought in his own work; his formal logic is independent of humans and floats apart from their strife and differences, an eternal and inherent framework of cognitive relations. Russell's suggestion that the whole universe is characterized as a "situation" was alien to Dewey's attempt to understand human knowledge as responding to sets of unique events, and addressed in a series of judgments regarding them.[3]

Dewey's theory of conflict was not presented in a unitary, dedicated text. His logic continues to be a controversial subject, especially among formal logicians, but even among Dewey's own followers the conflictual aspect has rarely been systematically addressed. Dewey described conflict in general abstract terms, often in language that is challenging to interpret as he struggled to define how society undertakes a "thinking" process. A new problem unites factual and moral issues and presents a normative dilemma or ethical conflict.

> [U]ncertainty and conflict are inherent in morals; it is characteristic of any situation properly called moral that one is ignorant of the end and of good consequences, of the right and just approach, of the direction of virtuous conduct, and that one must search for them.[4]

Conflict produces information in a continuous revelatory inquiry:

---

thinking is something going on, something which just as it stands is incomplete or unfulfilled. Its point, its meaning lies literally in what it is going to be, in how it is going to turn out." *Democracy and Education*, 151.

2 Bertrand Russell, "Dewey's New Logic," in *The Philosophy of John Dewey*, ed. P. A. Schilpp; *The Library of Living Philosophers* (Evanston and Chicago: Northwestern University Press, 1939), 1:137–156, 139–140.

3 John Dewey, *Studies in Logical Theory* (Chicago: University of Chicago Press, 1903), 50. This applies to natural phenomena, as an aspect of all logical inference, requiring a series of judgments, whether experiments in science or instances of legal decisions. "It is impossible to conceive of such a series of judgments as actually being made, unless each one represents a problematic situation and its determination." Dewey, *Studies in Logical Theory,* 125.

4 Dewey, "Three Independent Factors in Morals," 316; LW 5:280.

> I can only express, briefly and in passing, the idea that moral progress and the sharpening of character depend on the ability to make delicate distinctions, to perceive aspects of good and of evil not previously noticed, to take into account the fact that doubt and the need for choice impinge at every tum.[5]

More than one choice is presented over time:

> The essence of the moral situation is an internal and intrinsic conflict; the necessity for judgment and for choice comes from the fact that one has to manage forces with no common denominator.[6]

These passages are from Dewey's 1930 address "Three Independent Factors in Morals." His overall theory of reasoning applied to all categories of inquiry and is found in multiple works and contexts.

As was seen regarding deliberation and pluralism, Dewey scholarship has never been unanimous. About his view of logic and intelligence, Thomas Burke wrote in 1994 that

> Dewey's views on logic have been considered unorthodox if not rather obscure. . . . But to explain why his philosophy of logic so thoroughly slipped into oblivion, one could just as well argue that Dewey was working several decades ahead of his time.[7]

Failure to recognize the original "social" element of Dewey's "social intelligence" has a long history. James Gouinlock wrote in 1986 that "Dewey must shoulder part of the blame for confusions in interpretation."[8]

The uniquely social element of his logical theory has been indistinct. Dewey's theory of social intelligence is not thoroughly worked out. It is never presented systematically, and its meaning as a way of life is not elaborated at crucial junctures. Dewey repeats his advice that all phases of life should be directed by social intelligence, but he does not fully explain what this would mean. My purpose will be to clarify the social and agonistic element, how preferences aggregate and transform in extended disputes, by drawing on the

---

5 Dewey, "Three Independent Factors in Morals," 316; LW 5:280.

6 Dewey, "Three Independent Factors in Morals," 316; LW 5:280.

7 "By 1938, the new formal logic of Tarski, Godel, Church, et al., was beginning to achieve a full head of steam as a research paradigm, and Dewey's logical theory surely seemed irrelevant to these developments. Some highly negative criticisms at the time, particularly those of Bertrand Russell, did not add to Dewey's credibility. The net result has been that logicians in the last half-century have completely ignored Dewey's logic—many logicians these days have probably not even heard of Dewey, let alone forgotten him." Burke, *Deweys New Logic: A Reply to Russell* (Chicago: University of Chicago Press, 1994), 1.

8 James Gouinlock, *Excellence in Public Discourse: John Stuart Mill, John Dewey, and Social Intelligence* (New York: Teachers College Press, 1986), 68.

experience of historic and contemporary conflict as well as the evidence of conflict resolution in the domain of legal adjudication.

Dewey emphasized the element of distinctness or particularity in which shared conflicts first appear in human experience. When they involve broad problems, they are subject to incremental definition in a "series of judgments." Eventual resolution is associated with another characteristic often mentioned by Dewey, what he calls "unification." As with the specific events that galvanized the MeToo movement, separate occasions are compared in the succession of judgments for narrative similarity, prompting consideration of the various contexts in which they are found: various workplaces, attitudes, language, and patterns of response. Although they are first qualified by Dewey as unique, similar aspects in each instance can attach them to a "unified" vision and response.

This summary is consistent with the account of conflict found in the 1903 *Studies in Logical Theory*, which suggests distinct phases or stages. First, Dewey emphasizes the initial reality and specificity of individual conflicts.

> [T]here is always something unquestioned in any problematic situation at any stage of its process, even if it be only the fact of conflict or tension. For this is never mere tension at large. It is thoroughly qualified, or characteristically toned and colored, by the particular elements which are in strife. Hence it is *this* conflict, unique and irreplaceable. [Dewey's emphasis][9]

This language resists Russell's interpretation of a universal meaning to "situation." The next element described in 1903 is transformation through successive experience:

> [T]he distinction between fact and idea is one purely relative to the doubt-inquiry function. It has to do with the evolution of an experience as regards its conscious surety. It has its origin in problematic situations. Whatever appears to us as a problem appears as contrasted with a possible solution. Whatever objects of thought refer particularly to the problematic side are theories, ideas, hypotheses; whatever relates to the solution side is surety, unquestioned familiarity, fact. This point of view makes the distinctions entirely relative to the exigencies of the process of reflective transformation of experience.[10]

---

[9] Dewey, *Studies in Logical Theory*, 50.

[10] This serves to bring out "the correspondent character of datum and hypothesis, and the origin of the latter in a problematic situation and its consequent use as an instrument of unification and solution. Mill first points out that hypotheses are invented to enable the deductive method to be applied earlier to phenomena; that it does this by suppressing the first of the three steps, induction, ratiocination, and verification." Dewey, *Studies in Logical Theory*, 161.

Inquiry unites the dimensions of fact and idea in a continuum, in which the terms of disagreement, what I have called the "reasons environment," is subject to change. A later stage may involve "progressive determination of the ends of conduct."[11]

> In the last analysis the ultimate motive of all reflective thought is the progressive determination of the ends of conduct. Physical judgment, or, in psychological terms, reflective attention to objects in the physical world, is at every turn directed and controlled by reference to a gradually developing purpose, so that the process may also be described as one of bringing to fulness of definition an at first vaguely conceived purpose through ascertainment and determination of the means at hand. The problematic situation in which reflection takes its rise inevitably develops in this two-sided way into consciousness of a definite end on the one side, and of the means or conditions of attaining it on the other.[12]

The ultimate solution of a problem lies in its ethical or rule-based implications:

> Judgments of value are, then, objective in their import in the same sense as are the factual judgments in which the conditions of action are presented. The ideal problematic situation is, in the last resort, ethical, in the sense of requiring for its solution determination of the new end that has arisen with reference to existing standards. In structure and in function the judgment in which the outcome of this process is presented is knowledge, and objective in the only valid acceptation of the term.[13]

Transformation of the "problematic situation" extends to future patterns of conduct as well as of terminology and cognitive understanding. It is an ordering as well as a knowledge-production process, which Dewey attributed to both the social as well as the natural sciences. Conflict cannot be avoided; it is a necessary pathway toward the ideal of a justified order.

As with voluntary euthanasia, redescription exemplifies Dewey's term "transformation," extending to the reasons environment and potentially to embedded habits and practices that have resisted change and reinforced earlier responses. As judgments accumulate and a new order is found, what Dewey called "unification" will occur. This may embody an element of convergence of opposing preferences, such as a redefinition of attitudes for and against medical assistance to morbid patients, one that permits euthanasia under certain conditions. Whether the outcome is open to a convergence or even to one side appearing to win and the other to lose, there is an important

---

[11] "In the last analysis the ultimate motive of all reflective thought is the progressive determination of the ends of conduct." Dewey, *Studies in Logical Theory*, 269.

[12] Dewey, *Studies in Logical Theory*, 269.

[13] Dewey, *Studies in Logical Theory*, 317.

degree of a threefold transformation, cognitive, active, and verbal: of reasons, habits, and language.

Dewey's agonistic account appears more realistic for today's world than the static calculus of Kenneth Arrow. Democratic action has no mathematical formula or proof. Dewey's preference conflict theory illuminates the actual dynamic of democratic life: the boundary between inquiry and violence, in the polarization of aggregated opposing interests. It clarifies the actual but precarious path to a positive transformation in the continuum of inquiry, through which a specific problem can be democratically recognized, defined, and resolved by incremental preference adjustment, as concrete conditions are identified and remedial practices are adopted through stakeholder input, thereby outperforming ideology as a source of law.

James Buchanan challenged Arrow's finding of an overall *social* preference derived from individual preferences. He asked "Can the rationality of the social organism be evaluated in accordance with any value ordering other than its own?"[14] Yet Buchanan hesitated to challenge Arrow's overall view of rational preference calculation: he saw avoidance of Arrow's conclusion as possible through "unanimity" in reconciling diverse preferences for social order. This seems excessively optimistic in a society riven with conflicts. Yet Buchanan's question remains: What might be the *actual* "rationality of the social organism"?

THE "POINT OF VIEW OF THE UNIVERSE"

Dewey's agonistic conception implies a distinctive viewpoint. His approach derives not from a hypothetical instant omniscient observer like Arrow's but recognizes a multitude of possible observation points relating to any one of a number of specific problems, each also (at any given moment) being a stage in a succession of possible viewpoints. Instead of Arrow's set of distinct individual preferences, Dewey's alternative "model," if we can call it that, involves a mix of problems in various stages.[15] How is a constantly changing world subject to an overall utilitarian assessment?

---

14 Buchanan, "Social Choice, Democracy, and Free Markets," 116.

15 I have used the term *synchronic* for Arrow's model, opposing it to Dewey's *diachronic* one. Arrow is envisioning an omniscient picture, an entire display of preferences at a given moment (not unlike the entire display of utility or happiness that classical utilitarianism seeks to maximize). It is a *universal synchronic epistemic* picture (or *ontology*) and leads Arrow to a static rational calculus. Dewey's problematic perspective is focused on particular problematic issues, or topics. As he wrote in 1903, "This point of view makes the distinctions entirely relative to the exigencies of the process of reflective transformation of experience." As such it might be defined as a *topical problematic epistemic ontology and rationality. Studies in Logical Theory*, 164.

In examining a theory like Arrow's, the urge to naturalize asks more precisely: What is the observation point and method, and how is it justified? Arrow, as the author of *Social Choice and Individual Values*, is the observer writing the text, but he is writing as if he and the reader are not only in the same place of observation, observing a similar complex of distinct stable preferences among the individual members of any group, but occupy a universally omniscient place, in the sense used by classical utilitarian theorists. It is comparable to what contemporary authorities on utilitarianism, like Peter Singer and Katarzyna de Lazari-Radek in 2014 (following Henry Sidgwick in 1874), have called "The Point of View of the Universe."[16]

Sidgwick used this phrase in his authoritative 1874 treatise on utilitarianism, *Methods of Ethics,* in the context of considering a fundamental tension between what J. S. Mill called "psychological" and "ethical" hedonism, or what Sidgwick called the "Dualism of Practical Reason."[17] How should an actor balance individual welfare with the general welfare, self-interest versus benevolence? Singer and Lazari-Radek, in *The Point of View of the Universe: Sidgwick and Contemporary Ethics*, have renewed classical utilitarianism with a careful reassessment of Sidgwick's dualism: If an action is subject to the calculation of maximum welfare, there are two opposing principles for any actor, one being that of her *personal* welfare, and the other being the *general* welfare. The problem is, in assessing an action pursuant to the utilitarian principle of greatest happiness, how is benevolence to be balanced with self-interest? As Sidgwick had written,

> I quite admit that when the painful necessity comes for another man to choose between his own happiness and the general happiness, he must as a reasonable being prefer his own, i.e. it is right for him to do this on my principle. No doubt, as I probably do not sympathise with him in particular any more than with other persons, I as a disengaged spectator should like him to sacrifice himself to the general good: but I do not expect him to do it, any more than I should do it myself in his place.[18]

---

[16] Peter Singer and Katarzyna de Lazari-Radek, *The Point of View of the Universe: Sidgwick and Contemporary Ethics* (Oxford: Oxford University Press, 2014).

[17] "The two elements of Mill's view which I am accustomed to distinguish as Psychological Hedonism [that each man does seek his own Happiness] and Ethical Hedonism [that each man ought to seek the general Happiness] both attracted me, and I did not at first perceive their incoherence." Henry Sidgwick, *The Methods of Ethics* (Indianapolis: Hackett Pub. Co., 1981 [1874]), xvii. Derek Parfit in *Reasons and Persons* (Oxford: Clarendon Press, 1984), 30, writes, "According to C [self-interest consequentialism], each of us should try to do what would make the outcome best, given what others will actually do. And each of us should try to have one of the possible sets of motives whose effects would be best, given the actual sets of motives that will be had by others. Each of us should ask: 'Is there some other set of motives that is both possible for me and is such that, if I had this set, the outcome would be better?' Our answers would depend on what we know, or can predict, about the sets of motives that will be had by others."

[18] Sidgwick, *Methods of Ethics*, xix–xx.

When the question is presented in the abstract, it has no clear answer. Singer and Lazari-Radek now argue that "the point of view of the universe is the perspective of a rational being, in a way that alternative perspectives, such as that of egoism, are not." While they claim that Sidgwick would have welcomed their argument, they agree with him that "cracks in the coherence of ethics caused by the dualism of practical reason are serious, and threaten to bring down the entire structure."[19]

The tension suggests an unnatural conception of optimum welfare. When the question of optimum utility is applied to a specific problem in Dewey's fully naturalized diachronic context, the tension between personal and general preferences is not only recognized but also addressed by the progress of inquiry. Reconciling the opposing principles of personal and general welfare in each specific context is part of the "unification" that Dewey sees as occupying possible common ground. Information regarding personal advantage is *required* for a full account of the conditions of resolution. The ultimate resolution itself must appear as one of both general advantage and of personal utility or prudence. Benevolence is thereby reconciled with self-interest—*locally*, and not *globally,* as required by the classical utilitarian "viewpoint of the universe."[20]

Dewey's universe is not *one immediate abstract question or problem*, but a mixture of ongoing and *developing problems.* A dappled and diachronic world, rather than a static synchronic one, is the context in which Dewey's organic democracy must be conceived as applying any *actual* welfare calculus. Thus Dewey's question, unlike Singer's, Lazari-Radek's and Sidgwick's, would be the granular inquiry, "What *might* the universe recognize as the optimum utility in each of its ongoing problems," rather than utilitarianism's *abstract* question, "What does the universe (at some given moment) recognize as the greatest happiness of the greatest number?" Moreover, for Dewey, the universe cannot know or guess the outcomes, as preferences and utilities must adjust and transform.

One cannot answer the second question as simply "solution of all problems," as that would ignore that many older problems are yet unsettled and many new problems lie ahead. It would defy the notion of defining the *maximization* of overall well-being. For certain problems, like abusive messages

---

[19] Singer and Lazari-Radek, *The Point of View of the Universe*, 378, 173.

[20] "When, however, the Egoist puts forward, implicitly or explicitly, the proposition that his happiness or pleasure is Good, not only *for him* but from the point of view of the Universe,—as (*e.g.*) by saying that 'nature designed him to seek his own happiness,'—it then becomes relevant to point out to him that *his* happiness cannot be a more important part of Good, taken universally, than the equal happiness of any other person. And thus, starting with his own principle, he may be brought to accept Universal happiness or pleasure as that which is absolutely and without qualification Good or Desirable: as an end, therefore, to which the action of a reasonable agent as such ought to be directed." Sidgwick, *Methods of Ethics,* 420–421.

on digital social media, the problem of a line between, say, free expression and invasion of privacy (perhaps by bullying or trolling) was at first unobserved and later (and still as of this writing) recognized but uncertain. Utilities and preferences surrounding the issue have emerged in one form and led to others; they are still unstable and yet undefinable. Optimum well-being involves a balance of changing factors and adjusting practices that has yet to be clarified, much less struck. In certain cases, a final balance may never be attained. The universe is blind to its utilitarian future, under any description of the actual process.

Stability is an aspect of Dewey's "unification." His hoped-for "ethical" outcome is a new regime of practices yet unknown. The maximization principle of classical utilitarianism has no immediate meaning when ongoing conflict has yet to (in Dewey's words) "manage forces with no common denominator." The late professor Frederic Schick of Rutgers University advanced an insight in "Under Which Description?" in *Utilitarianism and Beyond*, the critical 1982 collection of essays edited by Amartya Sen and Bernard Williams. He writes that the utility we assign to something depends on its propositional form. Events "do not have unique propositions corresponding to them."[21] The very concept of utility is "descriptively relative"; for example, E. M. Forster put the question of whether in a crisis "one should betray one's friend or one's country." Schick replies:

> Someone more patriotically minded would complain that Forster put it badly: his question should have been whether or not he would betray his country. A third person might hold that he should have asked whether or not he would betray his friend. Does it matter which way this is put? It matters to a utilitarian of the nonconsequentialist sort. For he must look to how people feel about the actions an agent might take, and people may set different values on different propositions that report the same actions.[22]

Dewey would view the issue differently: as described by both Forster and Schick, it is too abstract to be settled, and demands more experience, in the retrospective analysis of concrete instances.

Only through specific instances, such as concrete cases regarding the misuse of classified documents, are abstract questions unified or resolved. As adjudications of such cases display diverse aspects of a general problem experienced in succession, an ethical practice distinct to the problem may emerge. For instance, drawing on recent experience, former public officials have retained classified documents in private offices or residences. The

---

[21] Frederic Schick, "Under Which Description?" in *Utilitarianism and Beyond* (Cambridge: Cambridge University Press, 1982), 251–560, 253.

[22] Schick, "Under Which Description?" 257.

circumstances in each case are different, and at this writing, new examples are still occurring. The problem of document retention by former high-level officials has several yet unexplored aspects, including the underlying question of how official documents become classified, and why.[23]

Given the actual world of ongoing disputed problems, conventional utilitarian maximization appears to be meaningless, just as Sidgwick's dualism of practical reason is meaningless when applied to actual inquiries. The very purpose of conflict resolution is to reconcile personal preferences with general ones, or to evaluate and specify the meaning of "utility" or "well-being" in any given particular context. Mill's well-known ranking of different kinds of happiness has long been a matter of debate over the application of the universal maximizing principle. As with the problem of benevolence versus self-interest, disputants in a real conflict bring differences over "kinds of utility" to any particularized inquiry, where a workable balance must be addressed and—after transformation—hopefully unified.

Dewey's problematic continuum enables the particularized reconciliation of traditional utility puzzles through the actual process of negotiation and adjustment. Instead of problematizing egoism, the continuum relies on it for the presentation of arguments necessary to successful outcomes. The degree of benevolence must be calibrated toward a balanced resolution. To portray shifting preferences graphically, one might use letter symbols for Dewey's shared problems. Compared to Arrow's x, y, and z for individual preferences, they might be represented in stages, such as Pa1 (for Problem *a,* stage 1), Pa2, Pa3, and so on, as well as (for another problem) Pb1, Pb2, Pb3, and so on. Such a model does not envision an entire immediate universe of identifiable preferences but rather a multiple process in which similar preferences aggregate (and potentially change) around a set of diverse particular problems, which are themselves in a constant process of emergence, definition, and redefinition, eventually seeking unification or resolution.

Some issues, like the status of women and racial minorities, have long recurred, arriving within new contexts. Some problems are local, like town governance issues. Some are derivative, like contractual transactions on the internet. Some are old, but recently more threatening, like those of the climate and environment. While all shared social problems are different in detail, a particular problem begins amid a context of established customary practices and preferences, and presents a threat to already existing practices and preferences (like the first stage of Problem *a*, shown as "Pa1" above). An

[23] See e.g. Matthew Connelly, *The Declassification Engine: What History Reveals About America's Top Secrets* (New York: Penguin Random House, 2023), making the case that, unless the classification process is reformed, unnecessarily large numbers of historical documents will never be declassified and opened to public access.

illustrative response is the comment of a white resident of Alabama during the 1961 Freedom Rides, seeking to integrate segregated southern bus stations, that met with organized violence on the arrival of buses from Washington, DC, to New Orleans: "They are trying to change the way we live."[24]

Existing preferences define the welfare of society in Arrow's thesis. For Dewey, social welfare is in constant redefinition as successive problems are addressed. An emergent problem is recognized and defined by a succession of events—similar injuries in a new factory, similar problems of affordable housing in Silicon Valley, similar twenty-first-century assaults on women, blacks, or children—and opposing preferences aggregate around prior lines of conduct that usually resist change. While many problems defy resolution, it is characteristic of those that do not that the nature of initial relevant preferences (and perceived utilities) have adjusted (or "transformed," as Dewey put it). The rights of organized labor were not resolved by legislation alone but by long and difficult struggle (see chapter 8 *infra*).

Initial judgments, when they emerge, are often marked by confusion and obscurity and can be derailed by ideological responses reflecting ethical and religious values often viewed as "incommensurable." Preferences are formed and aggregated in relation to various aspects of the situation: opposing assumptions, descriptions, and prospects for resolution. As inquiry proceeds, disputes invite new information, forcing new judgments and new descriptions of the overall problem. Given the stakes, changing the way people live, it is little wonder that massive efforts are made to divert and disrupt a "rational conversational" process.

The preferences (and perceived utilities) that dominated the trial of Dr. Kevorkian in 1999 were adjusted from the initial nature of "suicide" and "homicide" through intervention from the medical and legal professions as well as patients and their families (and other interested groups). The initial preferences that may dominate a town controversy over new construction, climate conservation or energy technology, have visibly adjusted where such controversies have been resolved. The original attitudes toward workers' rights, gays, women, and blacks, have nevertheless undergone transformations, even while resisting wholesale resolution.

To succeed, the adjustment process must take into account the claims and perceived preferences of stakeholders or constituents: the often numberless individuals who, over the course of a problem, are involved in redirecting

[24] The original group of thirteen Freedom Riders—seven African Americans and six whites—left Washington, D.C., on a Greyhound bus on May 4, 1961. Their plan was to reach New Orleans, Louisiana, on May 17 to commemorate the seventh anniversary of the Supreme Court's *Brown v. Board of Education* decision, which ruled that segregation of the nation's public schools was unconstitutional. The group first traveled through Virginia and North Carolina, drawing little public notice. The first violent incident occurred on May 12 in Rock Hill, South Carolina.

its course. Their disparate views regarding its resolution are not the idealized preferences that classical utilitarians might identify as appealing to a benevolent universal mind, or to the best versions of individual preferences, but they are gathered from diverse corners of the affected population and are placed in a real competition with each other. Legal battles are instrumental in producing both information and incentives.

It is common for renters to save money on living expenses, and it is common for landlords to maximize income. The two are inherently in conflict, but for the most part the conflict can be settled through adjusted practices. A comparable opposition of practices, broadly defined, is that of the interests of employers and employees, which has led to strikes and picketing. The history of gender inequality can be viewed as one of oppositions of habit and practice, as are reproductive rights and medical assistance to patient death.

In Dewey's continuum, contested preferences yield to the adjustment of practices for resolution. If deliberation is to be fully understood as taking place in conflict, deliberation itself must be fully naturalized. How does naturalized deliberation begin? Many problems are inherited and gradually transformed not through convening, like French President Macron, a national conference. Dewey emphasized the succession of judgments in specific conflicts, leading to the unification of a general question. This can be put in symbolic form, distinguishing what Dewey refers to as the specific instance or question (represented by a small cap "q") from the emergent "situation" (represented by a capital "Q" for the more general question).

When events reflect the arrival of a new particular *q*, the full nature of a possibly extended *Q* remains yet unspecified. An example is assisted death, which has often been conceived as a standoff between suicide and homicide.[25] Dr. Kevorkian sought to raise a broader question (and energize the continuum of inquiry) by devising a device for minimal medical assistance accessing mortal choice for a severely ill patient, for which he was prosecuted and imprisoned in 1999. His case was an early "*q*." A generation later, after extended social inquiry into many instances of what is now the complex and painful question of assisted death forced open by Kevorkian, the larger issue (the "*Q*") has acquired a new utility analysis on both sides. Suicide and homicide no longer dominate the conversation. A specific inquiry *today* (yet another *q*) will take place within a transformed reasons environment. Earlier reasons regarding expected utility have been retired and replaced.

Hence any original *q*, or indeed any given particular inquiry during the extended period, may be an *inquiry within an inquiry*, a point that is critical to understanding social inductivism and its bearing on utilitarian theory.

---

[25] See, e.g., Weir, *Physician Assisted Suicide* and Young, *Medically Assisted Death.*

This has an important impact on the notion of rules and rule formation. The retrospective utility calculus for Q will be different from the earlier reasons calculus of q, in ways yet invisible at the earlier camera-flash moment. Adaptation and the revision of practices will occur during the social continuum of inquiry, in some matters more readily than in others.[26] Yet, as should be evident, the stages of inquiry and transformation are invisible to a hypothetical instant utility camera.

Rather than applying an instantaneous consequentialism, Dewey's pragmatism assumes that the analysis of any given controversial moral question may be influenced by its relative position or stage in the discovery and completion of a broader and more general question. Inquiry into the specific ethical question q (what is right in this case to do *now*) often comes *within* an extended continuum, a Q, representing inquiry into what will be viewed as right after exploration of the more general question, in which the individual q may actually be early or late in the larger and longer extended social inquiry.

Preferences change as reasons change, in a transformation of the "reasons environment." Dewey rejected the immediate (sometimes referred to as Aristotelian) model of induction for an extended model which I have called "social inductivism."[27] Conflict reveals and addresses preferences and opposing perceptions of utility; assessment takes place in the continuum. The problems that have been resolved consist of a set of stable preferences that are now accepted as new or revised practices, or ethical standards. They are, as Dewey wrote in "Three Independent Factors," then reflected as *duties*. Those problems that are yet unresolved are surrounded by competing assessments of the overall utility situation.

Given Dewey's version of Peirce's radical naturalism, what does Sidgwick's hypothetical benevolent universe "see" when its current problems consist of the entire set of developing individual preferences at any given moment? The picture does not contain fixed but rather *evolving* preferences and forms of "utility." In resolving a shared problem, personal interests motivate the consideration of overall interests. For a conflict to be resolved, a solution must be generally agreeable, and new habits and practices must have emerged. Completed forms of utility arrive at the end of the inquiry.

I will suggest in the following chapter that Dewey's viewpoint is not so much an *anti*-utilitarianism as a radical *naturalist* utilitarianism. Instead of a global universal preference maximization principle, it views social welfare as guided by a local and problem-oriented agonistic preference adjustment

---

26 See Edward Levi, *Introduction to Legal Reasoning* (Chicago: University of Chicago Press, 1949), 1–6, 8–27, describing the century-long continuum of inquiry into the concept of "dangerous instrumentality," chapter 5 *infra.*

27 Frederic R. Kellogg, *Oliver Wendell Holmes Jr. and Legal Logic* (Chicago: Chicago University Press, 2018).

principle. As both Sidgwick, Singer, and others have noted at length, classical utilitarianism presents basic conceptual problems like reconciling the good of all with the good of the individual and the nature of general well-being. It also lacks a realistic account of rules, given the debates over act versus rule utilitarianism. To that question I now turn.

Chapter 4

Dewey's Naturalized Utilitarianism

> *Utilitarianism, whether as a moral or as a social doctrine, lacks a psychology and a politics. The questions that need to be pressed are "How could it be lived by anyone?" "How could it be lived here and now and in the foreseeable future?" "What institutions would it need?—in particular, institutions that could be formed, adapted or introduced by us?"*
>
> –Amartya Sen and Bernard Williams, 1982, *Utilitarianism and Beyond,* 21

The above comment is from the Introduction to Amartya Sen and Bernard Williams' critical edition of essays on the contemporary problems and prospects of classical utilitarianism.[1] They contend that the universal maximization principle "can't be lived." It presents basic conceptual problems, like Sidgwick's dualism of practical reason (of reconciling the good of all with the good of the individual) and Mill's concern with the diverse and controversial nature of aspects of utility or well-being.

It also needs a realistic account of rules and social order, as can be seen from unresolved debates over act utilitarianism versus rule utilitarianism. The previous chapter concluded that instead of a global universal preference maximization principle, Dewey views social welfare as guided by a local, problem-oriented, agonistic preference adjustment principle. This chapter will attempt to illustrate this, as well as explore the distinctive form of order and rules inherent in Dewey's "naturalized utilitarianism." Not only *can* his

[1] The quoted passage continues: "One such question, a central one, is presented in [Amy] Gutman's paper on education ["What's the Use of Going to School?"]: 'How could a utilitarian society replicate itself though learning?".

local principle be "lived," it is already *being* lived to a degree, and once fully understood, can be *improved.*

It is easy to see how classical utilitarianism "can't be lived" even without Kenneth Arrow's famous 1951 demonstration based on the assumption of a society of fixed individual preferences. Classical utilitarianism is an ideal theory, tied by Arrow to a fixed model of preferences in society. Summing up the "goodness of any act" leads to a major problem: the sum total of all acts, in the production of maximum happiness, justifies *too much.* Should a judge sentence an innocent man to death to quell a riot or stop a crime wave? If people explicitly adopted utilitarianism (or "consequentialism," as it is now often known) and tried to follow it (not punishing offenders during crime waves), things might very well go worse, even as judged by a utilitarian, than if people adopted and tried to follow rules instead.

How do utility-derived rules work? Classical rule utilitarianism (now often called "rule-consequentialism") is another instantaneous model that ignores the fluid nature of a society's changing preferences. It was long thought that some combination of ranking both acts and rules together could establish a workable utilitarian (or "consequentialist") model. But analysis of precisely how the consequences of a *rule* relate to the consequences of individual *acts* reveals that, under a global maximization calculus, act and rule utilitarianism have the same practical "extension," thereby questioning the very plausibility of a regime of rules, including faith in a rule of law.[2]

The utilitarian account of rules was carefully examined by John Rawls in his 1955 essay, "Two Concepts of Rules." Rawls offered an interpretation preventing utilitarianism from justifying too much, "by stating utilitarianism in a way which accounts for the distinction between the justification of an institution and the justification of a particular act falling under it."[3] He did so by distinguishing two distinct utilitarian conceptions of rules, the summary and practice views. In the former, "rules are pictured as summaries of past decisions arrived at by the *direct* application of the utilitarian principle to

[2] As one writer has put it, "act-consequentialists deny rules have a role in the criterion of moral rightness. Prescribing a decision procedure dominated by rules and then denying rules a role in the criterion of rightness can be problematic." Brad Hooker, "The Role(s) of Rules in Consequentialist Ethics," in *The Oxford Handbook of Consequentialism*, Douglas W. Portmore, ed. (Oxford: Oxford University Press, 2020), 441.

[3] "The real question, however, [writes Rawls] is whether the utilitarian, in justifying punishment, hasn't used arguments which commit him to accepting the infliction of suffering on innocent persons if it is for the good of society (whether or not one calls this punishment). More generally, isn't the utilitarian committed in principle to accepting many practices which he, as a morally sensitive person, wouldn't want to accept? Retributionists are inclined to hold that there is no way to stop the utilitarian principle from justifying too much except by adding to it a principle which distributes certain rights to individuals. Then the amended criterion is not the greatest benefit of society simpliciter, but the greatest benefit of society subject to the constraint that no one's rights may be violated." Rawls, "Two Concepts of Rules," *The Philosophical Review,* vol. 64, no. 1 (January 1955), 3–32, 9.

particular cases." In this view, particular cases are logically prior to rules, whereas in the latter view, institutions and practices are prior.

The summary view fails to resolve the problem of punishing innocent offenders, as it refers to collecting into a rule those acts that have maximized happiness, and this could *defend* a rule of punishing the innocent. Under the *practice* rule, however, punishment of offenders would be assessed within the concept of an institutionalized practice in the justice system, which itself is recognized as having been adopted for overriding utilitarian considerations. So also with practices like promising, or not stealing, for their high-maximizing utilitarian value. However, as David Lyons argued in 1965, the question would still arise as to whether and how *exceptions* should be evaluated by the utilitarian calculus, even for the practice theory of rules. The issue of exceptions to a utilitarian rule is critical to understanding the *actual* nature of rule formation, particularly in the continuum that is implicit in Dewey's theory.

What about the problem raised by a possible act that is opposed to an accepted practice, but which would *still* bring about greater overall utility? Rawls, according to Lyons, addressed exceptions to rules by using an "escape clause." To illustrate, Rawls notes that one answer to "why should I keep my promise" is that "doing so in *this* case will have the best consequences." Rawls concedes that "it is always necessary to take into account the effect which our action will have on the practice of making promises." He recognized that the strict act-utilitarian may yet observe that there might be a case where the promisor could argue that, even calculating the utility of the practice, "breaking the promise would lead to a better state of affairs on the whole . . . no matter how slight the advantage won by breaking the promise." Hence, the non-conforming action would be best in view of all utilitarian considerations *including* the importance of the practice.[4]

Rawls's "escape clause" *defended* rule utilitarianism from this objection, by arguing

> One is inclined to think it would either turn out that such a case came under an exception defined by the practice itself, . . . or it would happen that the circumstances were so peculiar that the conditions which the practice presupposes no longer obtained.[5]

But Lyons in 1965 pressed the objection further, arguing that this *still* failed to save a rule from collapsing into act utilitarianism. Lyons called Rawls's escape clause inadequate as it was nothing but a "ceteris paribus" (all other things being equal). Rules like "do not break promises" could be viewed as

[4] Rawls, "Two Concepts of Rules," 14.
[5] Rawls, "Two Concepts of Rules," 15.

> elliptical formulations of *ceteris paribus* rules . . . the suppressed *ceteris paribus* condition can in each and every case be taken in terms of the *escape clause*: "except when you know or are quite certain that the effects of not following the main body of the rule would be better."

He explained:

> The considerations which justify using the de facto moral rules to begin with, and those which determine justifiable exceptions to them, are all of one piece. If one accepts Act-Utilitarianism one can view the de facto moral rules as if they have the (AU) escape clause as an implicit qualification.[6]

Thus Lyons' argument challenged the very foundation of rule utilitarianism, by claiming that there is no *extensional* difference between act and rule utilitarianism.

This extensionalist challenge to the utilitarian tradition can hardly be underestimated (though it is a problem only for analytical theory, not for pragmatism). Brad Hooker recently summarized it as follows:

> In other words, for every situation where compliance with some rule would not produce the greatest expected good, rule-consequentialism seems driven to favor instead compliance with some amended rule that does not miss out on producing the greatest expected good in the case at hand. But if rule-consequentialism operates this way, then in practice it will end up requiring the very same acts that act-consequentialism requires.[7]

I will refer to this point as "extensional equivalence," or simply "extensionalism." It would appear to be fatal to any utilitarian account of a rule-based regime of law or morals:

> If rule-consequentialism ends up requiring the very same acts that act-consequentialism requires, then rule-consequentialism is indeed in terrible trouble. Rule-consequentialism is the more complicated of the two theories. This leads to the following objection. What is the point of rule-consequentialism with its infinitely amended rules if we can get the same practical result much more efficiently with the simpler act-consequentialism?[8]

The above is a condensed summary of an important turn in the history of utilitarianism. It has energized academic writers, notably Brad Hooker and

---

6 David Lyons, *Forms and Limits of Utilitarianism* (Oxford: Clarendon Press, 1965), 180.

7 Brad Hooker, "Rule Consequentialism," *Stanford Encyclopedia of Philosophy* (2023), https://plato.stanford.edu/entries/consequentialism-rule/.

8 Hooker, "Rule Consequentialism," section 8.

Michael Ridge, committed to further revising rule utilitarianism following Lyons's extensionalist challenge. Rule-consequentialism has tested the basic assumptions underlying utilitarian moral theory and its relation to the work of analytical moral theorists like Derek Parfit. I need not discuss other new views of utilitarianism here, as my brief summary of the extensionalist challenge provides an opening for better understanding the yet-ignored pragmatist critique, its continuum of inquiry, and the fundamentally diachronic character of normative inquiry. My task is to show that a *pragmatic* moral philosophy, with its own *distinctive* account of grounding rules (on a local rather than global and a naturalized rather than maximized utility balance), requires abandoning the momentary, flash-camera model of normative reality that dominates all maximizing theory.

The last chapter ended with the representation of a problematic continuum as a series (or succession) of small q's, gradually giving content to an emergent large Q. The small q's are the successive judgments Dewey refers to in *Studies in Logical Theory,* that mobilize preferences in a dispute in the assessment of an immediate problem. This may be an early stage of a continuum of inquiry, where Dewey stresses the *specificity* of particular conflicts as preceding a potentially larger question. In the next stage, as successive exemplars (more q's) occur and contribute to an overall assessment of the situation, there is likely to be what he calls a "transformation through successive experience," including what I have called a "transformation in the reasons environment."

Continuing inquiry, focused on other specific aspects of a broader problem, serves (in Dewey's words) to bring out "the correspondent character of datum and hypothesis, and the origin of the latter in a problematic situation and its consequent use as an instrument of unification and solution."[9] Dewey used few concrete examples, so I need to illustrate how this structure of successive judgments works and affects the reasoning process, as this is critical to the originality of Dewey's "social intelligence." The nature of preferences changes along with practices in the continuum, and this also *transforms* perceptions of utility.

Classical utilitarianism holds that an act may be judged on immediate considerations of utility; but Dewey amends this instantaneous model with the natural occurrence of further events that contribute to defining and redefining the problematic situation. These lead to adjustments in reasoning and practice, as the larger problem (the large cap "Q") is increasingly defined; there are distinct *stages* in the development of a Q. Early stages depend heavily on consequentialist tests. But, as Dewey writes, later stages are open

---

9 Dewey, *Studies in Logical Theory*, 161. He adds that "Mill first points out that hypotheses are invented to enable the deductive method to be applied earlier to phenomena; that it does this by suppressing the first of the three steps, induction, ratiocination, and verification."

to "unification," which includes generalization of response through ethical judgment or emergent rule-making.

Early on in a problem, especially one that involves opposing and clashing habits and beliefs, it is often hard to see a path to a solution, as the problem itself has yet to be fully defined. How do practices adjust amidst conflict, and how are they affected by further conflict? I have already used the euthanasia example as an illustration of the adjustment and transformation process. How does a problem *transform*, one that is first defined as a dilemma opposing the right to, or sanctity of, human life, against the personal autonomy of the individual, into a stable regime where new medical technologies and legal conditions are applied to permit assisted death? The original dispute over the general issue of life versus privacy must devolve into the examination and adjudication of specific practices in which actual conditions bearing on the conflict are examined.[10]

There is a simpler example, of the conflict basis of normative development, found in the early writings of Justice Oliver Wendell Holmes Jr., who mentions in a 1873 paper the emergence of English "rule[s] of the road." Holmes observed that rules of the road are practices that have been "worked out" after a "sufficient amount of fighting."[11] To illustrate, we might imagine disputes over vehicular collisions for which at first there is no settled rule. With the emergence of vehicular traffic comes the problem of collisions at road crossings, and the invention of devices like signs, signals, and traffic circles. The yielding rule for vehicles already in a traffic circle derives first from conflict, then from practice, and then from law enforcement.

In America, we drive on the right; in Britain, they drive on the left. Those puzzling (to me) clockwise "roundabouts" emerged in England after a period of trial and error, but historical oversimplification helps me make a point. Let's ask what might have happened when a driver (call her Ms Quickly) first entered what might have been an *early* English roundabout, perhaps nothing but a monument in the middle of an intersection, and was struck by a truck

---

10 An early analysis of the problem of voluntary euthanasia before Dr. Kevorkian extended the debate into new territory is Philippa Foot, "Euthanasia," *Philosophy & Public Affairs,* vol. 6, no. 2 (Winter 1977), 85–112. See also Young, *Medically Assisted Death,* 1–7, regarding "the findings of various courts that have shaped the debate."

11 "A more modern example [Holmes had been discussing changes in the liability of innkeepers] is to be found in the rule of the road. After a sufficient amount of *fighting*, a practice is worked out, and a corresponding *expectation* generated. Then this is judicially noticed by the courts, and it is laid down as a rule of law that men are bound to in this instance what by general consent they are *expected* to do" (my italics). Holmes, "The Theory of Torts," *American Law Review, vol.* 7 (July 1873), 652, 657, in Frederic R. Kellogg, *The Formative Essays of Justice Holmes* (Westport: Greenwood Press, 1984), 117 at 122; Holmes, *Collected Works* (Chicago: University of Chicago Press, 1995), 1:326, 328. See also Kellogg, "The Snake and the Roundabout: Ethical Particularism and the Patterns of Normative Induction," *Duc in Altum Cadernos De Direito,* vol. 8, no. 16 (jul .dez-2016).

(or rather a "lorry"). The question of responsibility can't be established by the yielding rule. How should the responsibility to pay for the damages be allocated? A classical utilitarian calculus would have multiple dimensions of utility to evaluate.

This example serves to illustrate the nature of an early *q*, a new conflict over competing perceptions of utility. In the early or novel case, the list of properties relevant to a utilitarian calculus is long: just like Sidgwick's "viewpoint of the universe." All of the drivers of vehicles approaching an intersection have an individual happiness calculus, some presumptively higher than others. There are aggravating and mitigating factors everywhere you look, on both sides of a given accident. Holmes's point is that rules begin to be formed from within an environment of yet-unregulated disputes. Once a remedial practice, and then a reinforcing rule, establishes a presumptive right of way for any vehicle *already* in the roundabout, none of the earlier drivers' (or their lawyers') opposing consequentialist reasons will be relevant.

How did that happen? Basically, the smarter drivers started yielding, and the word (and example) got around that this was the safer practice. Meanwhile, other accident cases were being heard in the courts (and discussed in the streets), perhaps with Benthamite lawyers bringing up utilitarian reasons why their clients should win. As a shared sense of similarity develops, affecting the shapes of the enlarged roundabouts and the practices of safe drivers, these arguments are being rejected, even though grounded in different aspects of a general utility calculus. Early cases and judgments do not reflect and define the eventual problem. They will have been progressively disregarded or overruled as an ethical rule emerges and the general issue is judicially explored and resolved.[12]

You might say that clockwise yielding was an experiment that worked. Generalism in law is a product of establishing a commitment to finite expectations in a given problematic situation. It often occurs at a later stage of inquiry, if and when the relevant properties can be winnowed down to a formula.[13] Is there a preference aggregation here, between the drivers arriving

---

[12] Holmes used the figure of "Mrs. Quickly" to illustrate a similar point in "The Path of the Law": "The reason why a lawyer does not mention that his client wore a white hat when he made a contract, while Mrs. Quickly would be sure to dwell upon it along with the parcel gilt goblet and the sea-coal fire, is that he foresees that the public force will act in the same way whatever his client had upon his head." Holmes, *Collected Works,* 3:391.

[13] Holmes referred to the 1866 English case of *Beadel v Perry,* L.R. 3 Eq. 465, as reaching a "mathematical" formula. "To leave the question to the jury forever, is simply to leave the law uncertain. Accordingly, we read in a recent equity case that what was left at large to the jury fifty years ago has now become a mathematical rule; that a building cannot be complained of unless its height exceeds the distance of its base from the base of the ancient windows." Kellogg, *The Formative Essays of Justice Holmes,* 120; Holmes, *Collected Works,* 1:328. The following chapter illustrates this with Edward Levi's account of the rise and fall of the concept of dangerous instrumentality.

at a roundabout and the ones already in? Not concretely; but there is a *convergence of interests* in the sense that they are both better off yielding than continuing to crash and litigate. This process is different for every problem, but it is important to distinguish it from the way in which we saw how classical utilitarian theory approaches rules.

Other types of legal litigation have occurred for generations, between and among individuals who occupy competing roles in the economy: landlords and tenants, buyers and sellers, employers and employees, all of whom have interests that have clashed with each other in real life. With the internet introducing "Air B&B," where short-term room rentals are created with a few clicks on a computer screen, new disputes have to be resolved under new habits and practices. When disputes get to court, you will find the lawyers looking back to the history of landlord/tenant law, and arguing from opposing precedents (earlier appellate decisions) before Air B&B came into existence. Each side, the newly internet-minted "landlords" and "tenants," will need to "distinguish" any precedents that seem to rule against them by bringing up new aspects of utility, like considerations of travel and access or what-have-you. We may find further clarification in the legal process of rule formation in discrete areas like tort, crime, possession, and so on.[14]

This is how legal experience exemplifies normative experience in conflict resolution. Opposing sides in virtually any case (that gets to the higher courts of appeal) will submit written briefs replete with references to prior published decisions, not only from the court involved, but from other courts that have ruled in somewhat similar circumstances. The lawyers are buttressing their strongest factual claims with examples that have some arguable similarity. Historically, this has happened not just with everyday matters, but with major issues like race and gender discrimination and labor strikes and organization.

Using the traffic example, it's easy to show why both the summary and the practice views of classical utilitarianism are faulty. Let's imagine that a utilitarian judge in Ms Quickly's case ruled that her getting to church on time had more and better happiness or welfare than the lorry driver's delivery of scandalous literature in the back of his truck. Assuming this is a fair and accurate balance, the summary rule might then be that churchgoers in roundabout accidents would always be paid for damage by trucks carrying pornography. The same reasoning would apply to other rules like "punish

---

[14] An early Holmes example (the 1866 English case of *Beadel v. Perry*) involved neighboring landowners disputing construction near a property line affecting the neighboring property, an issue then not yet covered by local regulation. "The Theory of Torts," in Kellogg, *The Formative Essays of Justice Holmes,* 117; *Collected Works,* 1:326. Another example was "the process of specification" in application of the standard of negligence in tort adjudications. Holmes, "Trespass and Negligence," Kellogg, *The Formative Essays of Justice Holmes,* 225, 248f; Holmes, *Collected Works,* 3:92f.

offenders," "don't steal," and "keep your promises." Hardly any rule would survive the onslaught of exceptions where the utility balance favored them. Stealing would always be permissible when the balance favored the thief.

How about Rawls's practice view? Rawls defended it using the maximization principle, and that is what led to its downfall in the extensionalist critique, as it is no different from the summary view, or from act-utilitarianism itself, as every practice is subject to exceptions that will show it to be nothing but a *ceteris paribus* summary. In essence, Rawls failed to see how practices, *and* exceptions, are derived from transformed preferences and the retirement of previous utilitarian reasons.

How do exceptions arise? Let us assume that an early claim of exception comes from the local fire department. Of course, the rule must adapt to allow a general exception for fire equipment—but a conditional one, only when displaying lights and sirens. Here too, Holmes's remark suggests the prospect of further "fighting." Assume that the first fire department vehicles enter the roundabout *without* lights and sirens. Collisions occur, disputes will re-engage the continuum of inquiry, and the conditional exception will be worked out in a further convergence.

Dewey was not concerned with utilitarian theory per se, but rather with addressing the actual process of social intelligence. The insight to be emphasized is that, in an actively disputed legal context, any rule resolving a given dispute is indeed (as Rawls saw in 1955) rooted in a *practice;* but the practice in effect *replaces* an earlier unsettled calculus of opposing reasons—and this only happens upon successful *adaptation.* That is, a *real and often intractable conflict* has been at stake, and a potentially continuing one. Resolving conflicts has precedence over any immediate utilitarian balance, just as it does over Arrow's calculations. As noted above, the background of broader conflicts (many yet unresolved) is unrecognized by the analytical model of extensionalism. The varied and emergent nature of utility conflicts is simply invisible to, and unseen by, the instantaneous utility camera. What does this mean for Lyons's argument about Rawls's "escape clause"?

Rules that work in real life have a history, and are rooted in the survival instinct of society—what Friedrich Hayek called "custom" (a presumption that underlies Hayek's aversion to *de novo* legislation[15]). Consequentialists like Lyons, Hooker, and other writers wrestling with the extensionalist problem treat them as maximization formulas, hence the additional concern of current rule-consequentialism with explaining public acceptance and compliance.[16] They fail to recognize that *previously settled* conflicts underlie and explain both *acceptance* of, and *compliance* with, what extensionalism sees as "de facto"

[15] See chapter 10 *infra.*

[16] See Hooker, "The Role(s) of Rules in Consequentialist Ethics."

rules. Thus, for Dewey's continuum, any "exception to the rule" (which extensionalism still assumes to be based on the maximizing calculus) requires *further* convergence through the resolution of *further conflict*. In other words, Lyons's objection to the "escape clause" assumes that the reasons environment is static throughout the often extended process of dispute resolution, which itself has contributed, and continues to contribute, to the existence and redefinition of relevant practice. As I hope to demonstrate, this is not as intricate as it may sound.

What about Lyons's claim, that "The considerations which justify using the de facto moral rules to begin with, and those which determine justifiable exceptions to them, are all of one piece"? I suggest that they are *not at all* part of the same extensionalist "picture," as the private considerations of individual drivers, presumably argued in a succession of cases (in the continuum of inquiry), leading toward adoption of the practice and eventual rule, have progressively been dismissed and are ultimately no longer relevant to the adopted practice.

The convergence of opposing purposes is implicit in working out the rules of the road. So then, I ask, is an exception always already covered? According to Lyons, "If one accepts Act-Utilitarianism one can view the de facto moral rules as if they have the (AU) escape clause as an implicit qualification." If a claim of exception came from the local fire department, the rule must adapt to allow a general exception for fire equipment—but a *conditional* one, based on acceptance of a new practice, only when displaying lights and sirens. Here too, the exception might have met with extended dispute; the first fire department vehicles entered the roundabout *without* lights and sirens, collisions occurred, and the dispute re-engaged the continuum of inquiry to adopt the conditional exception in a further "convergence."

This ongoing process (which Holmes called "specification") may appear more efficient through legislation, but successful legislation on major questions in a democracy (like labor organization) has followed considerable dispute and outright conflict. Acceptance and compliance with new rules do not automatically follow legislative decisions, but must be established incrementally in successive judgments (the process of agonistic deliberation through extended conflict is the subject of the following chapter). Specification, through repetition of disputes and particular judgments, creates patterns of conduct that can be judicially recognized, as prophylactic practices are adopted and approved, and as broader standards of conduct emerge from retrospective judicial findings of similarity, in what Edward Levi in 1949 called a "moving classification system," resolving disputes and guiding public conduct.[17]

---

[17] Levi, *Introduction to Legal Reasoning*, 4.

Extensionalism, on the other hand, posits a sweeping and fatal (but woefully unexamined) challenge to any utilitarian regime of rules, recently summarized as follows by Hooker:

> Here is why some have thought rule-consequentialism collapses into practical equivalence with act-consequentialism. Consider a rule that rule-consequentialism purports to favor—e.g., "don't steal." Now suppose an agent is in some situation where stealing would produce more good than not stealing. If rule-consequentialism selects rules on the basis of their expected good, rule-consequentialism seems driven to admit that compliance with the rule "don't steal except when . . . or . . . or . . ." is better than compliance with the simpler "don't steal." This point generalizes. In other words, for every situation where compliance with some rule would not produce the greatest expected good, rule-consequentialism seems driven to favor instead compliance with some amended rule that does not miss out on producing the greatest expected good in the case at hand. But if rule-consequentialism operates this way, then in practice it will end up requiring the very same acts that act-consequentialism requires.[18]

Hooker's tacit acceptance of extensionalism, that "don't steal" is (in Lyons's phrase) an "elliptical formulation of a ceteris paribus rule" and therefore cannot be distinguished from an act-utilitarian scheme, misses the crucial point of *specification*. The overbroad "don't steal" generalization fails to reflect and define an actual specified rule-based practice. Stealing is constantly being specified. The problem of redefining theft continues today in disputes over newly digitized intellectual property, requiring specification of computer practices.

This account of rule formation implies an environment of constant development and revision, rather than an always static landscape of clear and detailed utilitarian permissibility and impermissibility. Deweyan rules emerge from extended normative inquiry and convergent practices that depend in detail on feedback from society in the resolution of recurring disputes. Multiple opposing arguments from utility will apply to early novel cases, before eventual classification makes them irrelevant, as similarities of conduct are established and accepted. Various "q"s are transformed by the adaptive convergent definitions of larger "Q"s.

The main difference between Dewey and conventional utilitarianism lies in the assumption by the latter of the existence of a "right answer" in every moral inquiry. This assumption continues until the present day, in studies of act- and rule-consequentialism. This will be the subject of the next chapter (as well as chapter 9) which will address the issues that are opened up by the

---

[18] Hooker, "Rule Consequentialism," *Stanford Encyclopedia of Philosophy* (2023), https://plato.stanford.edu/entries/consequentialism-rule/.

prospective nonexistence of an immediate right answer, where dispute and conflict are engaged in a new emergent problem.

For a pragmatist model of inquiry, the impingement of experience on moral knowledge begins with the necessity of a common need: the resolution of particular disputes that (when unresolved) threaten the social order. The new dispute is often first conceived as either novel or original, or as situated in a gray area equidistant from opposing prior precedents. Over time, further experience establishes both similarities and differences in the emerging sense of a core problem. While the original dispute may *suggest* a general problem, it must be more precisely determined (or specified) before a general rule can be adopted through accepted practice.

Resolution of the uncertain case requires revising an *actual* context, not just an immediate conceptual *sense* of context, because a complex larger problem may be implicated in the specific dispute. A *pragmatic* grounding of rules on utility requires abandoning the momentary, camera-flash model of normative reality. The camera cannot detect the broader *Q*s in different stages of completion. One might say that Dewey's normative ontology does not imply a fixed landscape, but something more like a variable and constantly changing seascape, with some areas of settled calm, and other areas of turbulence, a "dappled world," to borrow Nancy Cartwright's metaphor for the conceptual environment of natural science.[19]

Dewey's naturalized utilitarianism is exemplified by a study of law. It translates into a general normative theory, more empirically based than abstract utilitarianism. The process of convergence implies more than a purely cognitive dimension to the analyzing and reconciling process. There must also be a convergence of communal practice and *action*. This means that *compliance*, the incentivized tendency of actors to follow the particular rule, and *acceptance*, the belief that a given rule is necessary and correct, are generated locally on a piecemeal basis, rather than globally and uniformly, from reliance on a presumptive utility calculus, majestic Kantian or Rawlsian principle or principles, or an "ideal code," as Brad Hooker has proposed.[20]

In every situation where compliance with some rule would not produce the greatest expected good, rule-consequentialism seems driven to favor instead compliance with some rule, and ultimately with some *amended* rule, one that includes all of the possible exceptions. It does not want to miss producing the greatest expected good in every *possible* case. But if rule-consequentialism operates this way, then in practice it will end up requiring the very same acts

[19] Nancy Cartwright, *The Dappled World: A Study of the Boundaries of Science* (Cambridge: Cambridge University Press, 1999).

[20] Hooker, *Ideal Code Real World* (Oxford: Oxford University Press, 2000).

that act-consequentialism requires. So it really doesn't provide any support for rules at all.

This leads to trouble for the very idea of utilitarianism, as a moral balance and as a test for the right action in any circumstances. Dewey's viewpoint is not so much an *anti*-utilitarianism as a radical *naturalist* utilitarianism. As both Sidgwick and Singer have noted at length, classical utilitarianism presents basic conceptual problems, like reconciling the good of all with the good of the individual: the conflict of egoism and benevolence. Dewey's problematic continuum presents a potential particularized reconciliation of traditional puzzles through the actual process of negotiation and adjustment. Instead of viewing egoism as inherently opposed to benevolence, Dewey's continuum relies on it for the presentation (in particular problems) of comprehensive arguments required for stable outcomes. The degree of benevolence may then be calibrated toward the relative success of the resolution.

Dewey's fully naturalized utilitarianism in the problematic continuum opens up questions that the universal maximization principle ignores. I mentioned earlier that it is a *lived* utilitarianism, one that comes with and cannot be separated from constant conflicts over shared problems. I mentioned how legal experience exemplifies conflict resolution; opposing sides in a typical case that gets to the higher courts of appeal will submit written briefs replete with references to prior published cases, not only from the court involved, but from other courts that have ruled in somewhat similar circumstances. The lawyers are buttressing their strongest factual claims with examples that have some arguable similarity. Historically, this has happened not just with everyday matters, but with major issues like race and gender discrimination and labor strikes in organization.

I should add a caveat here, to the effect that the agonistic process as I have outlined it may sound more orderly and manageable than it is. My main concern is to identify and distinguish preference conflict from other models of group conflict that ignore the adjustments that characterize problem-solving in a free society. Although an orderly classical utilitarianism can't be lived, a more disorderly one is *being* lived.

It has often been suggested that "democracy is a sort of *applied* utilitarianism, possessing utilitarianism's weaknesses as well as its strengths." It is "an institutional way of determining the happiness of the greatest number," and "[d]emocratic laws generally tend to promote the welfare of the greatest possible number; for they emanate from the majority of the citizens, who are subject to error, but who cannot have an interest opposed to their own advantage."[21] But this view of democracy is unrealistic in the extreme,

[21] See Jonathan Riley, "Utilitarian Ethics and Democratic Government," *Ethics*, vol. 100, no. 2 (January 1990), 335–348.

distorted by the conception of a nonexistent "viewpoint of the universe." As argued above, there is no hypothetical omniscient universe to assess the immediate balance of self-interest and benevolence, of diverse personal and general forms of utility, happiness, or welfare, all of which are in constant dispute. The universal viewpoint must be abandoned, in the hope that actual humans can find a way to fairly and democratically solve their shared problems.

Chapter 5

Agonistic Deliberation

The term "agonistic deliberation," with which this chapter begins, presents a challenge to elucidate, but a necessary one. How do democratic communication and dialogue occur in the context of endemic, problematic situations? Philip Kitcher's eleven steps recognize that deliberation may begin with group "resentment," leading to recognition of a situation that is "prima facie problematic." It then seeks "proposals" for a "change in moral practice."[1] Resentment by an injured group can certainly serve to open a dispute, but it is hardly the only impulse driving preference aggregation.[2]

Kitcher is right that change in practice is necessary for resolution. Change in habit and practice requires more than "appropriate conversation" and "representative discussion." It has to lead, as he suggests, to the "ranking" of urgency among relevant conditions and the necessity of imposing restrictions on "ideals of the self." These are significant hurdles to overcome in a strictly conversational setting. There are other significant and often greater hurdles: ingrained and opposing habits that block consideration of each other's point of view. They will be unlikely to change only through a discrete conversation, however extended.

The phrase "agonistic deliberation" is not found in Dewey's writing, but it captures a key aspect of his social intelligence of problem-resolution. The term is a counterpoint to mainly dialogical models, like Kitcher's ideal conversation, John Rawls' reflective equilibrium, Richard Rorty's conversation,

---

[1] See chapter 2, *supra*.

[2] Axel Honneth explores this form of motivation in *The Struggle for Recognition: The Moral Grammar of Social Conflicts* (Cambridge: Polity Press, 1995). The sequence of disrespect, demand for recognition, and social change constitute his "developmental logic" of collective movements. This confines the notion of social conflict to a far smaller context than the broad agonism that Dewey considers, where many diverse motivations can drive the aggregation of opposing preferences. See chapter 10 *infra*.

and Juergen Habermas' communicative rationality. It refers to the diverse ways in which social intelligence reaches outcomes in multiple extended problematic situations. If classical utilitarianism can't be lived, agonistic deliberation captures the reality that humans *actually* live, and is how Dewey's *naturalized* version works. It is the mechanism through which competing preferences and conceptions evaluate and balance utility and value.

There are many different ways in which problems are recognized and defined, as disputes emerge and develop often over extended periods of time. The process is far from uniform or ideal, and is subject to disinformation, distortion, and manipulation. The very diversity of human problems in the last century complicated Dewey's contention that empirical evidence, or an analogy with natural science, should apply to social phenomena. At least since Robert Boyle's experimentalism in the eighteen century,[3] natural science has developed empirical practices, and Dewey sought to advance a comparable approach for ethics as part of his "empirical naturalism." It was never clear to his critics whether and how the practices of empiricism that had developed so successfully in matters of scientific utility could be applied to matters of ethics, welfare, and social utility.

What has been shown so far, with letter symbols (like P for problem, q for small questions, Q for large ones), is an approximate notation of the problematic continuum of inquiry. A distinguishing feature of agonistic deliberation in social conflicts is the nature of uncertainty. Uncertainty for an immediate problem, where the dimensions are fairly clear and the relevant facts are in existence, may permit stable resolution to be attained contemporaneously. Uncertainty for an extended problem, where the full dimensions are unclear and many relevant facts and adjusted practices are yet to be established, is subject only to hypothesis or experiment. If resolution depends on future-adjusted and transformed habits and beliefs, extending even to language and terminology, the degree of uncertainty is radically increased. Future agonistic uncertainty is *radical* in the sense of being fundamentally and qualitatively different from immediate uncertainty.[4]

---

[3] Steven Shapin and Simon Schaffer, *Leviathan and the Air-Pump: Hobbes, Boyle, and the Experimental Life* (Princeton: Princeton University Press, 1985).

[4] In the inquiry into social problems, resolution requires what Dewey often characterized as transformation in reasoning, as in the passage cited earlier describing the difficult and complex progress from the uncertainty of outright conflict to 'modified' understanding:

> Since transformation of a problematic situation (a confused situation whose constituents conflict with one another) is effected by interaction of specially discriminated existential conditions, facts have to be determined in their dual function as obstacles and as resources. . . . No existing situation can be modified without counteracting obstructive and deflecting forces that render a given situation confused and conflicting. Dewey, *Logic*, 499–500; LW 12:493.

Whereas empiricism in science is often associated with immediate observation, ethical empiricism involves more than calculation from known or available "facts." In ethical or normative matters, it involves adjusting opposing preferences and different conceptions of utility grounded in clashing habits and beliefs. For Dewey, the preferred term for evidence in this domain was "experience." Experience is acquired through successive judgments, supplying the kind of information that informs normative discovery. A specific dispute may first present both aspects of uncertainty. Stable resolution for a broad problem depends first on finding the dimensions of the problem at hand, represented by a small q. Dimensions of the larger problem (the large Q) are developed through the resolution of specific cases, leading to a more general definition and resolution.

As there is contestation at every stage, individual case determinations constitute the accessible framework of an *agonistic* deliberation, reflecting the degree to which any outcome may continue to be contested. Deliberation begins from case to case and is case-specific, while the larger question takes time and experience to define as well as to resolve. Self-preferential considerations must be modified to conform to a new practice meeting the needs of others engaged in the relevant domain of experience. This will require multiple judgments and experimentation with solutions. Competing aspects of utility, like Sidgwick's dualism of practical reason, must be worked out piecemeal and in many specific contexts.

Kitcher's requirement for change in moral practice highlights the importance of experiential inputs to a problem: its recognition, definition, and progress through stages of information and the gathering and assessment of relevant information. This is the process represented by Dewey's phrase "empirical naturalism" and the nature of his naturalized utilitarianism. An immediate settlement, even through legislation, may not fully represent all affected interests. As an example (prominent in the literature of jurisprudence), the Anglo-American law of product liability has a long history and, given changing technology, is still not settled to the satisfaction of manufacturers, distributors, and the consumer public.

Recovery for an injury from a product that injures a purchaser, like an exploding boiler, might be decided on its specific facts after investigation has established existing evidence of a mechanical flaw and negligence by the seller. However, the general question of liability for manufacturers or sellers of other "dangerous instrumentalities" and those in the chain of later ownership who may recover absent applicable warranties must await sufficient future experience. For this reason, general arguments appealing to cultural, moral, or religious values are hypothetical at an early stage and not dispositive.

This was illustrated in 1949 in Edward Levi's classic essay on the history of the "inherently dangerous" rule, by which the original provider of a product found to be inherently injurious could be held liable for loss to a third party, absent direct contractual relations between the defendant and the injured party. Levi's hundred-year story of this circuitous path of legal conceptualization begins in 1816 with the case of *Dixon v. Bell*, where damages were recovered for injury from a loaded firearm; the court found liability without attempting an explanatory classification. It continues with *Langridge v. Levy*, a defective gun that exploded in the plaintiff's hand, where a distinction was offered between "inherent" dangerousness and faulty construction. The distinction was again urged in *Winterbottom v. Wright*, the case of a defective coach, and was recognized as law in *Longmeid v. Holliday,* involving an exploding lamp.[5]

The next stage involved diverse applications where the distinction between "inherent" dangerousness and faulty construction was variously applied to cases of mislabeled poison, hair wash, a circular saw, an exploding boiler, and a painting scaffold. As courts struggled to make sense of it, other considerations such as due care, direct or indirect dealing with third-party litigants, and other factors were analyzed at length. The story famously ends with an expanded foreseeability test for liability by Judge Nathan Cardozo in *MacPherson v. Buick* (1916), involving a car that collapsed with a defective wheel. Levi's portrayal of the story is one of the continuing intrusion of social influences in the construction (and, in this case, the ultimate failure) of a legal phrase in a tentative and experimental process, drawn out over many years, as the meaning of "inherent" or "imminent" danger was applied in multiple contexts.

Successive stages in the inquiry were evident to Levi:

> The first stage is the creation of the legal concept which is built up as cases are compared. The period is one in which the court fumbles for a phrase. Several phrases may be tried out; the misuse or misunderstanding of words itself may have an effect. The concept sounds like another, and the jump to the second is made. The second stage is the period when the concept is more or less fixed, although reasoning by example continues to classify items inside and out of the concept. The third stage is the breakdown of the concept, as reasoning by example has moved so far ahead as to make it clear that the suggestive influence of the word is no longer desired.[6]

Levi's account provides insight into Dewey's observation of experience gathered through successive judgments to inform general understanding and

---

[5] Levi, *Introduction to Legal Reasoning,* 5f.

[6] Levi, *Introduction to Legal Reasoning*, 8–9.

normative necessity. Particular judgments force the inquiry forward, as they have in the matter of assisted euthanasia. As Dewey wrote in the 1938 *Logic*,

> There is continuity in inquiry. The conclusions reached in one inquiry become means, material and procedural, of carrying on further inquiries. In the latter, the results of earlier inquiries are taken and used without being re-subjected to examination.[7]

More than one choice is presented over time:

> The essence of the moral situation is an internal and intrinsic conflict; the necessity for judgment and for choice comes from the fact that one has to manage forces with no common denominator.[8]

Yet the path of judgment in a controversial problem can be cut short by the political process. The problem of controlling gun violence is now receiving a greater degree of public inquiry, as have the other areas of product liability, despite legislated protections for the firearms industry. The problem of personal injury from messages, images, and false information disseminated on digital social media has received limited legal inquiry due to Section 230 of the Communications Decency Act of 1996. At an early stage of the developing problem, Section 230 provided immunity for online computer services with respect to third-party content generated by their users by treating the services as "distributors" rather than "publishers."

These were arguably premature legislative conclusions that have foreclosed detailed inquiry into the dimensions of the problems and possible long-term solutions to them.[9] This doesn't mean that further inquiry into both of the problems is foreclosed, but only that it has been largely removed from litigation and hence further agonistic deliberation by lawyers in the courtroom.

While the distinction between early and later decisions appears in Levi's narrative, it is nevertheless unrecognized in contemporary legal theory and the philosophy of law. Legal uncertainty in academic circles has instead long been identified with the immediate question of how a given immediate case

---

7 Dewey, *Logic*, 140; LW 12:143.

8 Dewey, "Three Independent Factors in Morals," 316; LW 5:280.

9 Section 230(c)(2) further provides "Good Samaritan" protection from civil liability for operators of interactive computer services in the good faith removal or moderation of third-party material they deem "obscene, lewd, lascivious, filthy, excessively violent, harassing, or otherwise objectionable, whether or not such material is constitutionally protected." Section 230 was developed in response to a pair of lawsuits against online discussion platforms in the early 1990s that resulted in different interpretations of whether the service providers should be treated as publishers or, alternatively, as distributors of content created by their users. Its authors, Representatives Christopher Cox and Ron Wyden, believed interactive computer services should be treated as distributors, not liable for the content they distributed, as a means to protect the growing internet at the time.

is to be decided, no matter how complex and controversial, without regard to the obscurity of a larger problem. The last century defined the issue as one of "formalism" versus "realism." Formalism referred to deduction from accessible legal authorities, a conception of law as comprehensive, logically ordered, and determinate, while legal "realism" arose in reaction to the idea that judges could always find authority to engage in a deduction producing the right outcome.[10] Realism countered that judges actually decide according to their personal preferences and then *construct* a legal analysis to justify their desired outcome.[11]

The focus of both formalism and realism was on the judicial response to the individual case, not the larger problem. The influential Oxford University scholar Herbert Hart decried in 1983 the unedifying choice between the two, which he called an "oscillation" between judging according to personal preference and instead always finding a realm of deductive certainty. Hart commented that in addressing this American jurisprudence, it has oscillated between two extremes, which he called the "Nightmare" and the "Noble Dream":

> The Nightmare is this. Litigants in law cases consider themselves entitled to have from judges an application of the existing law to their disputes, not to have new law made for them. Of course it is accepted that what the existing law is need not be and very often is not obvious, and the trained expertise of the lawyer may be needed to extract it from the appropriate sources. But for conventional thought, the image of the judge, to use the phrase of an eminent English Judge, Lord Radcliffe, is that of the "objective, impartial, erudite, and experienced declarer of the law," not to be confused with the very different image of the legislator.[12]

Hart called this image of the judge an illusion in distinguishing him from the legislator, as the expectations which it excites are doomed to disappointment.

> In fact the most famous decisions of the Supreme Court have at once been so important and so controversial in character and so unlike what ordinary courts ordinarily do in deciding cases that no serious jurisprudence or philosophy of law could avoid asking with what general conception of the nature of law were such judicial powers compatible.[13]

---

[10] See Brian Tamanaha, *Beyond the Formalist-Realist Divide* (Princeton: Princeton University Press, 2010).

[11] Lewellyn, *The Common Law Tradition: Deciding Appeals* (Boston: Little Brown and Co., 1960), 118.

[12] Hart, "American Jurisprudence Through English Eyes: The Nightmare and the Noble Dream," *Georgia Law Review*, vol. 11, no. 5 (September 1977), 969, 972; in *Essays in Jurisprudence and Philosophy* (Oxford: Clarendon Press, 1983).

[13] Hart, "American Jurisprudence Through English Eyes: The Nightmare and the Noble Dream," 971.

Hart found himself agreeing with criticism of the Supreme Court as acting like a third legislative chamber when, in the period of the Supreme Court's activism between the Civil War and the New Deal, they ruled unconstitutional, under the due process clause, social and economic welfare legislation, such as statutes fixing maximum hours, minimum wages, and price controls. He noted the Court's decision in *Roe* in 1973,

> sweeping away legislation against abortion in many states of the union, on an issue where much moral opinion was against reform. It achieved at a single judicial blow more than the last of eight English parliamentary struggles over a period of fifty years secured in my country. And this was done in the name of a right of the mother to privacy which is nowhere mentioned in the Constitution but was read into the due process clause as a fundamental liberty.[14]

Given this history, it is not surprising that one branch of American jurisprudential thought should be concerned to present the Nightmare view that, in spite of pretensions to the contrary, judges make the law that they apply to litigants and are not impartial, objective declarers of existing law. What remains surprising is that in some variations of this jurisprudence, the Nightmare view should be presented by serious American jurists not merely as a feature of certain types of difficult adjudication—as in the case of constitutional adjudication, in which hugely general phrases like "due process" or "equal protection of the laws" somehow have to be fitted to particular cases—but as if adjudication were essentially a form of lawmaking, never a matter of declaring the existing law, and with the suggestion that until this truth was grasped and the conventional myths that obscured it dissipated, the nature of law could not be understood.

> In conclusion let me say this. I have portrayed American jurisprudence as beset by two extremes, the Nightmare and the Noble Dream: the view that judges always make and never find the law they impose on litigants, and the opposed view that they never make it. Like any other nightmare and any other dream, these two are, in my view, illusions, though they have much of value to teach the jurist in his waking hours. The truth, perhaps unexciting, is that sometimes judges do one and sometimes the other.[15]

Hart here comes tantalizingly close to the transformative continuum of legal inquiry in describing judges as sometimes appearing to do one thing and sometimes the other, but he sees no apparent reason. The actual reason is that an *early* case of a new problem is one in which the novelty of circumstances

[14] Hart, "American Jurisprudence Through English Eyes: The Nightmare and the Noble Dream," 973.
[15] Hart, "American Jurisprudence Through English Eyes: The Nightmare and the Noble Dream," 989.

often defies comparison with any previously settled rule, precedent, or analogy. Hence, there is an appearance of indeterminacy that must nevertheless be addressed in a judicial decision, but on its particular facts. At a *later* stage, sufficient similarity among separate judgments may have been sufficiently "unified," in Dewey's term, to permit the statement of a generality from which deduction is possible. So Hart is right that judges sometimes do one thing and sometimes the other: the indeterminacy aspect of realism relates to the early particular case, and the deductive aspect of formalism relates to cases in the later stage.

Hart's "oscillation" can be described as a "gestalt switch" caused by attempting to form a universal synchronic generalization amidst evidence of distinct, but local and diachronic, characteristics. The opposing positions of formalism and realism were, in essence, forms of legal *objectivism* and *relativism.* A related "oscillation" in philosophy, concerning the definition of truth, was decried in 1981 by Hilary Putnam as a perennial "gestalt switch" between metaphysical objectivism and relativism. Legal theory followed suit, failing to find importance for judicial policy of the continuum of inquiry in Levi's analysis, just as pragmatic philosophers like Hilary Putnam did not see that Dewey's transformative continuum might explain the *gestalt* as a failure to recognize that the very progress of human inquiry could explain a relation between two distinct forms of uncertainty. The idea of legal formalism, which assumes that general rules, once determined, remain fixed in application, was clearly rejected by Levi, who showed that rules change from case to case and are remade with each case. "Yet," he wrote,

> this change in the rules is the indispensable dynamic quality of law. It occurs because the scope of a rule of law, and therefore its meaning, depends upon a determination of what facts will be considered similar to those present when the rule was first announced. The finding of similarity or difference is the key step in the legal process. . . . Yet it is a system of rules; the rules are discovered in the process of determining similarity or difference.[16]

Once similarity is found, deduction is possible. This form of empirical discovery in law was illustrated in Dewey's *naturalized* utilitarianism, as rules are not adopted by an immediate calculation of maximum utility but by a search for similarity among successive judgments.

Crucial to problematic inquiry is a feedback loop whereby each decision introduces further relevant knowledge into ongoing practices within the relevant community of stakeholders, like manufacturers and consumers. As Dewey wrote in 1938, "The conclusions reached in one inquiry become

---

[16] Levi, *Introduction to Legal Reasoning*, 2–3.

means, material and procedural, of carrying on further inquiries." It is thus that the legal process responds over time to the relevant community's idea of fairness:

> Reasoning by example in the law is the key to many things. It indicates in part the hold which the law process has over the litigants. They have participated in the law-making. They are bound by something they helped to make. Moreover, the examples or analogies urged by the parties bring into the law the common ideals of the society. The ideas have their day in court, and they will have their day again. This is what makes the hearing fair, rather than any idea that the judge is completely impartial, for of course he cannot be completely so. Moreover, the hearing in a sense compels at least vicarious participation by all the citizens, for the rule which is made, even though ambiguous, will be law as to them.[17]

Thus, there is a gradual adaptation of liability to the changing social environment; the process is not purely judge-centric or a synchronic utility calculation. There is a broader problem that must go through iterations of definition and redefinition, and while lawyers and judges participate in the process, they do not control it, nor can they resolve the underlying conflicts.

Any fully accurate theory or philosophy of law should recognize that fact. If law is a process of inquiry into shared problems, however imperfect, then it is a mistake to treat "law" not as part of normative inquiry but as an autonomous or separate body of rules and authoritative texts. Yet that is exactly what contemporary theory still does, having failed to recognize the full import of Levi's analysis. That account was distinct from legal realism's myopic focus on the individual's difficult case.[18] As Dewey had already noted in *Studies in Logical Theory*, conjoint judgment is "directed and controlled by reference to a gradually developing purpose." Levi wrote in 1949:

> The existence of some facts in common brings into play the general rule. If this is really reasoning, then by common standards, thought of in terms of closed systems, it is imperfect unless some overall rule has announced that this common and ascertainable similarity is to be decisive. But no such fixed prior rule

[17] Levi, *Introduction to Legal Reasoning*, 5.

[18] Legal realists shared opposition to a "formalist" model of judicial decision, that judges arrive at their decisions by applying law to facts, and the processes of finding the law and finding the facts are mutually independent. The decision was thought to follow deductively as in the syllogism. Realists criticized this model in two ways: as failing to recognize that the two findings are linked, and as reversing the end result and the beginning of the process. Instead, conflicting patterns suggest themselves, judges await an intuitive flash of understanding, and work back from the conclusion to the reasons. Gerald Postema, *Treatise of Legal Philosophy and General Jurisprudence*, vol. 11 (Dordrecht: Springer Netherlands, 2011), 118–119.

> exists. . . . Therefore it appears that the kind of reasoning involved in the legal process is one in which the classification changes as the classification is made.[19]

As Levi described it, the common ideas of the society have a role in shaping the law.

> The concept is suggested in arguing difference or similarity in a brief, but wins no approval from the court. The idea achieves standing in the society. It is suggested again to a court. The court this time reinterprets the prior case and in doing so adopts the rejected idea. In subsequent cases, the idea is given further definition and is tied to other ideas which have been accepted by courts.
>
> It is now no longer the idea which was commonly held in the society. It becomes modified in subsequent cases. Ideas first rejected but which gradually have won acceptance now push what has become a legal category out of the system or convert it into something which may be its opposite. The process is one in which the ideas of the community and of the social sciences, whether correct or not, as they win acceptance in the community, control legal decisions. Erroneous ideas, of course, have played an enormous part in shaping the law. An idea, adopted by the court, is in a superior position to influence conduct and opinion in the community; judges, after all, are rulers. And the adoption of an idea by a court reflects the power structure of the community. But reasoning by example will operate to change the idea after it has been adopted.[20]

Edward Levi's painstaking analysis illustrates how agonistic reasoning in that context worked case by case as a shaping mechanism, responding to the necessity of compensation for injury and loss. As injury happens in a manner suggesting a non-accidental cause, recovery is sought; lawyers must simultaneously seek both recovery and explanatory justification. Where no warranty relation exists between the parties, the idea of dangerousness is proposed, specific to the case but with implicit relation to a prospective standard. The future conduct, of consumers, manufacturers, and distributors, is affected by each stage in the process. The very subject under "deliberation" or "dialogue" is not the same from case to case as stages of the inquiry proceed.

Similarly, voluntary euthanasia and the MeToo experience in gender discrimination began with unique cases that represented a new stage of an earlier problem. The movement toward educational affirmative action was a stage in addressing the discriminatory treatment of racial minorities. Legal litigation has been part of a broader social process of coming to understand and address an underlying problematic situation. There are winners and losers in particular judgments, but also a gradual transformation of future practices.

[19] Levi, *Introduction to Legal Reasoning*, 3–4.
[20] Levi, *Introduction to Legal Reasoning*, 5–6.

Product safety has been influenced by product distribution and corporate profit. Family and medical concerns and conditions now influence medical euthanasia. Protective conditions of employment for younger women are sought in MeToo litigation. Kitcher's ranking of interests occurs over time as new practices evolve toward a stage of greater stability.

Despite Levi's diachronic model of law as part of a broader normative inquiry, legal theory has failed to recognize its importance. Dewey's situational sense was recognized by the realist scholar Karl Llewellyn, but not its extended problematic aspect. Concerned with the relativist implications of the "nightmare" of legal realism, Llewellyn sought to respond to pervasive skepticism in the wake of writings to the effect that available rules allowed judges to support any outcome. He undertook a lengthy study of the appellate process to address what he saw as a crisis of confidence among practicing lawyers: "a new corrosiveness" over "whether there is any reckonability in the work of our appellate courts." Examining the development of case law and its relation to doctrine, he looked in particular at the question of what aspects of predictability might convince lawyers not to despair over the judicial process.

Llewellyn's analysis produced various "stabilizing factors" in the profession as a whole, but more persuasive was his identification of a common element underlying and organizing the often confused mass of legal precedents, something he called the "situation sense." Searching a wide range of appellate opinions, Llewellyn noted that the better decisions avoided a formal style of citation and analyzed "the differential impact of the facts of the individual case and the facts of the situation taken as a type." Within this situation-sense lay, in Llewellyn's view, the key to better appellate decisions, increasingly replacing the formal style. In these opinions, an "open willingness to recanvass a situation is present in an unusual degree, the result being now confirmation of the old, now the clearing up of divergent leads, now a new direction or position."[21]

Llewellyn's situation-sense suggests a practical purpose within the appellate process: the finding of an underlying functional similarity among diverse particular judgments, indispensable to a diachronic continuum, coordinating legal predication with the external feedback from evolving practices. Judges and juries look to the immediate outcome to assess what will work in the future. Llewellyn noted that this sense of similarity (he called it

[21] Lewellyn, *The Common Law Tradition,* 148–149: "We shall demonstrate that . . . sense and wisdom are thus used daily not only in application of doctrine or in choice among competing rules but in an area by no means frequently observed, to wit, in the on-going, careful readjustment of doctrine to needs by way of overt recourse to the sense which ought to control in the given type-situation. We shall show that this is not novel, but is old, is not occasional, but is standard, is not unsettling, but is stabilizing."

"reckonability") is elusive, "sometimes far from evident, though given, and is often enough not given at all, but requires to be formed or forged from materials that are raw or rough and can be scanty."

> The fact is that every opinion is in one aspect an argument, an argument prepared by a lawyer. It is an argument to the writer himself, is an argument to his brethren, it is an argument to bar or public or both. The fact is, moreover, that once a lawyer accepts an outcome, two things happen even though he may be stewing hard over how to shape the argument. The one of these things is that, without much work or thought, the facts reweigh, realign, recolor themselves, as has been noted above, into a familiar and therefore persuasive pattern or gestalt.[22]

As he examined this phenomenon in different jurisdictions, Llewellyn identified various competing factors, including personal ones, of collegiality as well as competing commercial and private visions. Finding and describing the situation-sense was a creative process.[23]

In the course of his exposition of the legal situation-sense, Llewellyn noted Levi's essay on the history of the "inherently dangerous" rule. Llewellyn's own comment on Levi is instructive as to why transformation in the feedback continuum, so essential to Dewey, was not fully recognized by legal scholars:

> His [Levi's] interest centers more than, at this point, mine does on the manner of rationalizing the case results and on the manner of their integration into lines for *future guidance* [my emphasis], but his picture is directly relevant to the processes of actual deciding: the guiding, limiting, and suggestive power of a concept label or slogan; the incursion of changing or changed community ideas and standards by way of shift in attitudes or in the language meaning of such a label; the impact of life conditions and of learned categories and meanings via "reasoning by example" on the legal classification of a novel problem-situation or of a novel variant.[24]

Llewellyn's reference to "the manner of rationalizing the case results and on the manner of their integration into lines for future guidance" suggests that he saw that Levi was interested in external sources of influence on the growth of legal knowledge, as it was developed case by case in a social continuum

22 Levi, *Introduction to Legal Reasoning*, 118.

23 "Beneath what looks on the page as 'mere' following . . . there swirls a constant current of creation. . . . This is the region in which the modern logician revels as he exposes the manipulation of the minor premise and watches the reasoned clamp some concept-label upon a still-amorphous mass of problem-facts and thereby haul 'the case' in under a major premise which may have no particular need in either history or reason to apply." Levi, *Introduction to Legal Reasoning*, 116.

24 Levi, *Introduction to Legal Reasoning*, 125.

of inquiry. Yet Llewelyn, even though aware of the social context in which it occurs, continued to focus only on the problem of deciding the immediate case on its own terms.

Writers in the prevailing traditions of jurisprudence have simply not been looking for a social continuum of inquiry in law. Formalism is basically deductivism, assuming an amplitude of general propositions into which all disputed conduct might fit, as if governed by an overall syllogism: (1) the law covers all cases; (2) this new dispute is a case; (3) the law covers this case. Against this, the realist model failed to propose a Deweyan alternative vision of empiricism in law. It did not view the succession of disputes as akin to the gathering of evidence.

Naturally, there are cases arising in many areas in which novelty is not a pronounced factor, cases fitting more comfortably within the terms of statutes or settled precedents. This context may be presumed to be mainly deductive. But the general realist focus on immediate uncertainty, rather than Levi's sense of extended inquiry into the larger problem, continued to hold the attention of legal scholars, creating what Grant Gilmore, in his famous Storrs Lecture of 1974, published as *The Ages of American Law*, called "The Age of Anxiety." Remarkably, the judge-centric and synchronic perspective on legal uncertainty continues to ignore the *extended* situation-sense, and views all legal uncertainty as an algorithmic positioning beyond a contemporaneous "foreground" of clear rules and texts. It ignores the positioning of cases in a diachronic relation to ongoing legal disputes and social problems, such as labor picketing in the late nineteenth century or assisted death in the late twentieth century.

The view of law as autonomous and self-contained, which characterized both formalism and realism, was reformulated with Herbert Hart's argument for a "positivist" separation of law and morals in his 1958 Oliver Wendell Holmes Lecture at Harvard, leading to his influential *The Concept of Law* of 1961. Ronald Dworkin countered Hart's defense of "positivist separation" with the claim that morals are included within the body of law as "rights" (in his *Taking Rights Seriously* of 1977). This would introduce the notion of judicial recourse to a *background* that is behind the body of rules but still open to judicial consideration. The background included principles that bear a "moral" character as a necessary resource for legal decisions in cases in which the "foreground" is disputed or indeterminate. The "background elements" of the legal system are the "principles and policies that lie behind the rules and texts that legal positivists emphasize."[25]

Meanwhile, a school of critical theorists (Roberto Unger, Duncan Kennedy, Mark Tushnet, and others) pressed the notion that the background has

[25] H. L. A. Hart, *The Concept of Law* (Oxford: Clarendon Press, 1961); Ronald Dworkin, *Taking Rights Seriously* (Cambridge: Harvard University Press, 1977).

no single author, its diverse perspectives deriving from continuing disagreement throughout the law's history. They posited a deep pluralism in the legal background: opposing principles found there are not only just rival tendencies but also incompatible visions or theories of what we owe to others and the collective life of our society.[26] Thus, Ronald Dworkin and the school known as Critical Legal Studies (CLS) *both* focused on the "background elements" of the legal system. According to CLS (taken as a general approach), the background is so riven with contradiction as to be capable of supporting any result and thus inadequate for definitive recourse.

The next chapter addresses the dominant conception of law as autonomous and separate, rather than part of a broader social intelligence that resolves problems through conflict, within and *outside* the law. What I have called "agonistic deliberation" is the phenomenon by which a free society conducts much of its social decision-making outside of electoral, representative, and bureaucratic mechanisms. It is distinct from the formal aspects of deliberation that characterize those mechanisms. Extended agonism is a discovery process and an adjustment process. It can be abbreviated by political decisions like Section 230 and by other premature generalizing options, such as ideological decisions by an appellate court. Recourse by appellate judges to "moral principles" risks the intrusion of personal ideology, overlooking the details of an emergent problem in favor of a sweeping universalizing decision.

---

[26] See Andrew Altman, *Critical Legal Studies: A Liberal Critique* (Princeton: Princeton University Press, 1990). Dworkin's position was that the presence of an array of decisions, riddled with contradictions, is itself already an "interpretation" of the background materials. The practice of interpretation plays a major role in Dworkin's later contribution to the broadened debate in *Justice for Hedgehogs* (Cambridge: The Belknap Press, 2011). Dworkin's interpretive "descriptive optimism" held that the background elements of a legal system like that of the United States are capable of bearing the heavy weight of determinate argument that Dworkin assigns to it in his theory of law. Jeremy Waldron contends that the comparison with CLS forces us to confront the question of how judges actually accomplish this—how do they choose from among the disparate body of principles and policies that are arguably embedded in legal texts and precedents. "Did Dworkin Ever Answer the Crits?" in *Exploring Law's Empire: The Jurisprudence of Ronald Dworkin*, ed. Scott Hershovitz (Oxford: Oxford Scholarship Online, 2009), 159ff. Along with their univocal view of hard cases, CLS and Dworkin privilege a judge-oriented individualist epistemology of legal principles. Against claims of difficulty, Dworkin invented a mythical super-judge "Hercules" to navigate the subtle and complex realm of principles, as knowable only (if at all) by an idealized judge.

Chapter 6

Uncertainty and Legal Theory

The distinguishing feature of deliberation in social conflicts is the radical nature of uncertainty, not so much for an immediate problem where the dimensions are clear and the relevant facts are in evidence, but for an extended problem where the dimensions are unclear and relevant facts and practices are yet to be established. Future agonistic uncertainty is radical in the sense of being fundamentally and qualitatively different from immediate uncertainty.

Of course, there are many court cases that do not involve a broader problem, where uncertainty is a mixture of unestablished facts as well as procedural complexity; lawyers have a talent for throwing massive amounts of legal and procedural complications into any dispute involving substantial stakes. My concern is with the uncertainty that involves broader problems of policy and value that are implicated by the specific issues raised in an actual contested case, like the 2014 Supreme Court case disputing an appropriate "buffer-zone" distance from abortion clinics to balance the rights of pro-life picketers against pregnant women seeking access to medical assistance. The broader issue of the right to abortion itself was not specifically raised by the pleadings, but was nevertheless implicated.[1]

John Dewey observed in his 1938 *Logic: The Theory of Inquiry* that a perceived problem is at first sufficiently ill-defined to be categorized as indeterminate: "Indeterminate situations are marked by confusion, obscurity, and conflict. An unsettled situation needs clarification because as it stands it gives no lead or cue to the way in which it may be resolved." This viewpoint

[1] The Supreme Court case is *McCullen v. Coakley*, 453 U.S. 199, 134 S. Ct. 2518 (2014), holding that Massachusetts' thirty-five-foot abortion buffer zones, established via amendments to that state's Reproductive Health Care Facilities Act, violated the First Amendment to the U.S. Constitution, because it limited free expression too broadly.

recognizes a danger implicit in any early judicial recourse to general principle: the influence of ideology and subjectivity in the judicial application of moral principles. That possibility is heightened by a tendency to applaud the unrestrained expression of time-honored values in times of public uncertainty and polarization. Dewey's experience with that phenomenon is discussed in the following chapter. From this vantage point, premature recourse to principle (and indeed to constitutional principle) may foreclose fact-based inquiry in unsettled controversies. This does not just mean factual testimony in the trial courts. Cass Sunstein explained in his 1999 book *One Case at a Time: Judicial Minimalism on the Supreme Court*, that the caution against premature generalization applies even to final constitutional courts of appeal.[2]

Principled resolution can foreclose inquiry into further experience. A judge's interpretive role is variably shared with the community at large and should properly exercise minimalist restraint in the exploratory stage of ongoing controversies. This presents a strong but largely unrecognized case for a judicially restrained jurisprudence, grounded in a participatory, or socialized, epistemology for legal principles. There must be ample space when appropriate for input from outside the adjudicatory system. When a dispute stands in relation to a broader and continuing controversy, the time for a principled decision may not be ripe. This highlights the distinct form of uncertainty that has, nevertheless, been commonly perceived as legal "indeterminacy."

Ronald Dworkin claimed that recourse to the background, in particular to certain principles that bear a "moral" character, affords a necessary resource for legal decisions in cases in which the foreground is disputed or indeterminate, and the background is, moreover, a sufficient resource for finding the right answer to any hard case. A leading example that he gave to demonstrate the legitimate legal embodiment of moral principle was the 1960 opinion in *Henningsen v. Bloomfield Motors, Inc.*, like *MacPherson v. Buick Motor Co.*, a lawsuit to recover for injuries caused by a defective automobile. Here, the plaintiff had signed a contract clearly limiting liability to the replacement of defective parts. In building his case against Herbert Hart's positivist separation of law and morals, Dworkin argued that a strict interpretation of the legal rules could only be overridden by general principle, and hence the court was obliged to appeal to a "moral principle," which Dworkin found in the court's recitation of an ancient maxim: "Is there any principle which is more familiar or more firmly embedded in the history of Anglo-American law than the basic doctrine that the courts will not permit themselves to be used as instruments of inequity and injustice?" The sweeping abstractness of this statement was only slightly improved by another remark by the court, "More specifically,

[2] *One Case at a Time: Judicial Minimalism on the Supreme Court* (Cambridge: Harvard University Press, 1999).

the courts generally refuse to lend themselves to the enforcement of a bargain in which one party had unjustly taken advantage of the economic necessities of another."[3]

Dworkin ignored the history of product liability in order to support his argument that principles are part of the law.[4] Edward Levi's account of *McPherson v. Buick Motor Co.* stands at odds with Dworkin's claim, viewing it as part of a long-sought solution to the problem of product injuries, rather than a conclusive demonstration of a moral element falling inside the boundary of law as a separate entity. Dworkin was thus able to argue in opposition to Hart that the analytical positivist boundary between law and morals is pierced by the real existence of moral principles. What it instead shows is that judicial opinions, like legal arguments, use the language of principle in strengthening a stable outcome to a broader problem. But Levi's history demonstrates that a long and intricate struggle, pitting consumers against sellers and manufacturers, lay behind the actual change in judicial language.

Dworkin argued at length in favor of the proposition that there is a uniquely correct answer to every legal question and that "the uniquely correct legal answer in every case is the uniquely correct moral response to the problem raised by the case."[5] As this issue arose after Dworkin's response to Hart's positivist separation of law and morals, and only then moved to the forefront of jurisprudence well after Dewey's death, he was never presented with it. His response would be that the articulation of a moral response depends on the stage of the relevant inquiry and the definition of the broader problem. Underlying the particular problem of a difficult case are the ingrained habits and prevailing practices in society and the divisions among preference holders toward *opposing* practices. That these can be articulated as opposing moral propositions is clear, as was the right to life opposing personal autonomy in Dr. Kevorkian's criminal trial in 1999. When opposing practices, that still maintain active existence, define the issue in a particular case,

---

3 Dworkin, *Taking Rights Seriously*, 22.

4 In his 1967 challenge to Hart, reprinted in *Taking Rights Seriously*, Dworkin removed *Henningsen* from its history; he records that the case decided "the important question of whether (or how much) an automobile manufacturer may limit his liability in case the automobile is defective. Plaintiff Henningsen had bought a car, and signed a contract which said that the manufacturer's liability for defects was limited to 'making good' defective parts." Henningsen argued that "the manufacturer ought not to be protected by this limitation" but "was not able to point to any statute, or to any established rule of law, that prevented the manufacturer from standing on the contract. The court nevertheless agreed with [the plaintiff] Henningsen." This interpretation supported Dworkin's claim that the case was decided according to the principle "that the courts will not permit themselves to be used as instruments of inequity and injustice." But Dworkin omits that the issue, of liability for injury from a defective automobile to a remote plaintiff, is the one that, according to Levi, took a century to resolve in the famous opinion of Judge Cardozo in *MacPherson v. Buick Motor Co.*, cited as an authority by Judge Francis in *Henningsen*. 32 N.J. 358, 386–387 (1960).

5 Matthew Kramer, "When is There Not one Right Answer?" *American Journal of Jurisprudence*, vol. 53, no. 1 (2008), 49.

Dewey's continuum of inquiry rules out a "uniquely correct moral response to the problem raised by the case." A moral conflict is a conflict of practices that cannot be resolved by current knowledge of morality.[6]

The argument in favor of a diachronic model of legal uncertainty requires reversing perceptions that have hardened since the influence of both Hart and Dworkin on analytical jurisprudence. The contemporary picture of the "hard case," lying outside the foreground of determinate legal authorities, should be understood in the context of Hart's unique place in twentieth-century jurisprudence. Hart confined legal indeterminacy to the "interstices" between verbal meanings, making it synchronic with existing legal texts and thus outside a contemporaneous foreground. He dismissed legal realist criticisms of formalist legal determinacy as "excesses."[7] In his comments on legal realism, Hart conceded that there was a degree of indeterminacy in the law but argued that it necessarily occupied a peripheral zone.

The law for Hart could nevertheless be conceptualized as a system of rules, with some cases in which the rules do not clearly specify the correct legal outcome. This was due to the ineliminable "open texture" of not just legal but natural language, for which Hart drew on the linguistic analysis of Frederick Waismann. All general terms have both a "core" of meaning and a "penumbra," or a range in which it is unclear and controversial as to whether the term applies to a specific case.

For Hart, this penumbral range was considerably smaller than the extension of the core. Hart used as an example the term "vehicle," as in a prohibition of "vehicles in the park"; baby-strollers would fall harmlessly into the "penumbra." For Hart, the nature of law's indeterminacy is limited to a periphery outside a system of rules that provides specific outcomes in most cases. But Hart gave little attention to showing that this was a full and fair account of the realist critique. Thus were the contentions of realism deflated, persuading many writers (that followed Hart) that realist claims had been "transcended." But Hart and many others had simply failed to appreciate Edward Levi's identification of the extended form of uncertainty as related to inquiry over time. This was a form of uncertainty that occurred when competing lines of precedent were applied to novel forms of experience. The dispute was viewed by Levi not simply from the standpoint of a judge in one case, but in the nature of its relation to an ongoing class of cases.

From the perspective of logical space between lines of authority over time, rather than occupying interstitial textual space in one definitive moment, we may picture a new case that is not "outside" a discrete set of rules or body of legal doctrine, but arguably "inside," yet drawn in competing directions,

---

6 See Kramer on moral conflicts, "When is There Not one Right Answer?" 53f.

7 Altman, *Critical Legal Studies: A Liberal Critique*, 206.

pulled equally toward two (or more) established lines of precedent—for example, whether an exploding coffee urn or a defective automobile is a dangerous instrumentality, or (in the realm of contract law) whether promise of a gift is sufficient consideration for an enforceable contract.

Hart's influence and Dworkin's subsequent challenge solidified the dominance of a static autonomous foreground and background model, highlighted by Jeremy Waldron in 2009. This model privileges the individual inquirer and ignores the ongoing process of negotiated classification by multiple inquirers. A novel case may at first appear indeterminate in the context of prior precedent. As it recurs, it is recognized as a new situation, compared, defined, and eventually clarified in relation to prior patterns of decision. Waldron rightly characterized this process and the role of judges, principles, and community as a "constructive" enterprise, albeit tentative and experimental.[8]

Dworkin made an extended argument in *Law's Empire* advancing the notion that the judicial role is to keep faith with a "community of principle."[9] Waldron found that this response failed to address the core position articulated by leading Critical Legal Studies (CLS) writers: the more Dworkin insisted on reaching creatively into the background to keep faith with the community of principle, the more he needed to confront or ignore arguments that the background is riven with inconsistency. In Waldron's words,

> the constructivism that Dworkin appeals to, in order to evade the CLS critique, succeeds (if it does) only at the cost of cutting loose of the idea that the community is in some sense already committed to a coherent and principled position which the Dworkinian lawyer has a responsibility to unearth.[10]

In this insight, Waldron connected legal difficulty to the broader issue of community experience.

We might ask how, precisely, Dworkin's method of principled adjudication is conceived to operate. Dworkin claimed that it takes place (within the judicial mind) in three stages, consisting of identification, justification, and reform. In the first (or pre-interpretive) stage, the judge identifies "the relevant rules and standards taken to provide the tentative content of the practice." The second (interpretive) stage is one of constructing a theory of "why a practice of that general shape is worth pursuing, if it is"; the judge must "settle on some general justification for the main elements of the practice." Dworkin ignores the possibility that competing or conflicting practices might be involved in a lawsuit; he says the judge must "see himself as interpreting

[8] Waldron, "Did Dworkin Ever Answer the Crits?"

[9] Ronald Dworkin, *Law's Empire* (Cambridge and London: The Belknap Press, 1986), 164–178.

[10] Waldron, "Did Dworkin Ever Answer the Crits?" 156.

that [singular] practice, not inventing a new one." The third stage is "reforming" and "post-interpretive"; the judge "adjusts his sense of what the practice 'really' requires, so as better to serve the justification he accepts at the interpretive stage." Here the judge puts "the practice," and the scheme of values or principles that "the" practice can be said to serve, in its "best light." The practice is what the best interpretive theory says it is.[11]

Dworkin emphasizes here the need for achieving "consensus" to resolve the "inevitable controversy, even among contemporaries," over the "exact dimensions of the practice they all interpret." This barely gives even lip service to the prospect that the "controversy" in a legal case has arisen from often bitterly opposed plural practices; he suggests quite improbably that these can be "interpreted" in a courtroom, all at once, as a judicial redescription of a singular practice. If that practice is what the best interpretive theory says it is, then Dworkin obliges the judge to settle any controversy by simply imposing a "theory."

Dworkin's stages of interpretation are comparable to what might, under favorable conditions, take place over time in the hoped-for convergence of Dewey's continuum of inquiry. Llewellyn described the best appellate decisions as successfully honing in on the appropriate "situation sense." This sounds similar to Dworkin's description of the first stage, in which the judge determines what informed and active participants say is paradigmatic of a practice. But Dworkin makes this sound plausible for articulation by an individual judge, in defining the situation as a singular practice rather than presented in a contested account recognizing the clash of alternative practices. His second or interpretive stage sounds like a further exploration of Llewellyn's "situation," putting the practice in its "best light." This stage includes assessing the competing eligible theories to see which "fits the data" and has a unique quality that Dworkin calls "moral appeal." But here, two distinct problems are elided: the sense of the situation is itself contested, then (as Edward Levi, and later Alexander Bickel, sought to demonstrate) further experience and choices have to be encountered before it is "identified in its best light."

The critical difference between Dworkin's "stages," in one judge's (or court's) inquiry, and the successive stages of Dewey is that, although Dworkin describes them as stages, they are part of an immediate judgment. There can be instances where the larger problem can be resolved at once,[12] but there are many more that require time and wider experience, both of which

---

11 Dworkin, *Law's Empire*, 66–67.

12 Legal problems that take place within a broader social continuum of inquiry are diverse, and while the duration may be extended, as in Levi's example of the inherently dangerous rule, it may be shorter in matters resolvable by the judiciary at an early instance.

are foreclosed even to the most omniscient judge. Dworkin overrelies on the opposition of legal arguments, which he presumes can bring every relevant consideration to bear, ignoring underlying conflicts that remain intransigeant. Dworkin's conceived resolution, mainly through the opposing arguments of lawyers, is insufficiently participatory and provides no mechanism for the adjustment of opposing practices.

Even if the arguments somehow included all relevant considerations, reasoning would still rely on the supremely unnatural powers of Dworkin's mythical judge "Hercules," capable of seeing any situation in its "best light" and articulating its consistency with Dworkin's idea of integrity. The need to invent an entirely mythical and idealized source of cognitive power should signal the inability, if not refusal, to naturalize any purported account of legal inquiry. Yet strangely, Dworkin's argument from principle has yet to encounter any strong resistance from the empirical tradition of Francis Bacon and J. S. Mill. The overwhelming acceptance of Dworkin's view among legal theorists of recourse to principle as a "datum" of law reflects an ill-articulated rhetorical form of metaphysical realism, that "principles" (ill-defined though they may be) have a present and causal existence simply because the legal profession deploys them in legal advocacy. Such a view assumes that any difficult judgment underlying the determination of whether the law applies to an uncertain case is always in some important degree deductive, open to comparison of propositional content (the "black letter" law, authoritative texts, or the background of legal and moral principles) to the facts at hand.

Dworkin does not escape the fundamental deductivism of an analytical positivist model, but depends upon it for his assumption that clear law in a hard case may simply "run out," giving lawyers and judges access to principles. This underlies his notion of constructive interpretation and his theory of law as grounded in "integrity."[13] Dworkin's view of law as enabling critical, justice-focused politics and providing a "forum of principle" for deciding

[13] Dworkin, *Law's Empire*, 225–275. In *Law's Empire,* Dworkin widened the scope of his criticism of Hart and proposed an alternative "third conception" of law, distinct from positivism in holding that the law is fundamentally argumentative, affecting all aspects of law including Hart's rule of recognition. While positivism held that law could be described by criterial semantics, Dworkin held that disagreement is common among lawyers about the ground rules—the very rules that are supposed to establish the grounds for propositions of law. Hartian positivism could accommodate principle by emphasizing method, or methodological positivism, based as it was on the rule of recognition, and also the distinction positivists made between neutral analytic jurisprudence and engaged moral inquiry and argument. To this, Dworkin responded that argument was pervasive and theoretical (in a "justificatory ascent" from particular cases and issues): "[N]o firm line divides jurisprudence from adjudication," which is the "silent prologue to any decision at law." Throughout its history, judges in the American legal system treated the techniques they use "for interpreting statutes and measuring precedent—even those no one challenges—not simply as tools handed down by the traditions of their ancient craft but as principles they assume can be justified in some deeper political theory, and when they come to doubt this, for whatever reason, they construct theories that seem to them better." Dworkin, *Law's Empire*, 139. Edward Levi, and by implication also John Dewey,

the most important issues of justice translates into turning responsibility for public reason over to the courts. Hard cases arise when the threshold test cannot discriminate between two or more interpretations of some statute or line of cases. Then the judge must choose between eligible interpretations by asking which one reveals the relevant community's structure of both institutions and decisions—supposedly constituting its public standards as a whole—in a better light from the standpoint of political morality.

The judge's own moral and political convictions are now directly engaged. But the political aspect of the judgment to be made is itself complex and will set one department of political morality against another; the decision will reflect not only the judge's subjective opinions about justice and fairness but also any higher-order convictions about how these ideals should be applied or compromised when they compete.[14]

The social networks of judges and lawyers will always be insulated from the concerns of much of the population. Tradition and practice prevent having a representative from every minority, much less every major economic or social interest group, represented in the federal circuit courts of appeal, much less on a nine-member Supreme Court. Dworkin extends the rule of judicial reason to its absolute limit, incorporating moral and political theory into the realm of adjudication.

Waldron suggested that there may be no resolution at the abstract level of the disagreement between CLS and Dworkin.[15] Given the background of the post-Hart model of uncertainty, we must instead look to the nature of legal uncertainty itself. Levi's classic essay on the history of "dangerous instrumentalities" portrays the social construction of a legal principle, and it also shows how tentative and experimental the process is, often drawn out over a period of many years, indeed going back over a century in the case of liability for injury from an object of imminent danger, eventually applied to

---

would view this emphasis on legal argument as evidence of the much larger role and dimension of a broader struggle, of the underlying agonistic continuum of inquiry.

14 Dworkin, *Law's Empire*, 255–256.

15 Dworkin gave little attention to the legal realists. Whereas CLS would later emphasize a "global" indeterminacy of a background riven with contradicting norms and principles, the realists focused on a "local" uncertainty, the immediate ambiguity of fact and alternative rules in the context of individual cases. As Andrew Altman argued in 1986, the realist perception of difficulty was far deeper and more pervasive than Hart's characterization. First, realist analysis perceived a "cluster" of rules relevant to the decision in any litigated case. In any single case, there were two or more potential points of doubt, rather than a single point deriving from the open texture of language. Second, many realists rejected the distinction between holding and dictum. While the "holding" referred to the essential grounds of a decision, the "dicta" putatively covered nonessential commentary that might include points of law not treated as basic to the outcome. The actual line suggested by this distinction was virtually impossible to identify, and hence, for practical purposes, vague, and shifting. Thus, judges writing subsequent opinions were not bound by any original perception of what was essential. Altman, *Critical Legal Studies: A Liberal Critique,* 208–209.

the automobile. I will adapt a historical example[16] as a necessary precursor to reevaluating Dworkin's argument.

Imagine a new common-law jurisdiction with minimal codes or regulations. Cases arise that involve abutting landowners, some of whom prefer open spaces, and others who prefer privacy. Many of the latter favor walls and structures close to their boundary, and because there are no zoning or building codes, they are limited only by their wills and desires. Lawsuits are brought by abutting plaintiffs claiming violation of their natural right to light and air by these neighbors' boundary walls and structures. Jury trials are granted, and the wall-builders counterclaim their right to free enjoyment of private property. Many of the cases are submitted to the jury, and some are bench-tried by district and superior court judges. They are decided entirely on their particular facts, and this is reflected in the court documents, local press, and judicial opinions. Some cases involve high walls and structures, others low ones, some wood, others stone, some are aesthetically pleasing, others ugly, and so on. Opposing preferences and conceptions of utility are considered, and many are rejected as the cases are decided.

Meanwhile, the successive judgments have the effect of shaping expectations and the future conduct of landowners. While the majority of the litigants appear satisfied with the results of their trials, some will find the results unsatisfactory and appeal to the regional Supreme Court. That Court reviews the initial judgments for procedural regularity to assure itself that the facts support the decision. Thus, if the trial court finds that there was no substantial blockage of light and air, and the decision so holds, the judgment is upheld. Certain claims are ruled irrelevant, such as whether the structure is wood or stone, nice or ugly. Eventually, the lawyers specializing in boundary cases make arguments drawn from the growing record. Predictably, the lawyers focus on the height of the wall and the distance from the common boundary, citing these dimensions in the cases that support their clients. Meanwhile, landowners engaged in new construction, aware of the developing court decisions, have adjusted their expectations and refrain from building without agreement at certain heights generally deemed excessive near property lines.

Reviewing the cases over time, the lawyers and eventually trial judges conclude that there is a workable relationship reflected in the pattern of judgments: walls that exceed a certain ratio of height to the distance to the boundary are increasingly found to violate the abutting landowner's right to light and air. This leads to a rule of law. After several years of considering

16 My example is based on an 1866 English case, *Beadel v. Perry*, first cited by Holmes in his edition of Kent's *Commentaries on American Law* and later developed in "The Theory of Torts" (1873), where his lifelong reference to judges "drawing lines" between opposing precedents in hard cases appears to originate.

various other factors, the Supreme Court eventually rules that a particular ratio of height and distance "respects the fundamental right of a property owner's freedom to prosper and enjoy his own land, while protecting that of his neighbor's access to the beauty and breezes." Henceforth, the ratio is a "safe harbor," and any wall built within it is legal. With this noted (and appropriately "principled") decision, the controversial boundary wall dispute is considered resolved.

At the initial stage of litigation in a new class of cases, there is a climate we may call indeterminacy. Use and enjoyment of private property imply two opposing rights: access to light and air and freedom of use. Being utterly general and at first without bodies of precedent, the two rights secured jurisdiction in the boundary-wall cases but gave no specific guidance. The early lawsuits were decided on the basis of particular facts—on what appeared fair to the triers of fact, whether jury or judge. Two bodies of precedent grew, one upholding and the other overturning walls and structures. These cases were relatively easy, such as where a high wall is built without agreement right against the adjoining property's edge. But some cases were close to a yet-emerging consensus. The cases seemingly balanced by the facts are the hardest to decide.

Facts may appear in balance between two opposing "rights," as well as lines of decision, with no judicial rule (or legislation)—yet to evaluate them. By the time a case where the facts seemed perfectly balanced reached the high court, there was an appearance of both local and global indeterminacy: local because the lawyers could cite the opposing bodies of precedent allowing and removing structures, and global because they could argue equally from the opposing global rights of free enjoyment of private property and the preservation of environmental values. To the individual judges, the close case may have seemed indeterminate. For the judicial system, it was a stage of inquiry, the resolution dependent on many factors leading to the eventual governing legal principle, where the eventual legal "line" is drawn.

Legal indeterminacy is based on a balance not just of opposing conceptions or legal texts but of actual habits and practices. As Levi recounted in 1949, adjusted practices and public perceptions are translated by counsel into legal arguments for and against the prospect of liability. Such is the actual process of "construction" highlighted by Waldron's critique of Dworkin. It is not the superjudge Hercules who must find the answer. Juries and judges import prevalent notions of fairness, practice, and technology from the parties engaged in the very disputes that create the appearance of indeterminacy. Construction takes place within a context of concern for basic values that seem in conflict. Yet the perceived conflict of basic values does not undermine or delegitimize the law. Conflicting values may seem "incommensurable" in the broadest sense, yet they may be commensurate in application.

This is how naturalized utilitarianism is successful: the preferences that were grounded in habits are adjusted to make self-interest compatible with benevolence through the adoption of a new general practice. Dewey emphasizes the resource of "experience," but this includes transformed experience informing a rationality of preference revision. Such are the normative implications of the so-called "diachronic model" of legal uncertainty. They dictate what should be indicated to a court where a case lies in the stages of a broader controversy and what guides judicial decision in the early as opposed to the later stage. Without Dewey's inquiry, problems fester and confidence in the law decreases.

Early cases are decided on particular grounds, not weighing competing principles. Over time, the courts may, if the matter is not resolved by legislation, reach a general solution. Applying a similar analysis to the Supreme Court of the United States, Cass Sustein has described this as a "minimalist" path, saying that "not always, but usually" makes sense "*when the Court is dealing with a constitutional issue of high complexity about which many people feel deeply and on which the nation is divided (on moral or other grounds).*"[17]

> The pretense that the law is a system of known rules applied by a judge has long been under attack. In an important sense legal rules are never entirely comprehensive. The mechanism accepts the differences of view and ambiguities of words. It provides for the participation of the community in resolving the ambiguity by providing a forum for the discussion of policy in the gap of ambiguity. . . . The mechanism is indispensable to peace in the community.[18]

Sunstein provides further grounds for Edward Levi's warning against premature appeal to general propositions and for his emphasis that the broader community is involved in the conflicts of litigation. Minimalism alone, however, does not address the later stage of controversy, when competing factors must be unified in a new standard of conduct.[19]

Both CLS and Dworkin have failed to appreciate that distinct forms of legal difficulty have varied theoretical implications for judicial recourse to general principles. Both privilege a judge-oriented individualist epistemology of legal principles (as Dworkin's mythical super-judge "Hercules" exemplifies). The view offered here rejects the univocal conception of a "hard case" as outside a determinate foreground. Legal uncertainty may be related to developing but yet unresolved aspects of an underlying problem. This suggests a restrained

---

17 Sunstein, *One Case at a Time*, 5 (italics in original).
18 Levi, *Introduction to Legal Reasoning*, 1.
19 In portraying the Supreme Court as a "catalyst," Sunstein observes that the minimalist decision can operate as a call for public attention to a problem without foreclosing public judgment, 120–121.

and participatory, or socialized, epistemology for legal principles, leaving space when appropriate for input from outside the adjudicatory system. This approach recognizes the need for adjustments of belief and conduct to resolve ongoing community conflicts.

Rather than appealing to antecedent general principles in all hard cases, judges properly exercise minimalist restraint in the earlier stages of ongoing controversies. The diachronic view undermines any universalized theory of immediate interpretive resolution by appealing to morals, principles, or values—and equally undermines universalizing the "impossibility" critique of CLS. The implication of Edward Levi's analysis is that public debate among legal and nonlegal scholars, as well as citizens, should play a role in the development of practical reasoning surrounding the broader controversy as well as the transformation of relevant practices. An obvious example is the controversy over medically assisted death.

Cass Sunstein characterized the "right to die" as a "new dilemma" and applauded that the Supreme Court had as yet refrained from a broadly defined resolution. The issue of physician-assisted death is even now engaging in intense discussion. Sunstein claimed in 1999 that it was far too early for courts to preempt those discussions, certainly if there should be no systematic barrier to a fair hearing from any affected group. Difficult questions have arisen, like, When does life begin and end? What are personal autonomy and invasion of privacy? When is medical treatment criminally responsible for the death of a suffering and morbid patient? These questions cannot be answered by abstract argument or by recourse to moral generalization.

Chapter 7

Legal Principles

The nature of Dewey's empirical naturalism, crucial as it is to understanding his approach to all aspects of human knowledge, encountered little acceptance and less understanding during his lifetime. Appearing as a distinct term in the second edition of *Experience and Nature,* it was wrongly associated with ethical noncognitivism[1] and attacked in the 1930s by the president of the University of Chicago, Robert Hutchins, in calling for a revamped curriculum grounded in "absolute" values. After Hutchins and Chicago philosophy professor Mortimer Adler had reorganized the university around the study of the "Great Books" of western culture, Adler blamed Dewey for a "moral disarmament" of American culture in the face of German fascism.[2]

The theory of general principles in legal inquiry cannot be ignorant of a tendency to applaud the unrestrained expression of time-honored values in times of public uncertainty.

Legal principles might be viewed in two contrary ways. They might either be seen as free-standing, unrevisable, and absolute, although frequently opposing one another in the context of a disputed matter; or they might be open-ended, tentative, and suggesting (though not always supporting) alternative options for the matter at hand. In the first view, they can appear irreconcilable, while according to the second, they are, in Edward Levi's words, part of a "moving classification system." In the first view, the conceptual space of principle is relatively fixed at the moment of decision, and the legal mind is free to roam among them, always at risk of a choice dictated more by subjective preference than logic.

---

[1] Ethical propositions cannot be true or false; see A. J. Ayer below.

[2] Robert Westbrook, *John Dewey and American Democracy* (Ithaca: Cornell University Press, 1991), 507; Dewey, *Experience and Nature,* 2nd ed. (New York: Dover Publications Inc, 1958 [1929]).

According to the second view, based on induction rather than deduction, the legal mind must always hesitate as to whether the matter at hand warrants a decision broader than the particular case, given the immediate complexity of circumstances. The two alternatives might be described as thinking and judging from principle or, as Alexander Bickel has shown, *toward* principle. What difference will that choice make, if such matters, while drily legal in appearance, are intimately connected with unresolved social conflict? Without that perspective, lost from view is the possibility that the structure of human thought, concerned with conceptual ordering, is contingent upon its own success. Without the presence of ubiquitous conflict in sight, the possibility is invisible that the enterprise of intelligent action is precarious and can fail.

An influential American turn to legal principles can reasonably be dated to Herbert Wechsler's "Toward Neutral Principles of Constitutional Law," the 1959 Oliver Wendell Holmes Lecture at Harvard Law School. The turn came as a reaction against two disparate views, first a doubt raised at Harvard in 1958 by Judge Learned Hand over Supreme Court "judicial review"—oversight of state and federal legislation under the sweeping but vague dispensation of the Constitution's Bill of Rights. The other was the abstract question now associated with legal positivism and, harking back to philosophies of law since ancient Greece, the question of whether law is inherently separate from morals, brought to Harvard the preceding year by Herbert Hart of Oxford. In arguing for a strict separation of law from morals, Hart prompted a response from Harvard Law School Professor Lon Fuller, defending an "inner morality" of law.[3]

More influential was the later response to Hart by Ronald Dworkin, which began with the assertion that judges, in hard cases where the "positive law" had no apparent answer, could, should, and did turn to "moral principles." Both Hand and Hart delivered their thoughts at consecutive Oliver Wendell Holmes Lectures, followed by Columbia law professor Herbert Wechsler in 1959 with his appeal to neutral principles. Even though his name was honored, Holmes's own view continued to be misread. In the decade after his death, he had been defined as a seminal "legal positivist" (separating law and morals) for his cautionary remarks on moral language in "The Path of the Law." Fuller had written in 1940 that:

> [c]ertainly it cannot be said that the positivism of his early essays was ever completely sloughed off during his career as a judge. . . . For him the notion that the law is something severable from one's notions of what it ought to be seems to

[3] Published as *The Morality of Law* (New Haven: Yale University Press, 1964).

> have had a real and inhibitive meaning. We may admire his fidelity to a faith. But was it for the ultimate good of our law? I think there is reason to doubt it.[4]

In the wake of Second World War, Fuller's criticism was joined by others and, taken with occasional "military" allusions extolling valor in Holmes's Memorial Day speeches and essays, led to the notion that Holmes was an authoritarian. In 1945, an article appeared in the *American Bar Association Journal* with the title "Holmes, Hobbes, and Hitler." Five years later, Westbrook Pegler referred to him as a "cynical and senile brutalitarian."[5]

Meanwhile, Wechsler, in his 1959 Holmes Lecture, sought to refute Judge Hand's doubts about the controversial increase in substantive jurisdiction in the Supreme Court under the Fourteenth Amendment's "due process" clause. Observing a growing trend, Hand in 1958 declared that he did not care to be governed "by a bevy of Platonic guardians, even if I knew how to choose them, which I assuredly do not."[6] His lectures set off a round of reassessment among legal scholars that has not died out as debate continues over the enormous power wielded by the Supreme Court in "judicial review."

Hand, the master guide and reliable illuminator of complicated litigation,[7] left his mark as an oracle of misgivings. The Constitution was to be regarded primarily as the embodiment of historical compromise, not a set of durable principles or a resource from which to strengthen or modify the morals of society. The notion of a discrete constitutional law of economic or personal rights knowable by judges, Hand maintained at the close of his career, was a fallacy. In his response, Wechsler advanced the claim that Hand's doubts could be "transcended" if the Court would only follow "neutral principles" of constitutional law. Dworkin's path to principle would develop later, eventually working out as an independent theory about the nature of legal interpretation.

---

4 Lon Fuller, *The Law in Quest of Itself* (Boston: Beacon Press, 1940), 62–63.

5 Holmes's dissents in the *Lochner* and *Abrams* cases, that the U.S. Constitution is made for people of many faiths, carried almost no counterweight to these evaluations. The irony is more profound in view of an as-yet-unrecognized and deep congeniality between Fuller's and Holmes's views of the importance of understanding law in its social context. For Fuller, law to be effective must depend on informal and implicit social rules, as well as interaction between legal officials and those subject to legal rule making. The positivist view to which he objected was that law was ontologically and methodologically separate from morals, a view he saw carried forward by legal realism in equating law with the acts of judges and legal officials. Fuller believed that judges could only impose sanctions upon parties to legal disputes if social norms supported their doing so, norms that must be accepted and practiced in the community at large. Holmes took a critical further step in a direction that Fuller could have approved, had he understood it. Both men recognized the role of law and lawyers in bringing the law into conformity with communal norms; Holmes saw that to accomplish this was to break away from the notion that judges should dominate the public debate over principle and control the outcome. See Kellogg, *Holmes and Legal Logic*, 125f.

6 Learned Hand, *The Bill of Rights* (Cambridge: Harvard University Press, 1958), 11.

7 Gerald Gunther, *Learned Hand: The Man and the Judge* (New York: Alfred Knopf, 1994).

The two developments are close in the chronology of twentieth-century jurisprudence and were matched by a new cycle of realist-inspired criticism: the claim of Critical Legal Scholars that principles are not the solution, but rather the problem: legal doctrine, especially considering the diverse "background" of maxims and theories, includes so many diverse "principles" that any outcome can be given a principled defense by judges in a close case. The social scientific component of legal realism had failed to light the way forward to an understanding of law, but its skeptical component was taken up and deepened by Critical Legal Studies (CLS).

What exactly are "legal principles"? Where does the judiciary find them? Reference to principle can amply be found in the literature of jurisprudence, but there is no clear and agreed definition. How do principles compare in law and science? Can a "principle" change? Legal principles come in different guises: Wechsler's principles of constitutional law are "neutral," while Dworkin's are "moral" and cover law in general as a therapy for legal indeterminacy. The very separate existence of legal principles has been questioned.[8] Their nature in legal theory has been more assumed than examined. Are legal principles necessary truths? What is the act or series of acts of the mind (or "minds") in constructing legal principles, and when constructed, in what manner do we rest in them as expressive of truth? Broad constitutional statements, as found in our Bill of Rights, may be read two ways: as a list of axioms or, more consistent with induction, as posing fundamental questions, which in litigation are always posed in a specific context.

Wechsler's "neutral" adjective suggests a sweeping inclusion of anticipated but unexamined particulars. He concedes that courts should decide "only the case they have before them," but their reasoning must be "tested not only by the instant application but by others that the principles imply." To decide on principle is to decide on "grounds of adequate neutrality and generality" and "to insist upon attending to such other cases, preferably those involving an opposing interest in evaluating any principle involved." Wechsler's response to Hand was to abandon a gradual case-by-case approach.

How did Wechsler reach this broad license—the conviction that judges could be virtually clairvoyant regarding even the future content of a general principle? He starts with the proposition that

> the Court by rule has defined standards for the exercise of its discretion, standards framed in neutral terms, like the importance of the question or a conflict

---

[8] See Larry Alexander and Kenneth Kress, "Against Legal Principles," 82 *Iowa L. Rev.* 739 (1996–1997). The contemporary moral particularist Jonathan Dancy writes: "Particularists think that moral judgement can get along perfectly well without any appeal to principles, indeed that there is no essential link between being a full moral agent and having principles." Dancy, *Ethics Without Principles* (Oxford: Clarendon Press, 2004), 1.

> of decisions. Only the maintenance and the improvement of such standards and, of course, their faithful application can, I say with deference, protect the Court against the danger of imputation of a bias favoring claims of one kind or another in the granting or denial of review.[9]

Wechsler took the Supreme Court's discretionary standards, whether to accept a case or controversy, as models of neutrality, but it is difficult to see how either "importance" or "conflict" of decisions among the lower courts can provide any support for deploying general propositions in all controversial cases. In his argument for neutral principle, Wechsler actually condemned the *un*principled particular decision as "fiat." According to this claim, the "neutral principle" provides the only alternative to an exercise of "naked power."

> The man who simply lets his judgment turn on the immediate result may not, however, realize that his position implies that the courts are free to function as a naked power organ, that it is an empty affirmation to regard them, as ambivalently he so often does, as courts of law.

Here, concern with the "immediate result" (presumably based upon reference to the unique facts of the actual case) is made equivalent to "fiat," and equating principle with neutrality in the sense of transparency.

In support of his claim that minimalism is fiat, Wechsler cited Lon Fuller's 1946 article in the *Harvard Law Review*, "Reason and Fiat in Case Law." Originally delivered as a lecture in honor of Justice Cardozo, Fuller proposed that the distinction between reason and fiat is an "antinomy" embedded in the law, an inherent contradiction between two opposing conceptions:

> For Cardozo the law embraced many antinomies, but one of the greatest and most pervasive of these was that of reason and fiat. . . . Cardozo did not follow the example of those who make relativism itself an absolute. If the common law had not attained the perfection of reason, it could be understood only as an unremitting quest for that perfection. His view rejected neither branch of the antinomy of reason and fiat. For him law was by its limitations fiat, by its aspirations reason, and the whole view of it involved a recognition of both its limitations and its aspirations.[10]

Fuller held that "this antinomy is in fact inescapable," a "state of unresolved conflict" that "it is better to accept frankly" than "to purchase consistency at the cost of needed premises."

[9] Kellogg, *Holmes and Legal Logic*, 127.
[10] Lon Fuller, "Reason and Fiat in Case Law," *Harvard Law Review,* vol. 59 (1946), 376–377.

To use the term "antinomy," denoting an immediate apprehension of final irreconcilability, is again to conflate the stages of legal inquiry, placing them in opposition rather than succession. The effect of its use is to demonize one perspective as less desirable than the other, characterizing even what is really an early stage of a problem as one requiring "fiat," not recognizing that there may yet, in the quest for resolution, come a later reconciliation with "reason."

The antinomy of fiat and reason draws from the same phenomenon that Herbert Hart in 1977 called the "oscillation" of legal formalism and legal realism: selective emphasis, which Dewey called a fallacy in *Experience and Nature*. Fuller and Weschler both failed to appreciate, if not to articulate, the manner in which reason itself is emergent through induction from specific experience, but more importantly, from social conflict, and still more importantly, from its resolution in the adjustment of human conduct. "Fiat" suggests a deductive prejudice against the necessity of choice in the context of unfamiliar experience. There is no antinomy between reason and fiat, so translated. To use the term is to stand upon a ground of unresolved cognitive conflict, and to do this is to obstruct the prospect of resolving real conflict.

The clash between Hand and Wechsler stirred another Hand-style conservative, Yale law professor Alexander Bickel, to take up Hand's doubts and seek to reconcile them with Wechsler's principles. Bickel began by recasting Hand's argument with a phrase that has changed the terms of the debate. Bickel characterized Hand's practical doubts as a democratic crisis: Supreme Court review under the due process clause raised a "countermajoritarian difficulty" as to how it could be squared with democratically enacted legislation. Having refined the problem, Bickel recited the deductive assumption that the judicial process is

> justified only if it injects into representative government something that is not already there: and that is principle, standards of action that derive their worth from a long view of society's spiritual and material needs, and that command adherence whether or not the immediate outcome is expedient or agreeable.[11]

But Bickel then set off on a different, inductive tack: principle is something less to be imposed than to be achieved. Examining a series of recent decisions, he asked whether they met Wechsler's neutrality test. He concluded that some had failed simply for lack of coherence: "A neutral principle is an intellectually coherent statement of the reason for a result which in like cases

---

[11] Alexander Bickel, *The Least Dangerous Branch* (Indianapolis and New York: Bobbs-Merrill Co., 1962), 58.

will produce a like result, whether or not it is immediately agreeable or expedient." But Bickel's analysis then posed a question ignored by Wechsler: can the "neutral principle" withstand the unknown future?

> Now the demand for neutral principles is carried further. It is that the court rest judgment only on principles that will be capable of application across the board and without compromise, in all relevant cases in the foreseeable future: absolute application of absolute—even if sometimes flexible—principles. The flexibility, if any, must be built into the principle itself.[12]

This future orientation led Bickel to a surprising conclusion on the Supreme Court's task. How can we know the future? For this, Bickel looked to the past. Instead of decrying the inevitable ad hoc, the raw "fiat," in law and politics, Bickel saw the problem as one of reconciling principled consistency with realistic pragmatism. This he called the "Lincolnian tension," as Lincoln had opposed all slavery in principle while accepting the Missouri Compromise as "born of necessity."[13]

> Our democratic system of government exists in this Lincolnian tension between principle and expediency, and within it judicial review must play its role. Mr. Wechsler's dilemma is a false one. The constitutional function of the court is to define values and proclaim principles. But this is not a function to be exercised with respect to some exceedingly few matters, while society is left wholly to its devices of expediency in dealing with the great number of its other concerns. For, as with the segregation problem and slavery before it, we require principle and expediency at once. The rule of the neutral principles would excise the courts' function of declaring principled goals.[14]

Our system, Bickel declared, calls for an adaptation of principles in novel circumstances. In this,

> courts have certain capacities for dealing with matters of principle that legislatures and executives do not possess. Judges have, or should have, the leisure, the training, and the insulation to follow the ways of the scholar in pursuing ends of government. This is crucial in sorting out the enduring values of a society.

The courts are always concerned with the "flesh and blood" of the actual case.

> This tends to modify, perhaps to lengthen, everyone's view. It also provides an extremely salutary proving ground for all abstractions. It is conducive, in a

---

[12] Bickel, *The Least Dangerous Branch*, 59.
[13] Bickel, *The Least Dangerous Branch*, 66.
[14] Bickel, *The Least Dangerous Branch*, 68–69.

phrase of Holmes, to thinking things, not words, and thus to the evolution of principle by a process that tests as it creates.[15]

In his description of a process "that tests as it creates," Bickel gave clarity to Holmes's inductive admonition to "think things, not words."[16] Bickel's account of principles is a correction to Wechsler's naive and dubious ambition. It gives priority not to judicial autonomy, but to the experience felt by all participants in the process through a continuum of inquiry. To be thinking "things, not words" avoids the danger of runaway rule by principle, of its *abuse*:

> The Court—if Mr. Wechsler is right—either has set out to be a third legislative chamber or is imposing on the country an absolute rule of absolute principle. Thus it is either totally at war with the theory and practice of democracy or, far from being a stabilizing influence, it is leading the country to ruin by intractable, doctrinaire stages of irrepressible conflict. Or both, for the absolute rule of principle is also at war with a democratic system. But Mr. Wechsler, I believe, is not right. No society, certainly not a large and heterogeneous one, can fail to explode if it is deprived of the arts of compromise, if it knows no ways of muddling through. No good society can be unprincipled; and no viable society can be principle-ridden. But it is not true in our society that we are generally governed wholly by principle in some matters and indulge a rule of expediency exclusively in others. There is no such neat dividing line.[17]

Bickel is among the very few writers to identify the problem of *abusing* principle through its own elevation.

To avoid such abuse, his initial reflection was entirely in accord with Dewey and Holmes:

> [That] any first case is always a poor one in which to pronounce new principles is no doubt an over-generalization. And yet it is not far wrong. A sound judicial instinct will generally favor deflecting the problem in one or more initial cases, for there is much to be gained from letting it simmer, so that a mounting number of instances exemplifying it may have a cumulative effect on the judicial minds as well as on public and professional opinion.[18]

---

15 Bickel, *The Least Dangerous Branch*, 26.

16 "We must think things not words, or at least we must constantly translate our words into the facts for which they stand, if we are to keep to the real and the true." "Law in Science and Science in Law," *Harvard Law Review, vol. 12* (1899), 443, 460, *CW* 3:415. For its relation to inductive logic, see Kellogg, *Holmes and Legal Logic,* 13–18.

17 Bickel, *The Least Dangerous Branch*, 64.

18 Bickel, *The Least Dangerous Branch*, 176.

But what about the urgent "first case," one that demands judgment when the courts are the only resort? It is Bickel's next suggestion that has failed to take hold as a realistic measure: he concluded that the Supreme Court should avoid deciding all "first cases." For this, he said, there is an "arsenal of techniques and devices . . . most of which are lumped roughly and often disingenuously together under the rubric of jurisdiction," like standing or ripeness, the political question doctrine allowing the court to recuse itself, or simply by denying review through the writ of certiorari.

Bickel conceived that this answer was not a dodge but rather a deference to extralegal avenues for resolving controversy. It was indeed a dodge, but Bickel sensed rightly that a continuum of inquiry existed, and that feedback from "political processes" was essential to it:

> When the Court, however, stays its hand, and makes clear that it is staying its hand and not legitimating, then the political processes are given relatively free play. . . . Most of [these techniques] are quite properly called techniques for eliciting answers, since so often they engage the court in a Socratic colloquy with the other institutions of government and with society as a whole concerning the necessity for this or that measure, for this or that compromise. All the while, the issue of principle remains in abeyance and ripens. "The most important thing we do," said Brandeis, "is not doing." He had in mind all the techniques, of which he was a past master, for staying the Court's hand. They are the most important thing, because they make possible performance of the court's grand function as proclaimer and protector of the goals. These are the techniques that allow leeway to expediency without abandoning principle. Therefore they make possible a principled government.[19]

Bickel's turn to the techniques of avoidance failed to gain a scholarly consensus, largely due to the urgency of controversies forced upon the federal courts and the reluctance of justices (perhaps not masters of avoidance like Brandeis) to exercise such an obviously evasive form of restraint. Instead, according to Cass Sunstein, the Court has moved in a direction away from both Bickel and Wechsler: toward "incompletely theorized agreements."

Sunstein claimed in 1999 that the contemporary Supreme Court had actually "embraced" judicial minimalism. When the court ruled that the Virginia Military Institute could not exclude women, it refused to say much about the legitimacy of other single-sex institutions, leaving the general question undecided. When it struck down the affirmative action program in Richmond,

---

[19] Bickel, *The Least Dangerous Branch*, 70–71. Bickel also noted (at 132): "It follows that the techniques and allied devices for staying the court's hand, as is avowedly true at least of certiorari, cannot themselves be principled in the sense in which we have a right to expect adjudications on the merits to be principled."

Virginia, it self-consciously refused to impose a broad ban on race-conscious programs. When it invalidated a Colorado law forbidding measures banning discrimination on the basis of sexual orientation, it said nothing about how the constitution bears on other issues involving homosexuality.[20]

Such breathing room for adjustment has expired with the current conservative majority, in overruling *Roe v. Wade* and redirecting the Court in other controversial areas. In favoring "incompletely theorized agreements," Sunstein observed that "The Court's minimalist judges try to keep their judgments as narrow and as incompletely theorized as possible, consistent with the obligation to offer reasons."[21] Sunstein described judicial minimalism as an alternative to "maximalism," by which he meant the flight to an overarching general principle; Justice Antonin Scalia's "originalism" (turning to the original intent of the constitution) is "a form of maximalism," which should be rejected on the ground that it does not promote democracy and is "judicial hubris masquerading as judicial modesty."

> Whether minimalism makes sense cannot be decided in the abstract; everything depends on context, prominently including assessments of comparative institutional competence. The case for minimalism is strongest when courts lack information that would justify confidence in a comprehensive ruling; when the need for planning is not especially insistent; when the decision costs, for later courts, of a minimalist approach do not seem high and when minimalist judgments do not create a serious risk of unequal treatment. Thus minimalism tends to be the appropriate course when the court is operating in the midst of reasonable pluralism or moral flux, when the circumstances are changing rapidly, or when the court is uncertain that a broad rule would make sense in future cases.[22]

This may sound close to Dewey's view, but the reference only to informational context, rather than to the place of a controversial case within an underlying conflict, suggests that Sunstein misses the clash of opposing underlying practices that may be resisting ultimate resolution.[23]

Importing Wechsler's and Dworkin's views to the European continent, the influential German jurist Robert Alexy has defended the notion that judges should appeal to principle in all cases where the law has an "open area." Open areas are created by "the vagaries of legal language, the possibility of norm

---

20 Sunstein, *One Case at a Time*, 3–4, citing *United States v. Virginia*, 518 U.S. 515 (1996), *Richmond v. Croson*, 488 U.S. 469 (1989), and *Romer v. Evans*, 517 U.S. 620 (1996).

21 Sunstein, *One Case at a Time,* 262.

22 Sunstein, *One Case at a Time,* 262–263.

23 Sunstein's position instead places excess reliance on the communicative ideal of deliberative democracy. *One Case at a Time,* 24: "the American constitutional system aspires not to simple majoritarianism, and not to aggregation of private "preferences," but to a system of deliberative democracy."

conflicts, the absence of a norm on which to base a decision, and, in certain cases, the possibility of making a decision even contrary to the literal reading of a norm." Reinforced by Alexy's influence, it is permissible for jurists on both shores of the Atlantic to refer to an "open area" of the positive law, existing to some degree in *every* legal system. This picture is rooted in the classical positivist position that since only the positive law is law, the judge must decide in open areas on the basis of "extra-legal" standards: "Accordingly," writes Alexy, "he is empowered to create new law essentially as a legislator does, on the basis of extra-legal standards."[24]

New cases may implicate emerging controversies. At an early stage, legal claims will not be fully representative of all relevant considerations, and public as well as expert attitudes have yet to form. When the "open area" is viewed in the context of other influences in the feedback loop, it is not purely an open area in the law alone; it is open also with regard to extra-legal opinion, practices, and understanding. The model of immediate reference to principles in all doubtful cases ignores the operation of a feedback loop in society, influenced by public knowledge and opinion. It assumes that legal principles are always already available for reference, whereas their form and language, according to Bickel, are dependent on the path through which the larger controversy is understood and resolved.

Another popular conception adopted by Alexy is that opposing principles can be "balanced" in the decision of controversial cases. Alexy writes that principles, as "optimizing" rather than "definitive" commands, must be "balanced" by the judge in a case where they appear to conflict:

> In undertaking to strike a balance, one necessarily appeals to principles for support. For it is necessary to strike a balance precisely when there are competing reasons, each of which is by itself a good reason for a decision and only fails to lead directly to a definitive decision because of the other reason, calling for another decision; reasons like this are either principles or supported by principles.[25]

This provides little guidance for a judge. Girardeau Spann writes that principles so conceived are "incommensurable," such that balancing is inevitably a subjective act:

---

24 A Deweyan analysis would note that if this area is open, it is not univocally open, with all openness of a uniform quality, since different legal controversies are in different stages of classification and resolution at any one time. Thus, at the very least, different degrees of generality of reasoning are appropriate for different stages of judicial inquiry. Moreover, when the open area is viewed in the context of other influences in the feedback loop, it is not only an open area in the law alone, but it is also open with regard to extralegal opinion, practices, and understanding.

25 Robert Alexy, *The Argument from Injustice*, trans. by Bonnie L. and Stanley L. Paulson (Oxford: Clarendon Press, 2002), 72.

> Judges cannot balance interests without recourse to their subjective preferences. Even judges with the best intentions will balance competing interests according to their views about both the relative importance of those interests and the degree to which each interest will be advanced or frustrated by particular outcomes in the case before the court. Because this activity is essentially unconstrained, however, it is difficult to see how a judge could possibly engage in it without recourse to subjective values.[26]

It should take more than Alexy's bland assertion to overcome doubt that any clear logical path exists to resolve a difficult case by "balancing."

In the alternative account, based on the agonistic reality of legal deliberation, context is critical, and legal principles must await a comprehensive encounter with experience. They are also time-variant, changing with attitudes, practices, and technology. Competing principles are not in collision but in transformation, where conventional principles are inapplicable due to the novelty of circumstances. A new formulation must be found through engagement with the community and its sense of proportion. The controversy over medically assisted death was one in which two powerful norms conflicted: the right of autonomy and privacy versus the prohibition against homicide. The metaphor of a balance suggests that cases of medically assisted death arrive somewhere along a fixed metric of varying distances from one extreme or the other, rather than a developing inquiry.

Alexy has recognized four different types of doubt or uncertainty: vagaries of legal language, norm conflicts, the absence of a controlling norm, and even the possibility of a case in which the facts run contrary to a literal reading of the relevant norm. In assuming an *a priori* list of relevant norms, none of these "types of doubt" recognize the relevance of any case to a continuing inquiry. Absence of a controlling norm may involve a case that fits nowhere because of the comprehensive novelty of the circumstances, having been unanticipated by the existing system of statute and prior decision. The case could be an anomaly, of the type never to be seen again. It could be what the common law has traditionally called a "case of first impression," which can mean the first of a new type, the result of innovation in business or technology, yet unregulated by statute, or even the result of an emergent social controversy over a human right such as equality or privacy. In such a

---

26 Girardeau A. Spann, in "Simple Justice": "When legal doctrine calls for interest balancing, therefore, it does something that is seemingly counterproductive. Because particular doctrinal applications are utterly dependent upon how the balance is struck, the subjective preferences that doctrine is designed to guard against necessarily drive application of the doctrinal rules. Once again, asking a judge to balance competing interests is a lot like asking a judge to prevent unjust discrimination." Spann, "Simple Justice," *Georgetown Law Journal,* vol. 73 (1985), 1041, 1060. See also Mark Tushnet, "Anti-Formalism in Recent Constitutional Theory," and Stephen E. Gottlieb, "The Paradox of Balancing Significant Interests."

case, the argument *against* principle is that the particular dispute between two parties may be less than fully representative of the "principles" that may in due course be recognized as more generally applicable, and the activities surrounding the controversy or innovation are still in a state of transition toward an eventual reconciliation of conflicting purposes, such that legal principles cannot yet be formulated and fixed.

In many doubtful cases, this classification process cannot be done immediately by synchronic analysis, where the courts have insufficient or unrepresentative exposure to the conditions relevant to formulating a rule by practical reasoning. New cases arise from technological innovations in digital communication, medicine, and biology, the growth and diversity of governmental and non-governmental institutions, changing population demographics, and the prolongation of life expectancy despite states of illness, pain, and morbidity. Arguments from principle are too often framed in value terms like "Is there a right to die?" In cases raising doubtful questions of legal rights and duties in a newly controversial area, practices affecting those rights are unsettled and inchoate, and opinions regarding appropriate practices are unsettled as well.

Legal claims and legal outcomes may in fact serve to focus on relevant practices and, over time, to encourage their refinement and transformation. In the early stages of a problem, it is not necessary for preliminary legal outcomes to prescribe practices; it is more characteristic that they focus attention on them. The varying practices involving particular drugs and precautions, specific legal permissions, and designated medical and administrative procedures are influenced by the attention focused on litigation. Meanwhile, opinions and attitudes are affected by the nature of the very cases made public through litigation. A voluminous literature of educated and expert opinion is part of the opinion-making process. Public and expert opinion affects, and is affected by, the refinement of practices. This is the feedback loop through which, as the name suggests, information about the result of an action is sent back to the input of the system, transforming the very nature of language about and understanding of the system.

Neither the metaphor of a scale, nor the inference of balancing from the appearance of indefinite reasons, accurately portrays what takes place as judges draw on facts to decide cases, and society responds to its decisions. Balancing is a static metaphor, in which a priori principles are available by immediate reference and operate through immediate balancing. No account of weighing or balancing principles through a boundary-and-content analysis of specific considerations can assimilate the fundamental role of interactive experience in formulating legal principles. Contemporary jurisprudence has drawn on a model of law as autonomous, exogenous, acting on and controlling society. The alternative model suggested here is endogenous, embedded, reflecting and modifying society as part of a broader process of social ordering. Dewey's agonistic model of inquiry implies a view of rights and principles under constructivist rather than deontological assumptions, emphasizing the accumulation by society of self-knowledge in its adjustment to new experience.[27]

As in science, that engagement must be experimental. The metaphor of a balancing scale inaccurately portrays what takes place as judges draw on facts to decide cases and as society responds to legal decisions. Balancing is a metaphor in which *a priori* principles are measurable and always available. To draw on general propositions in a novel case is, as Bickel wisely characterized it, an *abuse* of reasoning from principle.[28] The turn to principles, as exemplified by Herbert Wechsler and Ronald Dworkin in America, and by Robert Alexy in Europe, is a turn away from Dewey's social induction and toward a tendency to think deductively from unrevisable "axioms."

The inductive view in science and law was attributed by the early pragmatist Chauncey Wright, citing J. S. Mill and William Whewell, to the work of Francis Bacon, who in the interest of progress proposed, four centuries ago, his own revision of the tradition:

> [G]oing by my method is to derive axioms gradually, in a connected succession, so as only at the end to arrive at the most general; however, when they do come forth they are not purely speculative but are well-defined, and such as nature would really recognize as better known to herself, and which lie at the very marrow of things. But far the greatest change I make is in the very form of induction, and the judgment made from it. For the induction of which the logicians talk, which proceeds from simple enumeration, is a childish affair, unsafe in its conclusions, in danger from a contradictory influence, taking account only

---

27 Robert Alexy recognizes that what may appear to be judicial balancing is subject to competing interpretations, and he has addressed the question:

> A criterion for whether or not the judge appeals to principles for support is whether or not he undertakes to strike a balance. The following proposition seems to be true: in undertaking to strike a balance, one necessarily appeals to principles for support. For it is necessary to strike a balance precisely when there are competing reasons, each of which is by itself a good reason for a decision and only fails to lead directly to a definitive decision because of the other reason, calling for another decision; reasons like this are either principles or supported by principles." Alexy, *The Argument from Injustice*, 72

> Principles, it would appear from this passage, are to be identified as a relevant norm that a judge gives as a reason that is not definitive. In his article "On the Structure of Legal Principles," Alexy specifies that, in a particular case of the collision of principles (for example whether a trial may proceed where the accused is in danger of stroke or heart failure), "the court solves the problem by determining a conditional priority of one of the colliding principles over the other with respect to the circumstances of the case." Alexy, "On the Structure of Legal Principles," *Ratio Juris*, vol. 13, no. 3 (September 2000), 296.

28 "[T]he absolute rule of principle is also at war with a democratic system." Bickel, *The Least Dangerous Branch,* 64.

> of what is familiar, and leading to no result. Now what the sciences need is a form of induction that will analyze experience and take it apart, and through due exclusions and rejections necessarily come to a conclusion.[29]

The final sentence, Bacon's lasting contribution, implied a departure from the assumption that uniformities exist in nature, turning attention instead to the process of "exclusions and rejections" whereby experience is fully examined and "taken apart." Mill carried this emphasis further in his analysis of "comparison." It was left to Holmes and Dewey to recognize how comparison actually occurs in a contentious climate of conflict—how experience is "taken apart," but how it must then be reconstituted as new forms of action and practice.

Throughout its history, induction has been grounded in meliorist hope—the hope for human survival and progress. That hope is now conditioned by increasing evidence of precariousness, by an unabashed look at the reality of conflict, and by the association of agonistic deliberation with the real prospect of violence. Dewey's "unification" will depend upon keen attention to the social problems that are masked beneath rhetorical blaming, and by the piecemeal, continuous, and sane adjustments of practice in resolving them.

Charles Peirce's "first rule of reason" included the command "do not block the way of inquiry."[30] This is also the first principle of Dewey's still-misunderstood empirical naturalism, eschewing in *The Quest for Certainty* (1929) the appeal to values and ideology.[31] As fascism arose in Germany and Italy during the following decade, his criticism of misplaced philosophical certainty was mistaken for a malevolent influence, notwithstanding its caution against *all* ideology. Dewey's former student, Mortimer Adler, turned on him for alleged "moral disarmament" and giving comfort to Nazism, even claiming that he should be "liquidated."[32]

Explaining this extraordinary development is that Dewey had fallen victim to an unfortunate twist in the history of philosophy and science. His empirical naturalism was associated with the "logical positivism" brought to the United States after the First World War, which advanced a rigid distinction of "fact" from "value," and led to an extreme "emotivist" view that moral language

---

29 Francis Bacon, *Novum Organum*, trans. and ed. Peter Urbach and John Gibson (Chicago and La Salle: Open Court, 1994), 20–21.

30 "Upon this first, and in one sense this sole, rule of reason, that in order to learn you must desire to learn, and in so desiring not be satisfied with what you already incline to think, there follows one corollary which itself deserves to be inscribed upon every wall of the city of philosophy: Do not block the way of inquiry." *The Collected Papers of Charles Sanders Peirce,* vol. I (Cambridge: Belknap Press, 1978), 56.

31 Dewey, *The Quest for Certainty: A Study of the Relation of Knowledge and Action* (New York: Minton, Balch & Co., 1929); LW 4.

32 Westbrook, *John Dewey and American Democracy,* 520.

was "non-propositional" and hence meaningless beyond expressing human emotion. The approach had caught on in England with A. J. Ayer's 1936 *Language, Truth, and Logic* and in America with Charles L. Stevenson's 1944 *Ethics and Language*. Stevenson's mistaken association of Dewey with emotivism, and Dewey's own cumbersome critique of it, led Adler to associate Dewey with an emotivist "positivism of the professors."[33]

It is all the more imperative to flesh out the practical application of empirical naturalism in law. While its importance is illuminated by the keen analysis of Alexander Bickel, it remains challenging to explain. Although an essential element in his thought, Dewey made inadequate use of examples. His 1928 revision of *Experience and Nature* included an exposition that confounded even the sympathetic mind of the octogenarian Oliver Wendell Holmes Jr., who found the book brilliant but difficult to read. Yet Dewey and Holmes both remarked on their shared understanding of the logical method in philosophy. As Peirce had said of the study of logic in 1866, in a lecture apparently attended by Holmes,[34] "Our fate hangs upon it."

In search of hard and clear evidence of the practical meaning of empirical naturalism, I next turn the clock back to a younger Holmes at pivotal moments of his earlier life.

---

[33] Westbrook, *John Dewey and American Democracy,* 402–407, especially 407 n. 29; A. J. Ayer, *Language, Truth and Logic* (London: Victor Gallantz Ltd., 1936). Stevenson misconstrued Dewey's writing on ethics and values as consistent with emotivism, claiming "broad similarities" even while conceding "one wonders why Dewey . . . should have been so neglectful of emotive meaning." Charles L. Stevenson, *Ethics and Language* (New Haven: Yale University Press, 1944), 263. Failing to recognize Dewey's continuum of inquiry in ethics as well as science, Stevenson's conception of the relation of generalization to particular judgments is inconsistent with Dewey's extended transformative induction; see "Reflections on John Dewey's Ethics," *Proceedings of the Aristotelian Society*, New Series, vol. 62 (1961–1962), 77, 84: "Although he grants generalizations an importance, I wonder if he grants them quite enough importance."

[34] Kellogg, *Holmes and Legal Logic*, 37.

Chapter 8

Empirical Naturalism in Law

Dewey's empirical naturalism, the term expressing how raw experience influences human inference in normative as well as natural inquiries, has been given little attention by contemporary scholars. The notion was never welcomed during his lifetime, and Dewey did not provide clear examples. Instead, polarizing issues of national importance, including the two World Wars and Cold War anti-communism, drove many intellectuals toward an attitude regarding fundamental American "values" that obstructed Dewey's focus on specifying and particularizing public problems and their resolution.

The background of legal conflict helps to explain how this applies to ethical empiricism. The last chapter showed how premature recourse to principles prevents full and representative inquiry when the "way of inquiry" is found through a succession of judgments (represented by the small q) through which the larger problematic situation (represented by the capital Q) must be found and defined. The path of judgments must be inclusive, and it can be cut short by judicial overreach.

Just as legal history illustrates an unseen agonistic form of deliberation, it also provides insight into the abuse of principle. I turn to an example of conflict over early labor organization for elucidating the "way of inquiry" that Peirce sought *not* to block, in two Massachusetts cases, near the beginning of the last century. Oliver Wendell Holmes Jr. shared Dewey's pragmatist perspective of extended social inquiry, especially the radical uncertainty of conflict resolution, having drawn it from the same resource, the origins of pragmatism, in discussions with Peirce, James, and other Cambridge philosophers in the late 1860s after the American Civil War. Holmes's two dissents in early cases of labor organization, the second as Chief Justice of the Supreme Judicial Court of Massachusetts, highlight the importance of extending inquiry in a time of uncertainty and polarization.

Dewey praised Holmes extensively in *Experience and Nature* and in *The New Republic* of January 11, 1928, for

> three outstanding ideas: belief in the conclusions of intelligence as the final directive force in life; in freedom of thought and expression as a condition needed in order to realize this power of direction by thought, and in the experimental character of life and thought. These three ideas state the essence of one type, and to my mind the only enduring type, of liberal faith.[1]

Holmes had already written to Harold Laski (on December 4, 1926):

> I am reading a book by John Dewey, Experience and Nature. Wu put me on to it saying that it was a great book and mentioning that it had amiable words about me. I give you my word that it was this former remark that set me to reading it–and I think Wu was right. It is badly written in the sense that the style makes it more difficult than the thought—but even in the writing it gives me the feeling that Walt Whitman gives of the symphonic.[2]

It is well known that Holmes's most admired judicial stand was for free expression in times of war—the stirring 1919 dissent in *Abrams v. United States*. Perhaps his next most famous dissent is *Lochner v. New York* of 1902, in which the Supreme Court majority overruled a state law governing the working conditions of bakery workers as inconsistent with the contract clause of the fourteenth amendment to the U.S. Constitution.[3] His memorable phrase was "general propositions do not decide concrete cases." Yet the most illuminating examples come earlier, as a judge on the Massachusetts Supreme Judicial Court.

In 1896 Holmes dissented in the case of *Vegelahn v. Guntner,* 167 Mass. 92, over the majority's reliance on a comparable contract protection in the Massachusetts constitution, to outlaw picketing at a workplace in support of a strike by furniture workers.[4] Holmes wrote

---

1 Dewey praised Holmes and quoted him extensively in *Experience and Nature*, in chapter 10 on "Existence, Value and Criticism" 417–419, beginning with a passage from Holmes's 1915 essay "Ideals and Doubts" [CW 3:443]: "The mode in which the inevitable comes to pass is through effort. Consciously or unconsciously we all strive to make the kind of world that we like. And although with Spinoza we may regard criticism of the past as futile, there is every reason for doing all that we can to make a future such as we desire. . . there is every reason also for trying to make our desires intelligent." LW 1:295.

2 *Holmes-Laski Letters*, ed. M. Howe (Cambridge: Harvard University Press, 1953), 901.

3 Article I, Section 10, Clause 1: No State shall enter into any Treaty, Alliance, or Confederation; grant Letters of Marque and Reprisal; coin Money; emit Bills of Credit; make any Thing but gold and silver Coin a Tender in Payment of Debts; pass any Bill of Attainder, ex post facto Law, or Law impairing the Obligation of Contracts, or grant any Title of Nobility.

4 "An employer has a right to engage all persons who are willing to work for him, at such prices as may be mutually agreed upon; and persons employed or seeking employment have a corresponding

> The true grounds of decision are considerations of policy and of social advantage, and it is vain to suppose that solutions can be attained merely by logic and the general propositions of law which nobody disputes. Propositions as to public policy rarely are unanimously accepted, and still more rarely, if ever, are capable of unanswerable proof.[5]

The issue of organizing activities by labor unions returned to the Massachusetts high court again in 1900, in the case of *Plant v. Woods*, under different circumstances but raising the same question of whether such organizing activities were lawful. Holmes dissented again, but his explanation will help me exemplify empirical naturalism. Before the court had decided the second picketing case, the newly promoted Chief Justice Holmes apparently gave his brethren on that court a seminar on legal method, and it succeeded in an important regard. Holmes got the majority to concede that their prior resort to the contract rationale constituted improper judicial method. He basically told them to address the particular facts and base their rationale on similarity with legal precedent. They still didn't reverse themselves, but adopted the rationale that picketing was comparable to unlawful extortion. This may seem like no progress at all, but Holmes appears to celebrate it in his dissent:

> Much to my satisfaction, if I may say so, the court has seen fit to adopt a mode of approaching the question which I believe to be the correct one, and to open an issue which otherwise I might have thought closed. The difference between my brethren and me now seems to be a difference of degree, and the line of reasoning followed makes it proper for me to explain where the difference lies.[6]

The issue "which [he] otherwise might have thought closed" was placing union organizing efforts under a constitutional ban, and the new line of reasoning was still "open"—to further legal inquiry. For Holmes, in his dissent, the purpose was not directly concerned with wages; it was a degree more remote. The immediate object and motive were to strengthen the defendant's society as a preliminary means to enable it to make a better fight on questions of wages or other matters of clashing interests.

These two dissents offer crucial evidence for us. Why did he dissent? First, the case for him was not decided by a constitutional phrase protecting freedom of contract, because "general propositions do not decide concrete cases." His opinion suggests that this was an early case on an open and

---

right to enter into or remain in the employment of any person or corporation willing to employ them. These rights are secured by the Constitution itself." Majority opinion of Judge Allen, 167 Mass. at 97.

5 167 Mass. at 106.

6 *Vegelahn v. Guntner*, 167 Mass. 97, 105–106, 44 N.E. 1077, 1080 (1896) (Holmes, dissenting); *Plant v. Woods*, 176 Mass. 492, 504, 57 N.E. 1011, 1016 (1900) (Holmes, dissenting).

controversial matter. It was an early example of a prospectively broader inquiry, and all relevant experience was not yet on the table. The early case may not be fully representative, and the more general issue cannot be decided in advance. A decision on the constitutional contract rationale would have done exactly that.

Holmes was looking at the prospect of a longer view. Instead of being covered by immutable principle, he places this case on the borderline between opposing analogies. He concedes that judges can pick the wrong analogy in an early case, but still keep the issue open. He has faith in full community inquiry, that discovering and addressing facts and considerations derived from repeated relevant experience will produce the best legal outcome. He wants to give induction time and space to work.

In demonstrating this, I turned first to the 1890s, when Holmes was a judge on the Massachusetts Supreme Judicial Court, at the height of his ability, but before he was appointed to the U.S. Supreme Court. Later, I turn back thirty years to the 1860s and focus on his early reading and writing after returning from the Civil War. In the 1890s, beside the dissents I now consider two speeches, the famous "Path of the Law" to law students at Boston University in 1897, and another in 1899 to the New York State Bar Association, entitled "Law in Science and Science in Law."[7]

The principal criticisms of Holmes, that still distort his legacy, can be traced mainly to one source, "The Path of the Law." There he said that law is "the prediction of the incidence of the public force through the instrumentality of the courts." Note that he did *not* say that the law is whatever the judges say it is, which is what almost all scholars have taken away from the comment. He was talking here about the long term, not just the immediate decision, viewing law as a stream of problematic situations and not just the isolated detail of a particular case.

Another remark in "The Path of the Law" was his warning to the law students of "a confusion between morality and law which sometimes rises to the level of conscious theory." This line has been a greater troublemaker for Holmes, beginning in 1940 when Lon Fuller attacked him for *removing* morals from the law, reinforcing the charge of value relativism. This misses the real meaning of that warning as well as of the prediction comment. He was cautioning how law students should interpret legal terms that have moral overtones: you cannot assume they allow you to introduce morals into the hard case, as it will reflect your own *personal* morals.

[7] Reprinted at *CW* 3:391 and *CW* 3:406.

Moreover, contemporary misreading of this comment ignores an address he gave just two years later, with a notably different tone, speaking not to students but to the New York Bar Association. It also ignores what he wrote in the second dissenting opinion. When Holmes delivered the two addresses and wrote the two dissents he was in his late 50s, promoted in 1899 to Chief Justice of the Supreme Judicial Court of Massachusetts. So what was going on in the 1890s?

The situation was not unlike that of the present. Barbara Tuchman in *The Proud Tower* describes the western world in turmoil, riven by socialism and anarchism, and the two movements were readily associated with each other. Socialists were rallying for workers' strikes everywhere, and European heads of state were being attacked and assassinated by anarchists. In Chicago at the Haymarket bombing in 1886 a peaceful rally for striking workers was disrupted by an anarchist bomb that killed seven police officers. In 1892 Andrew Carnegie lowered wages at the Homestead, Ohio, steel plant, causing a strike. Carnegie brought in the Army and crushed the union, leading to twelve deaths.

Into all this came the legal issue of whether workplace organizing and picketing were permissible by unions seeking to enlist other workers. People knew picketing could lead to violence. When Holmes dissented he was not looking for promotion to a higher court. He took a position 180 degrees against common opinion, a decision that he knew would likely disqualify him for the U.S. Supreme Court. Yet Theodore Roosevelt appointed him in 1902, having become president due to the assassination of James A. Garfield.

The two lectures together elucidate his early work and his treatise on the common law. My last chapter claimed that premature recourse to principles can block the path of normative inquiry and the extended process required for the adjustment of rigid preferences. In law, this assures comprehensive and representative information in the decision process and ample space to transform a problematic situation. The origin and demonstration of this require an earlier look at his career, beginning with the post-Civil War diaries, his early reading in philosophy and science, discussions with peers like Peirce, William James, and Chauncey Wright, his response to lectures on logic and scientific induction by Peirce in 1866, and his own early essays probing and responding to John Stuart Mill's *A System of Logic*.[8]

The son of a doctor and a scientist, Holmes's first job out of Harvard College in 1860 was as a Union soldier, wounded three times in the American Civil War. Returning to Cambridge to study law, he was disappointed with

---

[8] See Kellogg, *Holmes and Legal Logic,* 36f.

Harvard Law School and started his own personal graduate school: one-on-one talks with other young Harvard graduates, engrossed not just in law, but in science and philosophy. Those talks were informed by western philosophy, English experimental science, and profound curiosity. We should picture the young Holmes in the years following the war discussing philosophy and science with William James and Charles Peirce.

The war was a failure of legal order; it was perhaps also a failure of European philosophy. It cast doubt on the naturalism of both Kant's categorical imperative and Hegel's historical synthesis. It focused Holmes on the question of whether there is a threshold for human success and failure, of its survival, and of the necessary conditions that would apply to the theory of law.

Like Dewey, misguided criticisms have dominated Holmes's legacy. They have come from a high academic level, from Harvard Law School Professor Lon Fuller in 1940, Yale Law Professor Grant Gilmore in the 1970s, and University of Chicago Professors Allan Bloom in the 1980s and Albert Alschuler in 1999. The conundrum of legal realism is still a problem, but Holmes is not responsible for it. He has remained the subject of criticism even today. A decade ago, in his Storrs Lecture at Yale, Columbia Law Professor Philip Bobbitt considered the opinion of Grant Gilmore that Holmes was responsible for the notion that law was simply (as Holmes had apparently said) judicial behavior. "If law was simply what the judges did," asked Bobbitt, "then how could they ever—from a legal point of view—be wrong? But judges often contradicted and reversed each other and themselves—so how could they ever be right?"[9]

But Holmes had not said that. The historical context reveals that what he actually said and thought was related to the continuum of inquiry found in Levi's 1949 essay, concerning the logical method of law. Rather than judicial behavior Holmes viewed legal adjudication as part of the struggle among active and opposing forces—a struggle not just between rules or even ideas but patterns of belief and conduct. Legal knowledge must be grounded, then, in the ultimate resolution of broad conflicts. Professors Bloom and Alschuler took the criticism a step further and insisted that Holmes was a relativist, denying fundamental truths. *Law Without Values* was the title of Alschuler's book; Lon Fuller claimed that Holmes had removed morals from the law.

---

[9] Grant Gilmore, *Ages of American Law* (New Haven and London: Yale University Press, 1977); Philip Bobbitt, "The Age of Consent," *Yale Law Journal,* vol. 123 (May 2014), 2334, 2336; Albert W. Alschuler, *Law without Values: The Life, Work and Legacy of Justice Holmes* (Chicago: University of Chicago Press, 1999); Alan Bloom, *The Closing of the American Mind: How Higher Education Has Failed Democracy and Impoverished the Souls of Today's Students* (New York: Simon & Schuster, 1987); Fuller, *The Law in Quest of Itself.*

The conundrum is rooted in logic. Classical logic since Aristotle has been framed by deduction and induction, governing the relation between (as Holmes would have put it) "generals and particulars." What, in a difficult legal case, is the logical problem? In an easy case, it is whether I brought my car to a complete stop at a stop sign; there is a clear rule and a clear act, a plain particular covered by a general, decided by deduction. Difficulty increases with the complexity of unanticipated acts that have combined to cause a claim of loss or harm.

Where deduction from existing rules is inconclusive, the question approaches an inductive one. Properly understood, induction seeks to find, from experience, the general rule that will resolve not just the case but the problem. The problem may be a new one, not yet covered by settled authority. Is medically assisted death suicide or murder? The relevant "particulars" are not just the particular facts of this new case, but (as Dewey wrote in 1938) the judgments, or *findings,* in a *succession* of cases, very like a succession of experiments in chemistry or physics.

An example of the analogy is the seventeenth-century debate in fluid dynamics: the appearance of an empty space in a test tube when filled with mercury and turned upside down, which was called after its discoverer the "Toricellian space." Regarding the space that unexpectedly appears between the tube's rounded bottom and the heavy liquid through which no air could have passed was the question of whether this is an *empty* space, or if there is some substance in that visible area. How, thought Thomas Hobbes in the seventeenth century, could such a space be "filled with *nothing*"? Hobbes was a "plenist," a view opposed to "vacuism," and he opposed the experimental scientist Robert Boyle, whose experiments with an air pump explored the problem on several grounds. While Boyle chose to do experiments Hobbes favored a deductive method. It took a *succession* of experiments to find an answer.[10]

Holmes had been deep into science thirty years earlier, and in a 1919 letter to Morris Cohen he said his cautious attitude came from the scientific way of looking at the world. This example will elucidate where Holmes was and is misunderstood, and why he is innocent of blame for the conundrum. Surely, when deduction works, the law is what the judges say it is. But where a new

[10] This is an oversimplification of a famous demonstration originally made by Evangelista Torricelli in 1644 (where the test tube would have been set within a dish of mercury), and refers to the question raised as to the nature of the "Torricellian space," and whether or not a true vacuum could exist in nature. The question also arose as to the cause of the suspension of the mercury above the dish. Hobbes was a "plenist," a view opposed to "vacuism," and opposed Robert Boyle's air-pump experiments to explore the complex controversy on several grounds, including Hobbes's favoring a "demonstrative" (and largely deductive) method of inquiry. Shapin and Shaffer, *Leviathan and the Air-Pump: Hobbes, Boyle, and the Experimental Life*, 21, 41f.

matter falls cleanly *outside* or *between* settled general rules and propositions, induction from experience is required to revise, or renew, prevalent belief and conduct. Sufficient experience may take time to gather and evaluate. That is when judges may understandably, and quite legitimately, appear to contradict and reverse themselves and each other, as have scientists at least since the eighteenth century, working on successions of experiments to see whether the empty space in the test tube is something we can now (often inexactly) call a "vacuum."

Like scientists, judges don't and shouldn't "choose first and rationalize," but rather, like juries, they must surely choose, but not *prematurely* rationalize, as did Hobbes in opposing (and actually denouncing) Robert Boyle's famous air-pump experiments. What scientists have used is an inductive process that Holmes and his friends knew to be grounded in Francis Bacon's seventeenth-century empiricism, and which they also knew had recently been reexamined by Mill and William Whewell in the 1840s. It was examined and refined again by Holmes in the years following the American Civil War.

The most profound and misleading criticism of Holmes has come from the idea that law and morals are separate. This was the legal positivism of John Austin in the nineteenth century and later Herbert Hart in the twentieth, a word transferred from science to law in the nineteenth century. Positivism is defined as a philosophical system that holds that every rationally justifiable assertion can be scientifically verified or is capable of logical or mathematical proof, rejecting metaphysics and theism. The Englishman John Austin, a utilitarian and friend of Jeremy Bentham, focused on defining law as the commands of a sovereign, which he saw as verifiable.

Austin's approach was criticized in the 1950s by Hart, who redefined legal positivism as a theory of law as a system of rules. Hart defined law as a system of primary and secondary rules: primary rules controlled conduct, and secondary governed the conduct of legal officials. Hart held that legal change takes place internally, according to the secondary rules of recognition, change, and adjudication. He accounted for legal difficulty with the notion that legal language is vague and has an "open texture." His positivism retained the hard, analytical boundary around the phenomenon of law, obscuring any notion of a transformative continuum.

Rather than assuming a hard boundary, Holmes clarified the dynamic relation between morals and law by showing how normative knowledge can be the product of conflict. There are three aspects: first, new normative knowledge is generated in conflict, of *conduct* as well as opinion; second, this requires extension in time and space, in time and within *society*. Normative inquiry is a product of broad experience and often requires considerable time to reach stability. Finally, it requires transformation of conduct as well as of discourse and persuasion to resolve serious conflicts if they are to be finally resolved at all.

His second speech in New York in 1899, a year before the second labor dissent, is filled with more relevant evidence, but it is indirect evidence. Instead of zooming in on legal language, Holmes first zooms out and sees the big picture in a sweeping history. Much of this speech is a recap of his famous 1881 treatise, *The Common Law*, but its title is "Law in Science and Science in Law." Why science? Because it's a grand analysis—a reflection on both legal and scientific knowledge, especially the question of uncertainty. Holmes asks how deep uncertainty is resolved in addressing human problems, scientific or legal.

Holmes saw law through conflict, and cases often came as part of a broad social controversy. He says in the 1899 lecture

> It seems to me well to remember that men begin with no theory at all and with no such generalization as contract. They begin with particular cases and even when they have generalized, they are often a long way from the final generalizations of a later time.

Where does this come from? From John Stuart Mill's 1843 *System of Logic*, which Holmes read in 1866 and discussed with his friends. Where did Mill get it? From Francis Bacon, the seventeenth-century English lawyer *and* scientist, whose empiricism was directed against all forms of conclusory thinking. It involves the early roots of logical questions, of treating generals and particulars.[11]

Holmes had explored this issue before writing his 1881 treatise on *The Common Law*.

The uncertain particular case occurs between two opposing but already established precedents—one might say in a space of contested reasons. In 1873 he described this process as follows:

> The growth of the law is very apt to take place in this way: two widely different cases suggest a general distinction, which is a clear one when stated broadly. But as new cases cluster around the opposite poles, and begin to approach each other, the distinction becomes more difficult to trace; the determinations are made one way or the other on a very slight preponderance of feeling, rather than articulate reason; and at last a mathematical line is arrived at by the contact of

[11] See Kellogg, *Holmes and Legal Logic*, 36f.

> contrary decisions, which is so far arbitrary that it might equally well have been drawn a little further to the one side or to the other.[12]

This graphic description suggests two precedential "poles," which we might mark A and B, each encompassing a cumulative formulation based on previous decisions, but now surrounded by new cases that "cluster" like marks on a graph, some nearer to one pole, some to the other, and still others in a space equidistant from both. The new cases are not decided independently as in 1870, but rather with an awareness of (if not explicit reference to) prior precedents that operate as the opposing "poles." New marks are being made on the graph, which we should visualize along a timeline, with choices in the middle area occasioning explanation with regard to the earlier poles. As time progresses, the new cases are "marked" on either side of a "line" that defines agreement with one pole or the other.

Taken together with the gradual, retrospective "successive approximation" process outlined in an 1870 essay, the implication is that, as more cases are decided in the space of contested reasons, the meanings of both A and B, that is, the conceptual understandings of earlier discrete judicial experience (in the prior "clusters"), are subject to being retrospectively tweaked or refined to accommodate the new problem. Holmes has added the image of a time-dependent and possibly meandering "line," engaging broad input from judges, lawyers, affected potential litigants in the relevant environment, as well as critics and scholars.

Holmes in 1870 and 1873 recognized stages, where a problematic situation has first to be defined, contingent and conflicting problems of policy sorted out, while the need to defer a final resolution still remains. In his 1870 account, the legal general must be sought amidst an often inarticulate succession of specific situations. Only gradually, in retrospective summaries of accumulated decisions, does it gain the foothold of predication and normative expression.

This observation addresses the manner in which patterns of conduct are found, reinforced, and adjusted by legal decisions as conflicts occur in society. It comes directly from his study of English and American cases while editing Kent's *Commentaries*. The case he cites for the remark, explaining his use of the term "mathematical," involves distance measurement where eighteenth-century English courts settled on a formula to resolve continuing litigation over the competing rights of neighboring landowners concerning the height of structures near a boundary. In the absence of local building codes (a later development), a formula was eventually worked out. A comparable

---

[12] Holmes, "The Theory of Torts," Kellogg, *Formative Essays of Justice Holmes*, 117, 119; CW 1:326, 327.

issue today might be the U.S. Supreme Court seeking an appropriate "buffer-zone" distance from abortion clinics to balance the rights of pro-life picketers against women seeking access to medical assistance.

The diaries and letters reveal Holmes turning his focus in 1868 increasingly to law in place of science and philosophy. References to line drawing would recur throughout his career.[13] Levi's account matches and illuminates Holmes's original 1870 model. Although he seems unaware of that essay and its importance for Holmes, Levi made explicit the implicit process of feedback from outside the legal profession and the adjudicatory system:

> [It] appears that the kind of reasoning involved in the legal process is one in which the classification changes as the classification is made. . . . In a sense all reasoning is of this type [citing Dewey's 1939 *Logic*], but here is an additional requirement which compels the legal process in this way. Not only do new situations arise but in addition peoples' wants change. The categories used in the legal process must be left ambiguous in order to permit the infusion of new ideas. And this is true even when legislation or a constitution is involved. The words used by the legislature or the constitutional convention must come to have new meanings. Furthermore, agreement on any other basis would be impossible.[14]

Holmes's 1873 notion of the drawing of lines between opposing poles is suggested by Levi's reflection:

> The law forum is the most explicit demonstration of the mechanism required for a moving classification system. . . . What does the law forum require? It requires the presentation of competing examples. The forum protects the parties and the community by making sure that the competing analogies are before the court. The rule which will be created arises out of a process in which the differences have been urged. In this sense the parties as well as the court participate in the law-making. In this sense, also, lawyers represent more than the litigants. (1949:4–5)

Holmes should be recognized for outlining a departure in the direction later taken by John Dewey in his 1938 *Logic: The Theory of Inquiry*. Broadly speaking, this entails seeing classical logic and its instant analytic view of uncertainty as insufficient to explain the process of growth and change. Rather than a strictly judge-centric view of legal growth, his approach focused on the larger problem implied by the difficult case, its interpretation of legal uncertainty within a transformative continuum, and its focus on the nature of entrenchment amidst the inevitability of change in the conceptual structure of law.

---

13 *McCullen v. Coakley*, 453 U.S. 199, 134 S. Ct. 2518 (2014).

14 Levi, *Introduction to Legal Reasoning*, 3–4.

Discussing legal change before the New York lawyers, Holmes takes pains to show the lingering influence of ancient practices on contemporary law, just as he did in *The Common Law*. This reveals three things. First, he sees the roots of litigation in replacing the practice of revenge, still evident in legal doctrine even today. Second, it raises the question: how does law change, including deep conceptual change? And third, he's talking about the hidden underlying importance of practices and patterns of conduct. The source of general legal conceptions lies in both ancient and newly changing practices. Thus, if the law is to solve big problems, practice and habit must flex along with legal language.

How about Mill? His concern in the 1843 *Logic* was the grounds of thought and the origin of conceptions. Mill had found this origin in the comparison of particulars. Any conception, wrote Mill, originally found its way to us as a result of direct comparison. Holmes disputed this as early as 1870 after his friend, the pragmatic philosopher Charles Peirce, had criticized it in 1866. Comparison is like a visual process. It assumes a single stable platform of observation as if with an omniscient observer or observing mind, not a messy real world like that of the law, which consists of many viewers, their opposing comparisons, and the elusive nature of opposing habits of interested parties.

Before writing *The Common Law*, Holmes had spent several years revising Chancellor James Kent's *Commentaries on American Law*, the legal encyclopedia of the day. He found stability throughout much of the common law emerging out of interaction among different points of view, albeit grounded in habits and conduct. When necessary they can converge, but rarely by immediate fiat. Legal thought originates in disputes over problems, and convergence may take time.

The empiricist Francis Bacon was key to his early research, especially Bacon's attack on bad intellectual habits. In the 1899 New York speech, Holmes turns to bad intellectual habits. He uses legal examples. His first example is the assumption of risk, a common way of deciding for an employer against an injured laborer. Even if a worker is injured by defective equipment, the employer can make the argument that the worker has assumed the risk. I'll quote Holmes:

> Lately have we not all been bored to death with *volenti non fit injuria*? I blush to say that I have been as guilty as the rest. Do we not hear every day of taking the risk, an expression which you never heard used until within a very few years?

Holmes is resisting the temper of the times. This is not an illiberal, cynical judge displaying a retrograde attitude toward workers. He's asking, what assumption, and what risk?[15]

---

[15] "Law in Science and Science in Law," 443, CW 3:415.

Here's Holmes again:

> When we say that a workman takes a certain risk as incident to his employment, we mean that on some general grounds of policy blindly felt, we read into his contract a term of which he never thought. And the real question in every case is, what are the grounds and how far do they extend?

Here we have an answer to why he dissented to the rulings against picketing. What was the actual activity complained of in picketing? What precisely was the harm? Legal logic is embedded in society. It works within society in solving real problems. Like science, it begins with particular judgments and puts them together into generalizations with professional care. How this care works was his obsession, and the analogy with science is plain.

Holmes explained his attack on accepted legal formulas. Like the assumption of risk, they "do not represent a final analysis, but dodge difficulty and responsibility with a rhetorical phrase." Difficulty and responsibility: what does that signify? What is *not* dodging difficulty and responsibility? The answer is, frankly, not conspicuous. But it becomes clear when examining where this attitude came from.

After Holmes had returned from the Civil War in 1864, he and other Harvard graduates, Peirce, James, Chauncey Wright, and John Chipman Gray, would get together and discuss American experience in the context of the history of western thought. They read Kant, Hegel, and the later English empiricists, but they all looked back to Bacon's 1620 *Novum Organum*, which said:

> There are two ways of inquiry into truth. The one flies from the senses and particulars to axioms of the most general kind and treats them as unshakable truth. And this is the method that is now in use. The other calls forth axioms from the senses and particulars by a gradual and continuous accent.[16]

Bacon's phrasing indicates that logical induction is extended over time. I think most lawyers and judges know this but they need to ground it, which is what Holmes does here and what contemporary legal philosophy does not. Why is it missing today? The late Justice Sandra Day O'Connor, known for her narrow fact-based opinions, was criticized for that very attitude by both liberal and conservative commentators.

To be fair to the critics of Holmes, Francis Bacon is missing in Holmes's later writings, and hence ignored by both his critics and his defenders. But if you look carefully Bacon is not missing from the historical record. He has

---

16 Bacon, *Novum Organum*, 110.

been overlooked in the set narrative about Holmes's influential, but usually shallow, place in American legal thought, a view rooted in attitudes that came after his death. Today H.L.A. Hart of Oxford is the truly profound thinker. But it is Bacon who illuminates Holmes's 1890 speeches and opinions.

Bacon explains the warning to the law students against moral language—the warning against premature use of principle, not against principled jurisprudence *per se*. When Holmes equates law with "predicting the public force through the courts" he means the outcome of an extended inductive process, in which principles come at the end.

Lon Fuller, in attacking Holmes in 1940, was standing up for American values, like Alschuler who attacked him in the 1999 *Law Without Values*. Legal principles at the end of inquiry are not bland, expressing what Holmes often called a "benevolent yearning." The great Yale scholar Alexander Bickel wrestled with defining legal principle, and eventually concluded that the high court should work *toward* principle, not *from* it. Yet he, too, was blocked from recourse to Holmes by the dominant criticism, and didn't profit from Holmes's keen insights. Instead, he quoted Abraham Lincoln: "As our case is new, so we must think anew and act anew." Lincoln is said to have read Bacon's essays while still in Springfield, Illinois.

Such is the profound effect of the Civil War on Holmes's philosophy. In adding conflict to Mill's comparison model, he brings logical theory into the real world. Mill was the great optimist: education was the key to progress. While concepts from Mill came from bald comparison, for Holmes, concepts, theories, and solutions all come from the clash of habits and practices. If the basis of induction is mere comparison, then education and dialogue is all you need. But if thought involves dispute and the adjustment of opposing habits and practices, it can take effort and time. This is not an easy message to sell. Much easier is the argument favoring "principled jurisprudence." The appeal to American values was employed against John Dewey. The vague idea of our fundamental values is comforting; Lincoln used the word "enthralling." Values parade as the case against relativism, that only principled judges can save the country.

Returning to Holmes's remark in the second picketing dissent: "[t]he difference between my brethren and me now seems to be a difference of degree." How can we accept that as an approach? Here again, the best explanation might be a response to criticism. Professor Richard Epstein of the NYU School of Law wrote a book in 2008 called *Supreme Neglect*, attacking Holmes for his 1922 opinion in *Pennsylvania Coal Company v. Mahon*.[17]

[17] *Pennsylvania Coal Co. v. Mahon*, 260 U.S. 390 (1922); Richard A. Epstein, *Supreme Neglect: How to Revive Constitutional Protection For Private Property* (Oxford: Oxford University Press, 2008).

That's the first case overruling what has come to be called a regulatory taking. That means, basically, classifying a particularly intrusive regulation as an unlawful taking of private property. This case involved a state law that limited liability for damage caused by mining operations in a case where houses actually collapsed. Holmes saw it as unique, nearly without precedent. Nevertheless, he said in 1922 that limiting liability on those specific facts just "went too far."

Epstein jumped on this. He writes, "[a]ll liability questions demand yes or no answers that are best obtained by bright line rules. . . . Holmes's 'too far' question turns a bright line question into a matter of degree for no good reason." Thus, "Holmes got to a sound result but by the wrong path, thus plunging the law of regulatory takings into intellectual incoherence from which it has never escaped." The *Mahon* case is the very first case of a regulatory taking when the term itself was yet uncoined and unimagined. *Mahon* was, like picketing in 1890, an early and figuratively borderline case. But Epstein complains that Holmes treats everything as a matter of degree, implicitly rejecting all principled distinctions in kind. Not so; Holmes only treated the early borderline case as a matter of degree. He based his decision in *Mahon* on the specific facts. Bright-line answers are not available to the country when, in Lincoln's apt phrase, our case is new. The very idea of regulatory takings is still controversial in terms of deeply challenging sovereignty and the view that democratic states have broad police powers.

Now, given that Epstein's principles have taken a while to gain momentum, what should we make of their present legal status? Are they now a set of moral principles available to Ronald Dworkin's idealized judge? I think if you ask an academic legal philosopher, liberal or conservative, the answer would be yes. Principles are part of what they often call the background. To say "no" here is inconsistent with the path of legal theory, at least since Hart's 1957 Holmes Lecture and Ronald Dworkin's moralizing response. One turns to the background when the foreground has no clear answer. Holmes's insight is simply this: Sure, the new case can implicate moral principles. Sure, they are relevant. But they are also in dispute. Epstein's principles may be better described, with Robert Boyle's experiments, as hypotheses, in the same sense as Holmes's controversial theory of contract,[18] the articles in the Yale Law Review, and the particle nature of light. They may, in the course of inquiry, supply an explanation. Holmes's contract theory eventually did; many theories in the law reviews did not; and the particle nature of light may still be in play. Without fresh ideas, the law cannot grow. Judges have a duty to the

[18] See Grant Gilmore, *The Death of Contract* (Columbus: Ohio State University Press, 1974).

future, not just the immediate future, but to the distant and yet un-envisioned future.

In controversial public matters, a succession of judgments may go either way, as a line is drawn with considerations of utility examined seriatim. If Holmes's concern with this process had been recognized, it might have made a difference in the jurisprudential debates since his death. Instead, new influences arrived to wrest the debate away from Levi's articulation of the common law continuum and toward a static perspective on the "essential nature" of law. A renewed faith in "textualism" now often supports a conservative approach to individual cases without regard to their place in the continuum of inquiry.[19]

I have compared Holmes to standard views that followed in his wake, legal realism, legal positivism, critical legal studies, and, especially, the turn toward "principles," a form of reasoning from general propositions advanced by Herbert Wechsler and Ronald Dworkin. Holmes's insights lie outside the neoorthodox theories. Nevertheless, aspects of the transformative "continuum" are identifiable in the literature, especially in classic works by Edward Levi, Karl Llewellyn, and Alexander Bickel. Recognition is obscured by the fact that the path of the law is often circuitous and clouded by technicalities, intricacies, and diversions. Judicial vision is understandably tempted toward premature generalizing, given that new problems brought to law from society are rarely presented in a dispassionate, antiseptic environment.

What of the fundamental values that have guided the ideals of equality and fairness in the American experiment? They were not inactive or ignored in the contest between labor and management that Holmes sought to protect from a constitutional blocking of judicial inquiry. As Dewey recognized, motivating influences competed in the struggle for fair working conditions. That very endeavor was and remains an active part of the public quest for "right" answers. If shared problems are the context for life, and conflict is part of their solutions, what is the standard of objectivity?

The next chapter addresses that question in the context of the still-active debate over objectivism and relativism. The previous three chapters have discussed agonistic deliberation, radical uncertainty, and premature deduction from principle. Those phrases and the topics they represent are largely unrecognized by contemporary writers in jurisprudence and philosophy.[20] They relate to the process Dewey identified as normative or ethical empiricism, which he referred to more generally as *empirical naturalism*, the *actual*

---

[19] See e.g. William Baude's Scalia Lecture "Beyond Textualism" at Harvard Law School: Neil H. Shah, *The Harvard Crimson*, February 28, 2023.

[20] For an alternative view on principles see Onora O'Neill, *From Principle to Practice: Normativity and Judgment in Ethics and Politics* (Cambridge: Cambridge University Press, 2018).

process of acquiring knowledge through social intelligence, and seeing beyond the *unnatural* assumptions of current theory and Dworkin's unnatural, idealized judge Hercules.

In his preface to the 1928 revision of *Experience and Nature,* Dewey inaugurated his new term: "The title of this volume, Experience and Nature, is intended to signify that the philosophy here presented may be termed either empirical naturalism or naturalistic empiricism, or, taking "experience" in its usual signification, naturalistic humanism." Nature, he complained (with supporting quotes from Holmes), "is said to be complete apart from experience." He sought to frame a theory that would not "degrade and deny the noble and ideal values that characterize experience." [21]

---

[21] Dewey, *Experience and Nature*, 1a; LW 1:10.

Chapter 9

Naturalizing Objectivity

> Our identification with our community—our society, our political tradition, our intellectual heritage—is heightened when we see this community as ours rather than nature's, shaped rather than found, one among many which men have made. In the end, the pragmatists tell us, what matters is our loyalty to other human beings clinging together against the dark, not our hope of *getting things right.* [my italics][1]

In the passage above, the pragmatist philosopher Richard Rorty deflates the notion of "getting things right" in philosophy, in lieu of focusing on a commitment to community and communication—keeping a vivid cognitive heritage through conversation. The lead essay of his 1991 *Objectivity, Relativism, and Truth* is titled "Solidarity or Objectivity?" and "announces a theme which is repeated with variations in most of the other essays. There I urge that whatever good the ideas of 'objectivity' and 'transcendence' have done for our culture can be attained equally well by the idea of a community which strives after both intersubjective agreement and novelty—a democratic, progressive, pluralist community of the sort of which Dewey dreamt."[2]

Dewey agreed with the goal of a democratic, progressive, pluralist community, but Rorty, in deflating "getting things right," missed the importance Dewey (whom he considered in 1979 one of his three philosophical heroes) gave to the critical, indeed existential, project of "getting things right" in problematic situations. "Right" for Dewey would refer to the always contingent unification of divided attitudes, beliefs, and approaches; and he would give importance not only to the meaning of "right" but also to the implication

---

[1] Richard Rorty, "Pragmatism, Relativism, and Irrationalism," in *The Rorty Reader, ed. Christopher Voparil and Richard Bernstein* (Chichester: Wiley-Blackwell, 2010), 115.

[2] Rorty, *Objectivity, Relativism, and Truth* (Cambridge: Cambridge University Press, 1991), 13.

of "getting." For Rorty, the meaning of getting is primarily cognitive, while for Dewey, it is wholly practical, the conjoint activity resulting from resolving a problem. Yet Rorty is right, and Dewey would agree, that philosophy continues a failed quest for global cognitive objectivity.[3]

This chapter addresses what I will call Dewey's *naturalized* objectivity. It follows from the previous chapters, beginning with Kenneth Arrow's image of a society of individual preferences, which he viewed from an immediate, omniscient external point of view. Instead of the image of a totality of preferences, a "social state" fixed at any moment of vision (even if it assumes a *succession* of "social states"), Dewey's vision is one of multiple problematic situations in which habits and beliefs drive preference aggregation around problems large and small. Preferences cannot be marked with letters as if they are unique, as they are constantly evolving along with developing problems, and individual preferences (and *utilities*, as was seen in chapter 4) are changing as problems lead to new patterns of conduct. Arrow's viewpoint is a global synchronic one, as is Henry Sidgwick's "point of view of the universe." Dewey's viewpoint is a local diachronic one, like Edward Levi's description of law as a vast "moving system of classifications" based on a mixture of ongoing, developing, and stabilized problems.

Moreover, Dewey's view recognizes the battles of opposing visions that underlie this system. No matter how disparate and radically opposed they are, they cannot be dismissed as not part of the overall picture. The opposing images of extortion and free association battled each other in the early litigation over workers' rights. The opposing images of women's roles at home or at work battled each other through the transformations of the First World War. It is misleading to formulate a unitary model of social cognition in the face of multiple conflicting social goals. This challenges any attempt to posit a universal mind viewing a separate reality.

Dewey's pragmatism is a depiction distinct from one that has dominated philosophy—a *universal synchronic* embodiment reflected in the still ongoing debates over *mind* and *world*, or how (in the abstract) a universal "mind" can derive or effectuate knowledge from or within a separate "world." John McDowell in *Mind and World* wrote that "we are prone to fall into an intolerable oscillation: in one phase we are drawn to an objective reality, and in the other phase we recoil into an appeal to the Given, which turns out to be useless." Wilfrid Sellars, in his 1956 essay "Empiricism and the Philosophy of Mind" (titled earlier as "The Myth of the Given"), had argued

3 There are comments by Rorty that suggest an associated practical meaning, such as "By an antirepresentationalist account I mean one which does not view knowledge as a matter of getting reality right, but rather as a matter of acquiring habits of action for coping with reality." Dewey would approve the notion of *adjusting* habits directed toward the resolution of conflicts. Rorty, *Objectivity, Relativism, and Truth,* 1.

against finding any basic "given" element or fixed extra-human aspect of reality. Dewey's "given" is both human and *un*fixed: shared problems are fundamental, formed around specific issues, in a *topical* and *diachronic problematic* embodiment.[4]

Herbert Hart decried the "oscillation" between legal realism and formalism, concerned with immediate right legal answers in difficult cases, rather than stages in a continuum of inquiry. A related "oscillation" in philosophy, concerning the definition of truth, was decried in 1981 by Hilary Putnam as a perennial "gestalt switch" between metaphysical objectivism and relativism. The gestalt switch is a useful analogy for attempts to characterize a developing universe as a fixed one. Dewey would attribute it to the fallacy of selective emphasis.[5] The legal realist focuses attention on dissimilar uncertain cases, and the formalist on those that have been united by experience as similar. The metaphysical relativist focuses on disorderly aspects of cognitive engagement with the world, and the objectivist on orderly ones. McDowell writes of an oscillation in "the difficulties we can fall into in our reflection about empirical judgment and knowledge if we try to accommodate the point that Kant makes by talking of spontaneity."[6]

McDowell refers here to the priority Immanuel Kant gave to the creative and constructive role of human cognition in putting together (or "constructing") an understanding of fundamental aspects of reality and justice, of the real and the right. Yet McDowell writes that granting human "spontaneity" slides too readily into doubts concerning its empirical basis:

> To accept [Kant's] point is to acknowledge that judging is an active employment of capacities that empower us to take charge of our thinking. But that threatens us with oscillating between two unpalatable alternatives. The initial threat is that we lose a connection between empirical thinking and independent reality, a connection that there must be if what is in question is to be recognizable as bearing an independent reality at all. The idea of spontaneity is an idea of freedom, and that threatens to make what was meant to be empirical thinking degenerate, in our picture, into a frictionless spinning in a void.[7]

---

4 John McDowell, *Mind and World* (Cambridge: Harvard University Press, 1994), 23; Wilfrid Sellars, "Empiricism and the Philosophy of Mind," in *Minneapolis Studies in the Philosophy of Science*, vol. 1, ed. Herbert Feigl and Michael Scriven (Minneapolis: University of Minnesota Press, 1956), 253–329.

5 The continuum discloses distinct phases that can be mistaken for universal conditions. Uncertainty and unification are easily mistaken as relativism and objectivism; in *Experience and Nature* they are "initiations" and "consummations." Dewey, *Experience and Nature,* xii, 27.

6 McDowell, *Mind and World,* 66.

7 McDowell, *Mind and World,* 66.

This passage helps to further distinguish the nature of Dewey's controversial empirical naturalism and how it escapes from the "two unpalatable alternatives." Dewey's escape derives from abandoning the construct of "mind," or "human cognition," as separate from the construct of "world." The alternative to McDowell's universal "mind" is closer to what Holmes in 1873 referred to as the actual and opposed "many minds" that advance competing viewpoints in legal litigation, and the agonistic process of working out solutions to a "world" replete with diverse problematic situations. Dewey's vision hardly undermines the Kantian notion of spontaneity or creative freedom, but rather views local creativity as necessary in surmounting difficulties as they become recognizable. Spontaneity is not separate from a factual world, but is a critical source of valuable factual experience.

Dewey's fully naturalized empiricism continuously promotes new action leading to new judgments and new "facts," as experience of a problem proceeds. His agonistic freedom does not "spin frictionless in a void," because dispute and conflict engage problems by means of the friction of successive encounters, including lawsuits, strikes, news articles, debates, columns, documentaries, new ventures and proposals, eventual legislation, and of course, elections. There is no less friction in this process than the friction of competition by a tackle football team seeking a championship. The need for comprehensive experience reinforces the imperative of avoiding premature recourse to moral principles. Principles are not *a priori* unconditional obligations. While they can be useful as hypothetical guides in novel cases, they find granular and contextual clarity as inquiry proceeds. The battles over workers' and women's rights have survived many appeals to foreclose transformation, based on American values and principles. Moral principles guiding the future lie in transformed habits and practices.

Interest in Dewey's original contributions to philosophy faded in the mid-twentieth century under a wave of formal logic and linguistic theory. As a brilliant scholar of these fields, Rorty revived interest in both Dewey and pragmatism in his 1979 *Philosophy and the Mirror of Nature*, characterizing Dewey as an "anti-foundationalist" along with Martin Heidegger and Ludwig Wittgenstein. All three were credited with reforming the philosophical tradition to abandon an illusory essence or definitive structure of philosophical truth.

There are many problematic situations that humans have solved, or "gotten right" in the practical sense, in ocean navigation, agriculture, architecture, weather prediction, air travel, many of which are taken for granted in daily life even while new problematic aspects constantly surface. Rorty would naturally agree, and says as much. Where then is the difference? Rorty claims that he and Dewey are on the same page regarding philosophy, and many Dewey scholars today would agree. The strongly agonistic account of

Dewey in this chapter is not a common opinion. It is an aspect of Dewey that addresses the practical side of democratic inquiry as well as how experience is developed and preferences transformed in the continuum. Insofar as it is unrecognized by pragmatists, it should be part of the continuing debate over pragmatism's future. Its value lies in exploring how *real* problems have reached real *rightness.* It has taken more than Rorty's conversational "free and open encounter" of opinions.

Dewey would agree with Rorty that professional philosophers are overly concerned with the *global* question of getting things right: the sense in which philosophers seek to define rightness and other concepts like essential "truth." Dewey's rejection of that goal is why Rorty admired him and why it is important to articulate how a society of constant preference conflicts avoids both objectivism and relativism. For Dewey the terminology itself is inapt, and is rarely applied to a specific problem. In the actual continuum, the meanings of objectivism and relativism would translate to Dewey's favored terms of the *stability* of a unified outcome, coming from the *uncertainty* of earlier novelty and confusion.

Dewey sought less to end philosophy than to redirect it toward a necessary and useful theory of inquiry. The full practical value of his characterization of truth as "warranted assertability" *in a continuum of inquiry* was missed by both Rorty and Hilary Putnam, two leading pragmatist philosophers of the late twentieth century. Both sought to fit Dewey's meaning into an *immediate context* that could be warrantably asserted. Neither recognized that the phrase implicates more than present assertion, but involves the transformed outcome of specific shared inquiries to stabilize dispute and conflict through conjoint action—through both renewed and modified ethical habit and belief. In the many areas where stability has been achieved through experience, warrant comes from transformed, *consensual* conduct, derived from full and representative exploration and experience, including the transformative experience and unification of conflicting notions, habits, and beliefs.

Deflating a global conception of truth can *inflate* a relativist one. If there is no essence, there may appear instead a deep and "essential" pluralism of rigid values, and even of possible *conceptions.* Rorty took Isaiah Berlin's vision of a deep pluralism embedded in social reality to a higher level, where the vision encompasses a *cognitive* reality: the available objective knowledge articulable in propositional language. Even while sharing Dewey's concern for human problems, Rorty drew American pragmatism away from Dewey's agonistic mechanics of human problem resolution in the continuum of inquiry, which he rarely mentions. Again, *deliberation* is his essence of democracy; Rorty writes "I read Dewey as saying that it suits such a society to have no views about truth save that it is more likely to be obtained in Milton's 'free and open encounter' of opinions than in any other way" and that Dewey's warranted assertability is "what our peers will, *ceteris paribus*, let us get away with saying." He described this as "epistemological behaviorism" or "the claim that philosophy will have no more to offer but common sense (supplemented by biology, history, etc.) about knowledge and truth."[8]

Rorty's idea of community, which is dominant in his writing, is not the polarized one of contemporary American experience. Although Rorty recognizes contingency, knowledge is what the relevant community is presently justified in believing.[9] Dewey's vision, cast in the wake of two world wars, was open to the prospect of massive polarization. It recognized that present standards reflect many resolved conflicts and transformed habits and conduct, yet the conflict never ends. Present standards are what we have, as Philip Kitcher rightly says, for moral progress. The friction of conflict has extended consensual understanding into previously unrecognized areas, and it continues. In a society of pragmatic conflict, in which justification occurs when problems are unified and standards like legal principles follow that success, fundamental principles are themselves strengthened and extended to further aspects of American experience.

Both Rorty and Putnam referred often to the tendency of philosophy to "seesaw" between objectivity and subjective relativism. A comparable "gestalt switch" is the oscillation that Herbert Hart decried in 1973, regarding legal realism and formalism, and the term Putnam used in his extended debate with Rorty on whether and how pragmatism could *avoid* relativism.[10] Neither took note of Dewey's attribution to the fallacy of selective emphasis. While Rorty took Dewey to be an epistemological behaviorist, Putnam, rather perfunctorily, put Dewey into a category called "objective relativism," following an article in 1927 by Arthur E. Murphy, who joined Dewey with Alfred North Whitehead as "prophets of a new gospel":

> The common tendency I shall term "objective relativism." . . . It attempts to unite two propositions which have uniformly been taken to be incompatible. (a) The objective facts of the world of nature and of reality are the very "apparent" and relative happenings directly disclosed to us in perception. (b) In spite (or because) of such objectivity such happenings remain ultimately and inescapably relative. Such relativity is hence an ultimate fact about the objective world.[11]

---

[8] Rorty, *Objectivism, Relativism and Truth,* 1; *Philosophy and the Mirror of Nature* (Princeton: Princeton University Press, 1979), 176.

[9] Rorty, *Objectivism, Relativism and Truth,* 29; *Philosophy and the Mirror of Nature*, 3, 178.

[10] In *Reason, Truth and History* (Cambridge: Cambridge University Press, 1981), ix, Putnam decried "the 'gestalt switching' when such a dichotomy as between objective and subjective has become accepted: "In the present work, the aim which I have in mind is to break the stranglehold which a number of dichotomies appear to have on the thinking of both philosophers and laymen. Chief among these is the dichotomy between objective and subjective views of truth and reason."

[11] Arthur E. Murphy, "Objective Relativism in Dewey and Whitehead," *The Philosophical Review*, vol. 36, no. 2 (March 1927), 122.

This characterization simply adopted both opposing global and cognitive propositions, ignoring Dewey's local meaning of practical stability or uncertainty. The idea that "relativity is an ultimate fact about the objective world" ignores Dewey's account of the *appearance* of relativity in the early stage of a problem; as such, it is hardly objective. Nevertheless, the appellation stuck, and led Hilary Putnam to adopt it in *Reason, Truth and History*.

> A relativist need not be concerned to undermine the rationality of all "value" judgments, or to defend Foucault's picture of history as a discontinuous series of "discourses" or "ideologies" which succeed one another for no rational reason. A more modest relativist might be happy to agree with Dewey [footnoting his *The Theory of Valuation*] that some values are objectively relative—i.e., rational *given the circumstances,* the nature and history, of those who make them. What is important, such a modest relativist maintains, is precisely the *relativity* of all values. The "objectivity" he is denying is not the objectivity Dewey was affirming, which is simply the objectivity of any judgment that is warranted in its actual existential setting, but it is rather the objectivity a Plato would affirm, the spurious objectivity (the relativist would say) that purports to speak from an absolute point of view, apart *from* all circumstances and valid *for* all circumstances. [Putnam's italics][12]

The "objectivity of any judgment that is warranted in its actual existential setting" again fails to recognize the friction that has defined the judgment and the continuing friction that it must endure as a resolution. Putnam then utterly misreads Dewey's meaning with the following comment:

> What is of concern is that Dewey's doctrine of "objective relativism" cannot handle the case of the Nazi (although Dewey would have disputed this). We want to say that the Nazi's goals were deeply wrong; and the claim that "this is true relative to your interests and false relative to the Nazi's interests" is just the kind of "moral relativism" we find repulsive. Objective relativism seems the *right* doctrine for many moral cases; but not for cases where rights and duties are manifest and sharp and the choice seems to us to be between right and wrong, good and evil.[13]

Here, Putnam too fails to see the contested element of Dewey's problematic inquiry that underlies all critical choices. Based upon the once popular belief in eugenics and applied to a horrific extreme, Naziism came to be recognized

---

[12] Putnam, *Reason, Truth, and History*, 167. Lawrence Cahoone has illuminated the history of objective relativism in "American Realism, Objective Relativism, Columbia Naturalism, and Justus Buchler," *Transactions of the Charles S. Peirce Society*, vol. 52, no. 3 (Summer 2016), 416–434 and "The Metaphysics of Morris R. Cohen," *Journal of the History of Ideas*, vol. 78, no. 3 (July 2017), 449–471.

[13] Putnam, *Reason, Truth and History*, 168.

in the global continuum under the ultimate measure of "right and wrong, good and evil." But it required conflict—not altogether globally finished—to establish a unified response.[14]

Putnam's misreading of Dewey's "rightness" as "warranted in its actual existential setting" ignores that settled and stable "rights" (for Dewey) *were previously* arrived at through struggle. Here again is another example of the fallacy of selective emphasis. Deep pluralists like Richard Rorty and Isaiah Berlin see (and describe) a society of multiple values, preferences, and ideas of utility. Assuming that this is a final static reality, they ignore the ongoing dynamic reality in which many are in contestation over specific application, whether in the nation, the neighborhood, or the workplace. A transformed scientific and ethical environment always lies ahead, always agonistic, and hence beyond the comprehension of current knowledge, no matter how encyclopedic our current artificial intelligence.

Putnam characterized Dewey's objective relativism as: "Certain things are right–*objectively right*–in certain circumstances and wrong–*objectively wrong*–in others, and the culture and the environment constitute relevant circumstances." The instantaneous view of the universe that Dewey rejected can hardly be more evident in this characterization. If shared problems are the context for social life, and conflict is part of their solutions, there must be a performative standard of rightness, resting on the ongoing and extended identification and solution of problems. This supports what was called (in chapter 4) a constantly developing local normative embodiment (a term preferable to the static "ontology") in which rightness and objectivity are in a plural problematic multi-stage transformation, not univocal and uniform as in the gestalt image. The terms relativism and objectivism are commonly used to describe abstract cognitive attitudes, but where shared problematic situations are concerned they mislead inquiry into the gestalt oscillation.

Dewey's position regards both terms as inconsistent with human striving. The appearance of relativism is confusion and conflict, as if nothing can be done to relieve it. The appearance of objectivity is their absence, as if nothing is necessary to achieve a stable outcome. Both look to the immediate as given, as if there is no future malleability. Both assume a given and fixed viewpoint. Dewey may have given up on the idea of global rightness, but only insofar as it reflects the immediate "point of view of the universe."

In Dewey's view of social welfare, guided by a local, problem-oriented, agonistic preference adjustment principle, humans "get things right" insofar as they identify and resolve shared problems. Legal knowledge is presented

---

[14] Justice Holmes, as is well known, had approved a somewhat less drastic application of eugenics in his inaptly worded opinion in *Buck v. Bell*, during a period when it had yet to be fully invalidated by experience.

here as representative of Dewey's social intelligence, to show how "objectivity" actually works as a standard of human conduct in the normative realm. It implies a distinctive form of order and rules, inherent in Dewey's "naturalized utilitarianism." The most important element of Dewey's standard of rightness is conjoint *action*. Because a stable resolution of a shared problem requires the adjustment of opposing habits and practices, Dewey's vision is distinct from the general commitment in philosophical inquiry to an immediate and purely *cognitive* objectivity. Dewey saw human conduct, its patterns, flexibility, and consequences, as the overriding concern. His naturalized utilitarianism implies a naturalized objectivism, in which the nature of the real and the right are ultimately and indefinitely subject to human responsibility.[15]

[15] W. V. Quine, in "Ontological Relativity" writes "[w]hen we recognize with Dewey that 'meaning . . . is primarily a property of behavior,' we recognize that there are no meanings, nor likenesses nor distinctions of meaning, beyond what are implicit in people's dispositions to overt behavior." *Ontological Relativity and Other Essays* (New York: Columbia University Press, 1969), 29.

Chapter 10

Dewey's Democracy and Conflict

The comparison with Kenneth Arrow's impossibility theorem shows how different Dewey's conceptions of both conflict and democracy are from the current literature. The notion of conflict is extended by Dewey to nearly every form of social life, and democratic values are shown to be implicit in all forms of interactive, conjoint conduct. Broadly defined, social conflict is a natural rather than dysfunctional form of human action; it is a form of social inquiry. Organic democracy is certainly not *confined* to conflict nor limited to it, as democratic life depends on cooperative and creative human activity. Yet preference conflict forces creative experimentation, and is the impulse toward the adjustment of ingrained habit.

Kenneth Arrow drew on the maximizing formula of classical utilitarianism to demonstrate the impossibility of ordering fixed preferences. Underlying his demonstration is the concept of "social state," drawn from economic theory and still influential in welfare economics. The social state is a hypothetical instantaneous universal perspective on putative individual vectors in society, not unlike what the nineteenth-century utilitarian theorist Henry Sidgwick famously termed a "point of view of the universe." Taking individual preferences to be fixed at the moment of inquiry, Arrow generalized the eighteenth-century "voting paradox" of Condorcet and proved in 1951 that no "rational system" of ordering, other than dictatorship, was possible for any domain of diverse individual preferences.

The social state diverts attention from preference formation and rules out indecision or fluidity during the moment of observation. If all possible options of social choice are determined by an instant overall analysis, the plausibility of democratic government through electoral mechanisms is placed in question. A related implausibility, displayed in chapter 4, is the consequentialist rule of law. The instant-maximizing analysis of rule-consequentialism fails to account for the unified habits and practices that underlie acceptance and compliance with practice-based and conflict-resilient rules. The instant view attempts to explain all rules according to a current account of utility and welfare considerations. Dewey's dynamic account looks to the responsive transformation of preferences (and conceptions of utility) for the ongoing effectiveness of a normative order.

When Arrow's theorem was written, Dewey had previously argued at length (in *The Public and Its Problems* and other works) that democracy itself is more than electoral mechanisms. Having died in 1952, he was never confronted with Arrow's theorem. Rather than a succession of social states, Dewey's philosophy views social welfare as grounded in "problematic situations," subject to constant and extended conflict over the definition and resolution of particular shared concerns. Applying Dewey's broad view of conflict forces the question, missing from economic theory, of how diverse preferences actually aggregate and whether they can adjust for common purposes. In recognizing these questions, Dewey opened an inquiry into how inclusive deliberation can take place amidst resistant disagreement.

Economic theory still supports Arrow's assumption of fixed preferences through the concept of "competitive equilibrium" underlying them. They are stabilized in supply and demand by the market conditions of convexity, perfect competition, and demand independence.[1] Arrow's theorem extends the definition of individual preference to the entire realm of individual values. This fails to recognize that problematic situations arise within the broad universe of *all* preferences. The constant and endemic phenomenon of conflict over shared problems is a constant source of disequilibrium, such that (in contemporary society) demand independence for otherwise rational individual preferences can be disrupted by political and ideological factors, and hence not stabilized by the putative equilibrium.[2]

Equilibrium theory in economics appears from the literature to have displaced the larger issue of preference formation and transformation, central to the Deweyan problematic situation, which extends over time. In problematic situations like the history of gender discrimination, opposing aggregated preferences on either side of a particular dispute, such as assaults of women in the workplace, influenced by noneconomic vectors such as habitual attitudes toward vulnerability, have unsettled any presumptive equilibrium and obstructed successful efforts to define and address the core problem.

Arrow's proof demonstrates that democracy itself cannot be analyzed in the abstract, such as the general question: "Is a society of opposing preferences

---

1 Arrow and Debreu, "Existence of an Equilibrium for a Competitive Economy."
2 See, e.g., Frank, *What's the Matter With Kansas*?

molded into a purposive entity through discussion of alternative agendas leading to a responsive collective choice?" The question assumes utilitarian rationality and an overall dispositive answer rather than an agonistic rationality and contingent and situational context. Dewey's agonism turns away from the abstract question toward a vision of society as a constant succession of judgments in specific shared problems. Meanwhile, the abstract approach has turned instead toward various models of conversational deliberation and communication, which Dewey's model predicts will be unavailable for hotly contested issues. He addresses two real and fundamental questions: how preferences actually aggregate, and how they are actually formed into common purposes.

An overly abstract approach dominates much of contemporary theory, including alternative models like classical liberalism, emphasizing individual freedom and a market-based or evolutionary order. Both approaches to democratic theory, one affirming and the other denying the efficacy of electoral mechanisms, carry a rationale that implies a basic inevitability. As Dewey wrote in *Liberalism and Social Action*, "Commitment to inevitability is always the fruit of dogma; intelligence does not pretend to know save as a result of experimentation, the opposite of preconceived dogma."[3] Dewey's broad definition of conflict, stressing the contingency of successful human ordering, puts his perspective in an entirely different logical space from both utilitarian welfare maximization (often associated with a progressive liberalism) and *classical* liberalism, which draws from Hayek's work. The former inflates social freedom over individual freedom and the latter individual freedom over social, deflating the prospect of purposive human control over the forms of social order, even over such fundamental problems as war and climate disaster.

Dewey's naturalized utilitarianism seeks a working balance between both freedoms in a competitive order. By placing the problematic situation at the core of democratic theory, all problems, no matter how daunting, can be addressed when consensually recognized, adequately defined, and purposefully addressed.

CONFLICT THEORY

The many forms of preference conflict are not immediately visible, as are manifestations of responses to group inequality and class antagonism. As Dewey neared the end of his life, conflict theory had progressed little

[3] Dewey, *Liberalism and Social Action* (New York: Putnam, 1935),78; LW 11:55.

from Max Weber and Karl Marx.[4] Marx drew from Hegel a dialectical materialist interpretation of history and assumed class uniformities of value and preference in a critical view of existing social arrangements. Dewey displaced the dogma of inevitable class struggle with his science-based empirical naturalism, problem solving through accumulated experience.

> [T]he rise of scientific method and of technology based upon it is the genuinely active force in producing the vast complex of changes the world is now undergoing, not the class struggle whose spirit and method are opposed to science. If we lay hold upon the cause of force exercised by this embodiment of intelligence we shall know where to turn for the means of directing further change.[5]

Dewey viewed recourse to theories of class warfare as a wholesale avoidance of scientific method, but the empirical naturalism on which it was based was largely misunderstood or ignored.

After Dewey's death in 1952, general sociological theory influenced by Talcott Parsons' translations of Max Weber supported a structural and functional "theory of action," identifying natural and permanent social characteristics that could explain consensus and integration. Largely in reaction, conflict theory was retooled to challenge the nature of assumed inherent social characteristics, particularly through the work of G. H. Mead[6] and Ralf Dahrendorf.[7] Subsequent conflict theory has focused on aspects of exclusion and resentment as driving motivation, as in the recognition theory of Axel Honneth. In Honneth's thesis the "moral force" responsible for development

4 "We hear a great deal in these days about class conflict. The past history of man is held up to us as almost exclusively a record of struggles between classes, ending in the victory of the class that has been oppressed and the transfer of power to it. It is difficult to avoid reading the past in terms of the contemporary scene. Indeed fundamentally it is impossible to avoid this course." Dewey, *Liberalism and Social Action*, 74; LW 11:52.

5 Dewey, *Liberalism and Social Action*, 74; LW 11:53.

6 George Herbert Mead advocated a constructive view of social conflict. "The object of constructive social conflict is 'such a reconstruction of the situation that different and enlarged and more adequate personalities may emerge.' The new social situation is truly reconstructed only if 'all the personal interests are adequately recognized' and if one has a 'new world harmonizing the conflicting interests into which enters the new self.' It is only under the conditions in which individuals assume roles integrated in a harmonious social whole that truly 'democratic consciousness' occurs." Andrew Feffer, "Sociability and Social Conflict in George Herbert Mead's Interactionism, 1900-1919," *Journal of the History of Ideas*, vol. 51, no. 2 (April–June 1990), 233–254, 247.

7 Dahrendorf attempted to synthesize the Marxian concepts of class, class interests, and class conflict on the one hand, and the methodology and concepts of Parsons' theory of action on the other. Authority replaced forms of action as the focus of social conflicts and played a dual role in social structures as both a fiat-based integrative force, itself a source of conflict. "Whereas Marx, as the principal exponent of conflict theory, is rejected by the prevalent positivistic school for his idealistic philosophy of history and the crudeness of his conceptual categories, modern structural-functional theory, when it concerns itself with conflict at all, has been unable to break loose from the constraints of its basic theoretical assumptions." Peter Weingart, "Beyond Parsons? A Critique of Ralf Dahrendorf's Conflict Theory," *Social Forces*, vol. 48, no. 2 (December 1969), 151.

and progress is a struggle for recognition; his dynamic is simply that when individuals are "structurally excluded" from privileged ways of life, hurt feelings provide a vocabulary for shared personal disappointment, as the "motivational impetus" for collective struggle for recognition and social action.[8]

Avoiding the abstract "inevitability" of leading conflict theories, Dewey's conception includes, but is hardly dependent upon, resentment, organized protest, and the generation of discrete social movements. He includes a far greater variety of motivations, actions, and expressions bearing on problems that retain vitality but may not reach a stage of organized protest, in every walk of life, family, neighborhood, school, career, and employment. Diverse motivations influence every process of aggregation, opposition, and the successive stages of resolution and transformation.

Widely grounded in all aspects of culture, preference aggregation underlies multiple levels of conflict and an array of motives including altruism, curiosity, recovery from harm, health, income, working conditions, role definition, individual and social goals and purposes, science and technology, aesthetics—the list is endless. To limit moral motivation to the struggle for recognition is to adopt a massively incomplete account of preference aggregation and the diverse paths toward resolution or unification. Resentment is certainly one, and likely to grow when a discrete problem has long been insufficiently defined and addressed. In such situations the increased level of resentment can define a threshold of resort to force and violence.

Dewey's conception of scientific method held that abstractions in inquiry are to be deferred in favor of evidence-based judgments in particular problems. He universalized Popper's characterization of scientific knowledge as a response to problems; his agonism is intimately associated with his logic, and applies everywhere, to transformations of doubt to belief through the formation of knowledge from extended experimental problem resolution. His analogy with the success of natural science is reinforced by Popper's account of scientific problems as extended and always partial resolutions. For both Dewey and Popper, knowledge is the embodiment of new habit.

> At this point, indeed, is located the conflict that underlies the confusions and uncertainties of the present scene. The conflict is between institutions and habits originating in the prescientific and pre-technological age and the new forces generated by science and technology. The application of science, to a considerable degree, even its growth, has been conditioned by the system to which the name of capitalism is given, a rough designation of a complex of political and legal arrangement centering about a particular mode of economic relations.[9]

---

8 *Honneth, The Struggle for Recognition.*

9 Dewey, *Liberalism and Social Action,* 75; LW 11:53.

Capitalism is not a monolith and is itself subject to transformation. Dewey saw aspects of social inequity as grounded less in laissez-faire dogma than in older habits:

> The argument drawn from past history that radical change must be affected by means of class struggle, culminating in open war, fails to discriminate between the two forces, one active, the other resistant and deflecting, and it produced the social scene in which we live. The active force is, as I have said, scientific method and technological application. The opposite force is that of older institutions and the habits that have grown up around them.[10]

Dewey's broadening of the conception of conflict recognized violence as a *threshold* of failure of intelligent therapeutic action, given its vulnerability to polarization and the use of brute force.

> For, be it noted, the issue is not whether the same amount of violence will accompany the effectuation of radical change of institutions. The question is whether force or intelligence is to be that method upon which we consistently rely and whose promotion we devote our energies. Insistence that the use of violent force is inevitable limits the use of available intelligence, for wherever the inevitable reigns intelligence cannot be used.[11]

Dewey's vision of agonistic preference aggregation is independent of the leading approaches to conflict in sociology and philosophy. It is not uniquely materialist, admits of many different motivations, and concedes no permanent classes or structures. All aspects of social life, including perceived social divisions, are open to problematic consideration and unification. His perspective opens social inquiry to a vast universe of preferences, values, and perceived utilities and to vastly more possibilities of social change

DEMOCRACY AND LIBERTARIANISM

Friedrich Hayek's insight into the knowledge-creating function of markets enabled him to formulate an argument against central economic planning and social legislation. He claimed that deliberative electoral mechanisms cannot overcome customary practices, built up over generations through natural market mechanisms and comparative group choices. Hence *de novo* legislation, based on what Hayek derisively called "constructive rationality," can only

---

[10] Dewey, *Liberalism and Social Action,* 75; LW 11:54.
[11] Dewey, *Liberalism and Social Action,* 78; LW 11:55.

fail and disrupt the natural social order. Hayek largely denied direct purposive human control. He writes in *Law, Legislation and Liberty:*

> [The] orderliness of society which greatly increased the effectiveness of individual action was not due solely to institutions and practices which had been invented or designed for that purpose, but was largely due to a process described at first as "growth" and later as "evolution," a process in which practices which had first been adopted for other reasons, or even purely accidentally, were preserved because they enabled the group in which they had arisen to prevail over others.[12]

Hayek's model of "evolution," drawing from the notion of species survival advanced by Charles Darwin, suggests that the prevailing system of rules has "been preserved" because "groups who practiced them displaced others."[13] Hayek also took another model, of individual self-regulation, from economic markets. Attention has focused on these two competing ideas, the claim first that social structures owe their persistence or extinction to their tendency to "increase or decrease the efficiency of the group as a whole"[14] and second that "orderly structures . . . are the product of the action of many men but are not the result of human design."[15] The two distinct ideas, one of group and the other of individual agency, have given rise to the claim of a "major flaw" in his reasoning, that his "appeal to a process of cultural evolution operating at the group level as such stands in contrast to his explicit methodological individualism."[16]

If indeed Hayek proposed incompatible accounts of the social order, one privileging local adjustments by individuals unintentionally giving rise to social institutions, and another the adaptation by macro-level properties in intergroup competition, he doesn't explain how his mechanisms combine in structuring society toward positive ends at any stage of history.[17] The conception that they simply represent a mysterious "invisible hand" collides with

---

[12] Hayek, *Law Legislation and Liberty* (Chicago: University of Chicago Press, 1973), 1:9.

[13] Hayek, *Law Legislation and Liberty*, 1:18.

[14] Hayek, "Notes on the Evolution of Systems of Rules of Conduct," in *The Market and Other Orders*, ed. Bruce Caldwell (Chicago: Chicago University Press, 2014), 283.

[15] Hayek, *Law Legislation and Liberty*, 1:37.

[16] Viktor Vanberg, "Spontaneous Market Order and Social Rules: A Critical Examination of F. A. Hayek's Theory of Cultural Evolution," *Economics & Philosophy,* vol. 2, no. 1 (1986), 75–100, 85. See Alexander Shaefer, "Hayek's Twin Ideas: Reconciling Methodological Individualism and Group Selection," *Cambridge Journal of Economics* vol. 45, no. 6 (November 2021), 209.

[17] Social structures "arose from unintentionally conforming to certain traditional and largely moral practices, many of which men tend to dislike, whose significance they usually fail to understand, whose validity they cannot prove, and which have nonetheless fairly rapidly spread by means of an evolutionary selection—the comparative increase of population and wealth—of those groups that happened to follow them." Hayek, *The Fatal Conceit: The Errors of Socialism* (Chicago: University of Chicago Press, 1988), 6.

Dewey's objection that "commitment to inevitability is always the fruit of dogma."

Dewey has addressed any supposed mystery of preference formation and aggregation with a theory of continuous problematic conflict resolution. Rather than providing an account of how rejected group practices yield to successful ones, and how conflicts among them were (or still are) settled, Hayek's argument pivots toward discrediting an opposing "constructive" model of order:

> I attempt to show that certain widely held scientific as well as political views are dependent on a particular conception of the formation of social institutions, which I shall call "constructivist rationalism"—a conception which assumes that all social institutions are, and ought to be the product of deliberate design.[18]

The label implies that Hayek's conception of representative legislation is always *de novo*, with all relevant facts having to be recognized and addressed at once rather than drawing upon paths of prior detailed inquiry. Hayek identifies custom as the alternative to "constructivist rationalism":

> Many of the institutions of society which are indispensable conditions for the successful pursuit of our conscious aims are in fact the result of customs, habits or practices which have been neither invented nor are observed with any such purpose in view.[19]

But Hayek's account of custom has no explanation for the emergence of specific rules.

> We live in a society in which we can successfully orientate ourselves, and in which our actions have a good chance of achieving their aims, not only because our fellows are governed by known aims or known connections between means and ends, but because they are also confined by rules whose purpose or origin we often do not know and of whose very existence we are often not aware.[20]

Studies of law can illuminate how such rules have emerged and adapted, and their putatively "unknown" history. Legal history has shown how habits and practices, if not custom itself, are subject to incremental transformation through ordered judgment.

---

18 Hayek, *Law Legislation and Liberty*, 5.
19 Hayek, *Law Legislation and Liberty*, 1:11.
20 Hayek, *Law Legislation and Liberty*, 1:11.

Nevertheless, there seems room for a piecemeal form of public choice within Hayek's own model. He asserts that a major reason why constructivism fails is the natural complexity of the matters subject to human ordering:

> [T]hough the use of spontaneous ordering forces enables us to induce the formation of an order of such a degree of complexity (namely comprising elements of such numbers, diversity and variety of conditions) as we could never master intellectually, or deliberately arrange, we will have less power over the details of such an order than we would of one which we produce by arrangement. . . . In consequence, the degree of power of control over the extended and more complex order will be much smaller than that which we could exercise over a made order or *taxis*.[21]

This complexity is such that no immediate encounter by a legislative body can grasp its extent and importance. A prime cause of Hayek's doubt lies also in his skeptical view of reliance on abstract formulas like "social justice" for the formulation of responses to social problems—a reliance that is primarily deductivist, detached from particular experience. But these difficulties are not applicable to a continuing process of incremental ordered judgment.

Potentially extending over sufficient time and experience to grasp and adapt to complex problems, incremental judgments analyze and address resistant disputes case by case. They generalize retrospectively, after they have, in multiple disputed situations, encountered, identified and addressed critical elements and conditions bearing on ultimate resolution. Moreover, they can incrementally effect gradual preference adjustment and revision of resistant habits and practices along with the process of inquiry. Indeed, Hayek mentions "practices" in a context that suggests that they are in fact subject to change:

> The important insight to which an understanding of the process of evolution of law leads is that the rules which will emerge from it will of necessity possess certain attributes which laws invented or designed by a ruler may but need not possess, and are likely to possess only if they are modelled after the kind of rules which spring from the articulation of *previously existing practices.* [my italics][22]

Yet, other than by "spontaneous evolution," Hayek offers no account of how such practices *might* have changed.[23]

---

[21] Hayek, *Law Legislation and Liberty*, 1:41–42.

[22] Hayek, *Law Legislation and Liberty*, 1:85.

[23] Rules for Hayek promote no known or unified goal: "the natural selection of rules will operate on the bases of the greater or lesser efficiency of the resulting order of the group." Rules are not tailored to achieve some pre-specified goal and "not the result of all the factors being taken into account by a single centre" but rather are "produced by the responses of the individual elements to their respective surroundings." Hayek, "The Political Ideal and the Rule of Law," in *The Market*

Viktor Vanberg complained that Hayek's two inconsistent accounts of spontaneous ordering, individual advantage and group benefit, pull in opposite directions.[24] In Dewey's agonism, the adaptive strategies of both individuals and groups are resolved in a piecemeal practical convergence, as was shown in chapter 4 regarding Henry Sidgwick's "dualism of practical reason." Vanberg's complaint assumes that the individual vector is driven by market considerations and the group vector by Darwinian survival, hardly what Dewey would consider representative of the multiple facets of a fully naturalized utilitarianism. Even so, the continuum of inquiry into a particular problematic situation would not displace individual preferences in favor of group ones, or vice versa. The succession of judgments regarding voluntary euthanasia, the MeToo controversy, or other recent controversies has encompassed individual and group forms of consideration into proposals for resolution, even while remedial inquiry is continually disrupted by ideological manipulation.

The opposition of group and individual considerations raises the issue of opposing forms of individual and corporate freedom, privileged by different conceptions of democracy. Vanberg and Helmut Leipold questioned whether the classical liberalism influenced by Hayek has a clear role in contemporary democracy:

> The ideals of democracy and of (classical) liberalism do not appear to co-exist in easy harmony with each other. Advocates of liberalism emphasize the need to impose strict limitations on the authority of government in order to safeguard individual liberty, and they tend to look with suspicion at the tendency of democratic politics to extend the power of the state at the expense of the "private autonomy" of its citizens. Advocates of democracy, on the other hand, emphasize the priority of the principle of popular sovereignty, and they tend to regard liberal demands for the limitation of governmental authority as illegitimate attempts to pre-empt what should be rightly decided by the democratic process.[25]

Dewey's agonistic account does not encounter this antinomy. What is described here as the "popular sovereignty" idea of democracy depends heavily on the primacy of the electoral process and representative government in justifying legislation. But before votes are taken and counted, a hierarchy of

and Other Orders, ed. Caldwell, 160–161. The rules that underlie spontaneous orders "must be independent of purpose and be the same, if not necessarily for all members, at least for whole classes of members not individually designated by name" and these rules are "applied by the individuals in the light of their respective knowledge and purposes; and their application will be independent of any common purpose." Hayek, *Law Legislation and Liberty*, 1:50.

24 Vanberg, "Spontaneous Market Order and Social Rules."

25 Viktor Vanberg and Helmut Leipold, "On the Complementarity of Liberalism and Democracy: A Reading of F. A. Hayek and J. M. Buchanan," in *Ökonomische Analyse Politischer Institutionen, ed. Uwe Vollmer* (Berlin: Duncker & Humblot, 2010), 13. See also Peter J. Boettke and Peter T. Leeson, "Hayek, Arrow, and the Problems of Democratic Decision-Making," *Journal of Public Finance and Public Choice,* vol. 20, no. 1 (2002), 9.

multiple and often divisive problems has always already framed opinions, divisions, and options. The "safeguard of individual liberty" lies in the contingent, even though often unresolved, political clashes that are most evident in times of polarization, including resistance to extending the power of the state at the expense of private autonomy.

Political polarization is most evident when inclusive paths and sources of problem resolution have become least effective. When many controversial problems are locked in a condition that Dewey describes as confusion and uncertainty, the voting and representative process alone is least likely to bring them to a successful resolution. Beneath general and salient divisions lie more specific and often ill-defined ones, driven by embedded habits and beliefs that resist easy convergence. The most effective response to polarization lies in dedicated and persistent efforts to define and remediate the specific underlying conflicts.[26]

Dewey's broad analysis of conflict makes his account vastly more valuable than Arrow's for understanding the current era. He identifies the use of force as a threshold for the failure of empiricism. All social choices are necessarily contested in the development of their full inclusive dimensions. His original, pragmatist conflict theory points to a constant choice between empiricism and force, and the appeal to ideology lies in the volatile area between them. In seeing the possibilities of transformational convergence Dewey is able to dismiss attitudes of "impossibility" of solution and "incommensurability" of values as selective emphasis. Abstract analyses of social conditions, like the need for more legal rights, more civic republicanism, and more communitarianism, are ultimately what Holmes might have described as "benevolent yearning," compared to the granular efforts to address causes as a set of unsolved problems.[27] The social state analysis of Kenneth Arrow actually reinforces Dewey's agonism; it is a dispositive proof that a society of fixed and unyielding preferences must be ordered by fiat, dictatorial authority, by force. It also proves the importance of preference transformation. Recognizing the reasoning behind John Dewey's emphasis on the problematic situation may be the only avenue toward the survival and success of the human enterprise, especially in the face of polarization and its threat to successful democratic ordering.

---

[26] This indicates the importance of dedicated effort to define and advance recognition of the most important problems threatening human societies. The first climate change case at the European Court of Human Rights in Strasbourg was brought in early 2023, by a large group of Swiss female pensioners, claiming that their country's inaction in the face of rising temperatures puts them at risk of dying during heatwaves. Bold action from all segments of society is required in critical situations, as no problematic situation can be fully defined and addressed without broad recognition and acceptance, achieved only through inclusive and continued effort.

[27] See, e.g., Donald Kagan, *On the Origins of War and the Preservation of Peace* (New York: Doubleday, 1994).

Bibliography

Aikin, Scott F., and Robert B. Talisse. 2018. *Pragmatism, Pluralism, and the Nature of Philosophy*. London and New York: Routledge.

______. 2016. "Pragmatism and Pluralism Revisited." *Political Studies Review*, vol. 14, no. 1 (February 12).

______. 2005. "Why Pragmatists Cannot Be Pluralists." *Transactions of the Charles S. Peirce Society*, vol. XVI, no. 1 (Winter): 101.

Alexander, Larry, and Kenneth Kress. 1995. "Against Legal Principles." In *Law and Interpretation*, edited by Andrei Marmor, 279–327. Oxford: Clarendon Press.

Alexy, Robert. 2003. *The Argument from Injustice: A Reply to Legal Positivism*. Translated by L. Bonnie and Stanley L. Paulson. Oxford: Clarendon Press.

______. 2000. "On the Structure of Legal Principles." *Ratio Juris,* vol. 13, no. 3 (September): 294–305.

______. 1989. *A Theory of Legal Argumentation: The Theory of Rational Discourse as Theory of Legal Justification*. Translated by Neil MacCormick. Cambridge and Oxford: Oxford University Press.

Alschuler, Albert W. 1999. *Law without Values: The Life, Work and Legacy of Justice Holmes*. Chicago: University of Chicago Press.

Altman, Andrew. 1990. *Critical Legal Studies: A Liberal Critique*. Princeton: Princeton University Press.

______. 1986. "Legal Realism, Critical Legal Studies, and Dworkin." *Philosophy and Public Affairs*, vol. 15, no. 3: 205–235.

Arrow, Kenneth J. 1951. *Social Choice and Individual Values*. New Haven: Yale University Press.

______. 1950. "A Difficulty in the Concept of Social Welfare." *Journal of Political Economy*, vol. 58, no. 4 (August): 328–346

______, and Gerard Debreu. 1954. "Existence of an Equilibrium for a Competitive Economy." *Econometrica*, vol. 22, no. 3 (July): 265–290.

Athens, Lonnie. 2017. "The Belated Appearance of 'Radical Interactionism' on the American Sociological Stage: The Rise of G. H. Mead and Fall of Robert Park." *The American Sociologist*, vol. 48, no. 1 (March): 23–47.

______. 2012. "Mead's Analysis of Social Conflict: A Radical Interactionist's Critique." *The American Sociologist*, vol. 43, no. 4 (December): 428–447.

Austin, John. 1869. *Lectures on Jurisprudence; or, The Philosophy of Positive Law*. London: John Murray.

Backhouse, Roger. 2009. "Robbins and Welfare Economics: A Reappraisal." *The Journal of the History of Economic Thought* online (December 2009): 474.

Bacon, Francis. 1994. *Novum Organum*. Translated by Peter Urbach. Chicago: Open Court.

Barnes, Barry, David Bloor, and John Hanson. 1996. *Scientific Knowledge: A Sociological Analysis*. Chicago: University of Chicago Press.

Becker, Gary S., and George J. Stigler. 1977. "De Gustibus Non Est Disputandum." *American Economic Review*, vol. 67, no. 2 (March): 76–90.

Bercowitz Jacob. 2008. *Sage Handbook of Conflict Resolution*. Sage Publication.

Bernstein, Richard. 1987. "One Step Forward, Two Steps Backward: Richard Rorty on Liberal Democracy and Philosophy." *Political Theory*, vol. 15: 538.

______, ed. 1960. *On Experience, Nature, and Freedom*. Indianapolis: Bobbs-Merrill Co.

Bickel, Alex. 1962. *The Least Dangerous Branch*. Indianapolis and New York: Bobbs-Merrill Co.

Bix, Brian. 1993. *Law, Language, and Legal Determinacy*. Oxford: Clarendon Press.

Bloom, Alan. 1987. *The Closing of the American Mind: How Higher Education Has Failed Democracy and Impoverished the Souls of Today's Students*. New York: Simon & Schuster.

Bobbitt, Philip Chase. 2014. "The Age of Consent." *Yale Law Journal*, vol. 123 (May): 2334.

———. 1991. *Constitutional Interpretation*. Oxford and Cambridge: Blackwell.

———. 1982. *Constitutional Fate: Theory of the Constitution*. Oxford and New York: Oxford University Press.

Boettke, Peter J., and Peter T. Leeson. 2002. "Hayek, Arrow, and the Problems of Democratic Decision-Making." *Journal of Public Finance and Public Choice,* vol. 20, no. 1: 10.

Brandom, Robert. 2014. "A Hegelian Model of Concept Determination: The Normative Fine Structure of the Judges' Chain Novel." In *Pragmatism, Law, and Language*, edited by Graham Hubbs and Douglas Lind, 19. New York and London: Routledge.

______. 2011. *Perspectives on Pragmatism: Classical, Recent, and Contemporary*. Cambridge and London: Harvard University Press.

______. 2008. *Between Saying and Doing: Towards an Analytic Pragmatism*. Oxford: Oxford University Press.

———. 1976. "Truth and Assertibility." *The Journal of Philosophy*, vol. 73, no. 6 (March 25): 137–149.

Brent, Joseph. 1998. *Charles S. Peirce: A Life*. Bloomington and Indianapolis: Indiana University Press.

Brown, Matthew J. 1991. "The Concept of 'Situation' in John Dewey's Logic and Philosophy of Science." In *Pragmatism in Law and Society*, edited by Michael Brint and William Weaver. Boulder: Westview Press.

Buchanan James M. 1954. "Social Choice, Democracy, and Free Markets." *Journal of Political Economy*, vol. 62, no. 2 (April): 114–123.

Burke, Thomas. 2019. "Dewey's Chicago-Functionalist Conception of Logic." In *The Oxford Handbook of Dewey,* edited by Steven Fesmire, 507. Oxford: Oxford University Press.

______. 1994. *Dewey's New Logic: A Reply to Russell.* Chicago: University of Chicago Press.

Burns, J. H. 1959. "Utilitarianism and Democracy." *The Philosophical Quarterly*, vol. 9, no. 35 (April): 168–171.

Burton, Steven J. 2000. *The Path of the Law and Its Influence: The Legacy of Oliver Wendell Holmes, Jr.* Cambridge: Cambridge University Press.

Butler, Brian E. 2017. *The Democratic Constitution: Experimentalism and Interpretation.* Chicago: University of Chicago Press.

Cahoone, Lawrence. 2017. "The Metaphysics of Morris R. Cohen." *Journal of the History of Ideas*, vol. 78, no. 3 (July): 449–471.

______. 2016. "American Realism, Objective Relativism, Columbia Naturalism, and Justus Buchler." *Transactions of the Charles S. Peirce Society*, vol. 52, no. 3 (Summer): 416–434.

Calabresi, Guido. 2003. "An Introduction to Legal Thought: Four Approaches to Law and to the Allocation of Body Parts." *Stanford Law Review* 55: 2113.

———. 1982. *A Common Law for the Age of Statutes*. Cambridge: Harvard University Press.

Cane, Peter. 2010. *The Hart-Fuller Debate in the Twenty-First Century*. Oxford and Portland: Hart Publishing.

Cardozo, Benjamin N. 1921. *The Nature of the Judicial Process.* New Haven and London: Yale University Press.

Cartwright, Nancy. 1999. *The Dappled World: A Study of the Boundaries of Science.* Cambridge: Cambridge University Press.

Cohen, Adam. 2016. *Imbeciles: The Supreme Court, American Eugenics, and the Sterilization of Carrie Buck.* New York: Penguin Press.

Connelly, Matthew. 2023. *The Declassification Engine: What History Reveals About America's Top Secrets.* New York: Penguin Random House.

Coser, Lewis A. 1957. "Social Conflict and the Theory of Social Change." *The British Journal of Sociology*, vol. 8, no. 3 (September): 197–207.

Cross, Rupert. 1977. *Precedent in English Law*. Oxford: Clarendon Press.

Crowder George. 2017. "Value Pluralism vs. Relativism in Bernard Williams's 'Relativism of Distance'." *The Pluralist*, vol. 12, no. 3 (Fall): 114–138.

Dancy, Jonathan. 2004. *Ethics without Principles*. Oxford: Clarendon Press.

———. 1993. *Moral Reasons*. Oxford and Cambridge: Blackwell.

Dewey, John. 1958. *Experience and Nature*. New York: Dover Publications.

———. 1938. *Logic: The Theory of Inquiry*. New York: Henry Holt and Co.

______. 1927. *The Public and Its Problems.* New York: Henry Holt and Co.

———. 1924. "Logical Method and Law." *Cornell Law Review*, vol. 10: 17.

______. 1903. *Studies in Logical Theory*. Chicago: University of Chicago Press.

______and James H. Tufts. 1988. *Later Works*, vol. 14. Carbondale: Southern Illinois University Press.

______. 1932. *Ethics*. New York: Henry Holt & Co.

______. 1930. "Three Independent Factors in Morals." *The Later Works* (LW), vol. 5: 280.

Dreier, James, ed. 2006. *Contemporary Debates in Moral Theory*. Oxford and Cambridge: Blackwell.

Duxbury, Neil. 1995. *Patterns of American Jurisprudence*. Oxford: Clarendon Press.

Dworkin, Ronald. 2011. *Justice for Hedgehogs*. Cambridge and London: The Belknap Press.

______. 2006. *Justice in Robes*. Cambridge: Belknap Press.

______. 1986. *Law's Empire*. Cambridge and London: The Belknap Press.

______. 1977. *Taking Rights Seriously*. Cambridge: Harvard University Press.

Eldridge, Michael. 2005. "Why a Pragmatist May Be a Pluralist." *Transactions of the Charles S. Peirce Society*, vol. XLI, no. 1: 119–122.

Epstein, Richard A. 2008. *Supreme Neglect: How to Revive Constitutional Protection For Private Property*. Oxford: Oxford University Press.

Feffer, Andrew. 1990. "Sociability and Social Conflict in George Herbert Mead's Interactionism, 1900-1919." *Journal of the History of Ideas*, vol. 51, no. 2 (April–June): 233–254.

Feldman, Allan. 1980. *Welfare Economics and Social Choice Theory*. Boston: Martinus Nijhoff.

Field, Hartry. 2005. "Truth and the Absence of Fact." *Philosophical Studies: An International Journal for Philosophy in the Analytic Tradition*, vol. 124, no. 1 (May): 41–44.

______. 1972. "Tarski's Theory of Truth." *The Journal of Philosophy*, vol. 69, no. 13 (July 13): 347–375.

Fink, Clinton F. 1968. "Some Conceptual Difficulties in the Theory of Social Conflict." *Journal of Conflict Resolution*, vol. 12, no. 4, Special Review Issue (December): 412–460.

Fishkin, James. 2011. *When the People Speak*. Oxford: Oxford University Press.

Foot, Philippa. 1978. *Virtues and Vices*. Berkeley and Los Angeles: University of California Press.

______. 1977. "Euthanasia." *Philosophy & Public Affairs*, vol. 6, no. 2 (Winter): 85–112.

______. 1967. *Theories of Ethics*. Oxford: Oxford University Press.

Foucault, Michel. 1998. *The History of Sexuality: The Will to Knowledge*. London: Penguin.

Frank, Jerome. 1963. *Law and the Modern Mind*. New York: Doubleday and Co.

Frank, Thomas. 2005. *What's the Matter With Kansas?* New York: Macmillan Co.

Frega Roberto. 2014. "Between Pragmatism and Critical Theory: Social Philosophy Today." *Human Studies*, vol. 37, no. 1 (Spring): 57–82.

Friedmann, Wolfgang. 1967. *Legal Theory*. New York: Columbia University Press.

Friedrich, Carl Joachim. 1963. *The Philosophy of Law in Historical Perspective*. 2nd ed. Chicago: University of Chicago Press.

Fuller, Lon L. 2001. *The Principles of Social Order: Selected Essays of Lon L. Fuller*. Edited by Kenneth Winston. Oxford and Portland: Hart Publishing.

———. 1964. *The Morality of Law*. New Haven and London: Yale University Press.
______. 1954. "American Legal Philosophy at Mid-Century." *Journal of Legal Education*, vol. 6: 457–485.
______. 1946. "Reason and Fiat in Case Law." *Harvard Law Review*, vol. 59: 376–377.
______. 1940. *The Law in Quest of Itself*. Boston: Beacon Press.
Fuller, Steve. 2000. *Thomas Kuhn: A Philosophical History for Our Times*. Chicago and London: University of Chicago Press.
———. 1988. *Social Epistemology*. Bloomington and Indianapolis: Indiana University Press.
Gilmore, Grant. 1977. *Ages of American Law*. New Haven and London: Yale University Press.
______. 1974. *Death of Contract*. Columbus: Ohio State University Press.
Goldman, Alvin I. 1999. *Knowledge in a Social World*. Oxford: Clarendon Press.
Goldstein, Laurence, ed. 1987. *Precedent in Law*. New York and Oxford: Clarendon Press.
Goodman, Nelson. 1972. "Seven Strictures on Similarity." In Goodman, *Problems and Projects*, 437. Indianapolis and New York: Bobbs-Merrill Co.
Gordon, Robert W. 2012. "Critical Legal Histories Revisited: A Response." *Law & Social Inquiry*, vol. 37: 202.
———. 1997. "The Arrival of Critical Historicism." *Stanford Law Review*, vol. 49: 1023.
———. 1996. "The Past as Authority and as Social Critic." In *The Historic Turn in the Human Sciences*, edited by Terence McDonald. Ann Arbor: University of Michigan Press.
———. 1992. *The Legacy of Oliver Wendell Holmes Jr*. Edinburgh: Edinburgh University Press.
———. 1984. "Critical Legal Histories." *Stanford Law Review*, vol. 36: 57.
Gottlieb, Stephen E. 1994. "The Paradox of Balancing Significant Interests." *Hastings Law Journal*, vol. 45: 825.
———, ed. 1993. *Public Values in Constitutional Law*. Ann Arbor: University of Michigan Press.
Gouinlock, James. 1986. *Excellence in Public Discourse: John Stuart Mill, John Dewey, and Social Intelligence*. New York: Teachers College Press.
______. 1978. "Dewey's Theory of Moral Deliberation." *Ethics*, vol. 88, no. 3 (April): 218–228.
Gray, John Chipman. 1972. *The Nature and Sources of the Law*. Gloucester: Peter Smith.
Gunther, Gerald. 1994. *Learned Hand: The Man and the Judge*. New York: Alfred Knopf.
———. 1975. "Learned Hand and the Origins of Modern First Amendment Doctrine: Some Fragments of History." *Stanford Law Review*, vol. 27: 719.
Haack, Susan. 1978. *Philosophy of Logics*. Cambridge: Cambridge University Press.
Haakonssen, Knud. 1981. *The Science of a Legislator: The Natural Jurisprudence of David Hume and Adam Smith*. Cambridge: Cambridge University Press.

Habermas, Jurgen. 1996. *Between Facts and Norms: Contributions to a Discourse Theory of Law and Democracy*. Translated by William Rehg. Cambridge: MIT Press.

Hacking, Ian. 1999. *The Social Construction of What*? Cambridge: Harvard University Press.

Hampshire, Stuart. 2000. *Justice Is Conflict*. Princeton: Princeton University Press.

Hand, Learned. 1959. *The Spirit of Liberty: Papers and Addresses of Learned Hand*. New York: Vintage Books.

______. 1958. *The Bill of Rights*. Cambridge: Harvard University Press.

Hanson, N. R. 1958. *Patterns of Discovery: An Inquiry into the Conceptual Foundations of Science*. Cambridge: Cambridge University Press.

Hare, R. M. 1981. *Moral Thinking*. Oxford: Clarendon Press.

———. 1952. *The Language of Morals*. Oxford: Oxford University Press.

Hart, H. L. A. 2013. "Discretion." *Harvard Law Review*, vol. 127 (December): 636.

———. 1983. *Essays in Jurisprudence and Philosophy*. Oxford: Clarendon Press.

———. 1961. *The Concept of Law*. Oxford: Clarendon Press.

______. 1958. "Positivism and the Separation of Law and Morals." *Harvard Law Review*, vol. 71: 593.

Hayek, Friedrich. 2014. "Notes on the Evolution of Systems of Rules of Conduct." In *The Market and Other Orders*, edited by Bruce Caldwell, 283. Chicago: Chicago University Press.

______. 2002. "Competition as a Discovery Procedure." *Quarterly Journal of Austrian Economics*, vol. 5, no. 3 (Fall): 9–10; also in *New Studies in Philosophy Politics Economics and the History of Ideas*, 179–190. Chicago: Chicago University Press, 1978.

______. 1988. *The Fatal Conceit: The Errors of Socialism*. Chicago: University of Chicago Press.

______. 1978. *Law, Legislation and Liberty*. Chicago: University of Chicago Press.

Hegel, G. W. F. 1989. *Science of Logic*. Translated by A. V. Miller. Atlantic Highlands: Humanities Press International.

———. 1978. *Elements of the Philosophy of Right*. Translated by T. M. Knox. Oxford: Oxford University Press.

Herget, James E. 1990. *American Jurisprudence, 1870–1970: A History*. Houston: Rice University Press.

Hickman, Larry A., Stefan Neubert, and Kersten Reich. 2009. *John Dewey Between Pragmatism and Constructivism*. New York: Fordham University Press.

Hobbes, Thomas. 1962. *Leviathan; or, The Matter, Forme, and Power of a Commonwealth Ecclesiasticall and Civil*. New York: Collier Books.

Holmes, Oliver Wendell Jr. 1995. *The Collected Works of Justice Holmes: Complete Public Writings and Selected Opinions of Oliver Wendell Holmes*. Edited by Sheldon M. Novick. Chicago and London: University of Chicago Press.

———. 1881. *The Common Law*. Boston: Little Brown and Co.

______. 1873. "The Theory of Torts." *American Law Review*, vol. 7 (July): 652–663.

______. 1870. "Codes, and the Arrangement of the Law." *American Law Review*, vol. 5 (October): 1–13.
Honneth, Axel. 1995. *The Struggle for Recognition: The Moral Grammar of Social Conflicts*. Cambridge: Polity Press.
Hooker, Brad. 2020. "The Role(s) of Rules in Consequentialist Ethics." In *The Oxford Handbook of Consequentialism,* Douglas Portmore, ed. Oxford: Oxford University Press, 441.
_____. 2000. *Ideal Code Real World.* Oxford: Oxford University Press.
_____. 1990. "Rule Consequentialism." *Mind*, New Series, vol. 99, no. 393 (January): 67–77.
______, and Margaret Little, eds. 2000. *Moral Particularism*. Oxford and New York: Oxford University Press.
Howe, Mark de W., ed. 1962. *The Occasional Speeches of Justice Oliver Wendell Holmes*. Cambridge: Harvard University Press.
______. 1961. *Holmes-Pollock Letters*. Cambridge: Harvard University Press.
______. 1957. *Justice Oliver Wendell Holmes: The Shaping Years 1841-1870.* Cambridge: Harvard University Press.
______. 1953. *Holmes-Laski Letters.* Cambridge: Harvard University Press.
Hubbs, Graham, and Douglas Lind, eds. 2014. *Pragmatism, Law, and Language*. New York and London: Routledge.
Hume, David. 1896. *A Treatise of Human Nature*. Oxford: Clarendon Press.
______. 1751. *An Enquiry concerning the Principles of Morals*. London: A. Miller.
Hutchinson, Allan. 1989. "The Three 'Rs': Reading/ Rorty/ Radically." *Harvard Law Review*, vol. 103: 555.
James, William. 1975. "Pragmatism." In *The Works of William James*, edited by Frederick H. Burkhardt, et al. Cambridge: Harvard University Press.
______. 1912. *A Pluralistic Universe*. London: Longmans, Green & Co.
Kagan, Donald. 1994. *On the Origins of War and the Preservation of Peace*. New York: Doubleday.
Kellogg, Frederic R. 2018. *Oliver Wendell Holmes Jr. and Legal Logic*. Chicago and London: Chicago University Press.
———. 2016. "The Snake and the Roundabout: Ethical Particularism and the Patterns of Normative Induction." *Duc in Altum Cadernos de Direito*, vol. 8, no. 16: 5.
———. 2013. "What Precisely Is a 'Hard' Case? Waldron, Dworkin and Judicial Recourse to Principle." Social Science Research Network. https://papers.ssrn.com/sol3/papers.cfm?abstract_id=2220839.
______. 2011. "The Abuse of Principle: Analytical Philosophy and the Doubtful Case." *Archiv fur Rechts und Sozialphilosophie*, vol. 97: 218.
———. 2010. "Hobbes, Holmes, and Dewey: Pragmatism and the Problem of Order." Social Science Research Network. https://ssrn.com/abstract=1655307.
______. 2007. *Oliver Wendell Holmes Jr., Legal Theory, and Judicial Restraint.* Cambridge: Cambridge University Press.
———. 2004. "Holistic Pragmatism and Law: Morton White on Justice Oliver Wendell Holmes," with reply by White, "Holmes and Hart on Prediction and Legal Obligation." *Transactions of the Charles S. Peirce Society*, vol. 60 (Fall 2004): 559.

———. 1992. "Who Owns Pragmatism?" *Journal of Speculative Philosophy*, n.s., vol. 6: 67–80.

______. 1987. "Holmes, Pragmatism, and the Deconstruction of Utilitarianism." *Transactions of the Charles S Peirce Soc'y*, vol. 23: 99.

———. 1987. "Learned Hand and the Great Train Ride." *American Scholar*, vol. 56 (Autumn): 471.

———. 1984. *The Formative Essays of Justice Holmes: The Making of an American Legal Philosophy*. Westport and London: Greenwood Press.

Kennedy, Duncan. 1994. "A Semiotics of Legal Argument." In *Academy of European Law*, Collected Courses of the Academy of European Law, vol. III, Book 2, 309. Netherlands: Kluwer Academic Publishers.

______. 1983. "The Political Significance of the Structure of the Law School Curriculum." *Seton Hall Law Review*, vol. 14, issue 1: 15.

______. 1982. "Legal Education as Training for Hierarchy." In *The Politics of Law: A Progressive Critique*, vol. 47, edited by D. Kairys.

Kitcher, Philip. 2021. *Moral Progress*. Oxford: Oxford University Press.

______. 2001. *The Ethical Project*. Cambridge: Harvard University Press.

Koopman, Colin, 2010. "Revising Foucault: The History and Critique of Modernity," *Philosophy and Social Criticism*, vol. 36, no. 5 (August): 545.

Kornbluth, Hilary. 1996. *Inductive Inference and its Natural Ground: An Essay in Naturalistic Epistemology*. Cambridge and London: MIT Press.

Kreps, David M. 2021. "Not Every Couple Should Have a Prenup: How the Context and History of Exchange Affects Personal Preferences, and Why This Matters Both to Economic Theory and to Practical Human Resource Management." Kenneth Arrow Lecture.

______, and Robert Wilson. 1982. "Sequential Equilibria." *Econometrica*, vol. 50, no. 4 (July).

Kuklick, Bruce. 1977. *The Rise of American Philosophy*. New Haven: Yale University Press.

Leib, Ethan. 2009. *Deliberative Democracy in America*. University Park: Penn State Press.

Leiter, Brian. 1995. "Legal Indeterminacy." *Legal Theory*, vol. 1: 481–492.

Levi, Edward H. 1949. *An Introduction to Legal Reasoning*. Chicago and London: Chicago University Press.

Lewellyn, Karl N. 2011. *The Theory of Rules*. Edited by Frederick Schauer. Chicago: University of Chicago Press.

______. 1999. "Open Texture and the Possibility of Legal Interpretation." *Legal Philosophy*, vol. 18: 297–309.

———. 1962. *Jurisprudence: Realism in Theory and Practice*. Chicago: University of Chicago Press.

______. 1960a. *The Common Law Tradition: Deciding Appeals*. Boston: Little Brown and Co.

______. 1960b. *The Bramble Bush: Our Law and Its Study*. New York: Oceana.

Lyons, David. 1965. *Forms and Limits of Utilitarianism*. Oxford: Clarendon Press.

Madden, Edward H. 1963. *Chauncey Wright and the Foundations of Pragmatism*. Seattle: University of Washington Press.

Margolis, Joseph. 2012. *Pragmatism Ascendent*. Stanford: Stanford University Press.

———. 2010. *Pragmatism's Advantage*. Stanford: Stanford University Press.

Marmor, Andrei. 1992. *Interpretation and Legal Theory*. Oxford: Clarendon Press.

Maskin, Eric, Amartya Sen, Kenneth J. Arrow, Partha Dasgupta, Prasanta K. Pattanaik, and Joseph E. Stiglitz. 2014. *The Arrow Impossibility Theorem*. New York: Columbia University Press.

McDowell, John. 1998. *Mind, Value and Reality*. Cambridge and London: Harvard University Press.

———. 1994. *Mind and World*. Cambridge and London: Harvard University Press.

Mead, G. H. 1934. *Mind, Self and Society*. Chicago: Chicago University Press.

Mendenhall, Allen. 2017. *Oliver Wendell Holmes Jr., Pragmatism, and the Jurisprudence of Agon: Aesthetic Dissent and the Common Law*. Lewisburg: Bucknell University Press.

Mensch, Elizabeth. 1982. "The History of Mainstream Legal Thought." In *The Politics of Law: A Progressive Critique*, edited by D. Kairys, 23. New York: Basic Books.

Mill, John Stuart. 2001a [1861]. *Representative Government*. Ontario: Batoche Books.

______. 2001b [1863]. *Utilitarianism*. Ontario: Batoche Books.

______. 1963–1991. *The Collected Works of John Stuart Mill*, edited by John Robson. 33 vols. Toronto: University of Toronto Press; London: Routledge and Kegan Paul.

———. 1843. *A System of Logic Ratiocinative and Inductive*. 2 vols. London: Longmans, Green, Reader and Dyer, 1872.

Milsom, S. F. C. 1969. *Historical Foundations of the Common Law*. London: Butterworths.

Misak, Cheryl. 2013. *The American Pragmatists*. Oxford and New York: Oxford University Press.

______. 2005. "Pragmatism and Pluralism." *Transactions of the Charles S. Peirce Society*, vol. 41, no. 1 (Winter): 129–135.

Mouffe, Chantal, and Ernest Laclau. 2001. *Hegemony and Socialist Strategy: Towards a Radical Democratic Politics*. Revised edition. London and New York: Verso.

Murphy, Arthur E. 1927. "Objective Relativism in Dewey and Whitehead." *The Philosophical Review*, vol. 36, no. 2 (March): 122.

Nagel, Thomas. 1986. *The View From Nowhere*. New York and Oxford: Oxford University Press.

Novick, Sheldon M., ed. 1995. *The Collected Works of Justice Holmes: Complete Public Writings and Selected Opinions of Oliver Wendell Holmes*. Chicago and London: University of Chicago Press.

Oberschall, Anthony. 1978. "Theories of Social Conflict." *Annual Review of Sociology*, vol. 4: 291.

Okrent, Mark. 1988. *Heidegger's Pragmatism: Understanding, Being, and the Critique of Metaphysics*. Ithaca: Cornell University Press.

O'Neill, Onora. 2018. *From Principle to Practice: Normativity and Judgment in Ethics and Politics.* Cambridge: Cambridge University Press.

Owen, G. E. L. 1986. *Logic, Science and Dialectic.* Edited by Martha Nussbaum. Ithaca: Cornell University Press.

———, ed. 1968. *Aristotle on Dialectic, The Topics: Proceedings of the Third Symposium Aristotelicum.* Oxford: Clarendon Press.

Parfit, Derek. 1984. *Reasons and Persons.* Oxford: Clarendon Press.

Peirce, Charles. 1982. *Writings of Charles S. Peirce: A Chronological Edition, 1857-1866.* Bloomington: Indiana University Press.

______. 1978. *Collected Papers of Charles Sanders Peirce.* Edited by Charles Hartshorne and Paul Weiss. Cambridge: Belknap Press.

Pohlman, H. L. 1984. *Justice Oliver Wendell Holmes and Utilitarian Jurisprudence.* Cambridge and London: Harvard University Press.

Point, Christophe. 2018. "What's the Use of Conflict in Dewey? Toward a Pedagogy of Compromise." *Education and Culture*, vol. 34, no. 2: 69.

Popp Jerome A. 2008. "John Dewey's Ethical Naturalism." *Contemporary Pragmatism*, vol. 5, no. 2 (December): 149–163.

Popper, Karl. 1962. *Conjectures and Refutations: The Growth of Scientific Knowledge.* New York: Basic Books.

Posner, Richard. 2013. *Reflections on Judging.* Cambridge and London: Harvard University Press.

______. 2003. *Law, Pragmatism, and Democracy.* Cambridge and London: Harvard University Press.

______. 1990. *The Problems of Jurisprudence.* Cambridge and London: Harvard University Press.

Postema, Gerald J. 2011. *A Treatise of Legal Philosophy and General Jurisprudence.* Dordrecht: Springer Netherlands.

______. 1986. *Bentham and the Common Law Tradition.* Oxford: Clarendon Press.

Pound, Roscoe. 1921. *The Spirit of the Common Law.* Boston: Beacon Press.

Putnam, Hilary. 2002. *The Collapse of the Fact/Value Dichotomy.* Cambridge and London: Harvard University Press.

______. 1994. "Rethinking Mathematical Necessity." In *Words and Life.* Cambridge and London: Harvard University Press.

______. 1983. *Realism and Reason: Philosophical Papers.* Vol. 3. Cambridge and London: Cambridge University Press.

_____. 1981. *Reason, Truth and History.* Cambridge: Cambridge University Press.

______. 1978. *Meaning and the Moral Sciences.* Boston and London: Routledge and Kegan Paul.

______. 1975. *Mind, Language and Reality.* Cambridge and London: Harvard University Press.

_____. 1971. *Philosophy of Logic.* New York: Harper & Row.

Quine, W. V. 1976. *The Ways of Paradox and Other Essays.* Cambridge: Harvard University Press.

______. 1970. *Philosophy of Logic.* Cambridge: Harvard University Press.

______. 1969. *Ontological Relativity and Other Essays.* New York: Columbia University Press.

______. 1966. *Elements of Logic.* Cambridge: Harvard University Press.

______. 1960. *Word and Object.* Cambridge: Harvard University Press.

Ralston, Shane. 2010. "Dewey's Model of Moral (and Political) Deliberation Unfiltered." *Education and Culture*, vol. 26, no. 1: 23–43.

Rawls, John. 2000. *Lectures on the History of Moral Philosophy.* Cambridge and London: Harvard University Press.

_____. 1971. *A Theory of Justice.* Cambridge and London: Harvard University Press.

_____. 1967. "Two Concepts of Rules." In *Theories of Ethics*, edited by Foot. Oxford: Oxford University Press.

Ridge, Michael. 2009. "Climb Every Mountain." *Ratio* (new series), vol. XXII, no. 1: 22.

Riley, Jonathan. 1990. "Utilitarian Ethics and Democratic Government." *Ethics*, vol. 100, no. 2 (January): 335–348.

Rogers, Melvin L. 2009. "Dewey, Pluralism, and Democracy: A Response to Robert Talisse." *Transactions of the Charles S. Peirce Society*, vol. 41, no. 1: 75.

______. 2009. *The Undiscovered Dewey.* New York: Columbia University Press.

Rorty, Richard. 2010. "Pragmatism, Relativism, and Irrationalism." In *The Rorty Reader*, edited by Christopher Voparil and Richard Bernstein, 115. Chichester: Wiley-Blackwell.

______. 1999. *Philosophy and Social Hope.* New York: Penguin Books.

______. 1991. *Objectivity, Relativism, and Truth.* Cambridge, Cambridge University Press.

______. 1990. "The Banality of Pragmatism and the Poetry of Justice." *Southern California Law Review*, vol. 63: 1811–1819.

______. 1989. *Contingency, Irony and Solidarity.* Cambridge: Cambridge University Press.

______. 1987. "Thugs and Theorists: A Reply to Bernstein." *Political Theory*, vol. 15: 564.

______. 1982. *Consequences of Pragmatism.* Minneapolis: University of Minnesota Press.

______. 1979. *Philosophy and the Mirror of Nature.* Princeton: Princeton University Press.

Russell, Bertrand. 1939. "Dewey's New Logic." In *The Philosophy of John Dewey*, edited by P. A. Schilpp, *The Library of Living Philosophers.* Evanston and Chicago: Northwestern University Press.

______. 1914. "Logic as the Essence of Philosophy." In Russell, *Our Knowledge of the External World*, 33. London: Allen & Unwin.

Ryle, Gilbert. 1968. "Dialectic in the Academy." In *Aristotle on Dialectic, The Topics: Proceedings of the Third Symposium Aristotelicum*, edited by G. E. L. Owen, 73. Oxford: Clarendon Press.

Samuelson, Paul. 1948. "Consumption Theory in Terms of Revealed Preference." *Economica*, vol. 15: 243–253.

Sandel, Michael. 1982. *Liberalism and the Limits of Justice*. Cambridge: Cambridge University Press.

Scalia, Antonin. 1989. "Originalism: The Lesser Evil." *University of Cincinnati Law Review*, vol. 57: 849, 852–865.

Schauer, Frederick. 2013. "Legal Realism Untamed." *Texas Law Review*, vol. 91: 749.

———. 2008. "A Critical Guide to Vehicles in the Park." *New York University Law Review*, vol. 83, no. 4 (October): 1109.

———. 2006. "Do Cases Make Bad Law?" *University of Chicago Law Review*, vol. 73 (Summer): 883.

———. 1991. *Playing by the Rules: A Philosophical Examination of Rule-Based Decision Making in Law and Life*. Oxford: Clarendon Press.

Schlegel, John Henry. 1995. *American Legal Realism and Empirical Social Science*. Chapel Hill and London: University of North Carolina Press.

Schneewind, Jerome B. 1977. *Sidgwick's Ethics and Victorian Moral Philosophy*. Oxford: Clarendon Press.

Schneider, Herbert. 1946. *A History of American Philosophy*. New York: Liberal Arts Press.

Schneider, Joseph W. 1985. "Social Problems Theory: The Constructionist View." *Annual Review of Sociology*, vol. 11: 209–229.

Sellars, Wilfrid. 1997. *Empiricism and the Philosophy of Mind.* Cambridge: Harvard University Press.

______. 1962. "Philosophy and the Scientific Image of Man." In *Frontiers of Science and Philosophy*, edited by Robert Colodny. Pittsburgh: University of Pittsburgh Press.

______. 1956. "Empiricism and the Philosophy of Mind." In *Minneapolis Studies in the Philosophy of Science*, vol. 1, edited by Herbert Feigl and Michael Scriven, 253–329. Minneapolis: University of Minnesota Press.

———. 1949. "Language, Rules and Behavior." In *John Dewey: Philosopher of Science and Freedom; A Symposium*, edīted by Sidney Hook, 289–315. New York: Barnes and Noble.

Sen, Amartya K. 2009. *The Idea of Justice*. London and New York: Allen Lane.

______, and Bernard Williams. 1982. *Utilitarianism and Beyond.* Cambridge: Cambridge University Press.

______. 1970. *Collective Choice and Social Welfare.* San Francisco: Holden-Day Inc.

Shaefer, Alexander. 2021. "Hayek's Twin Ideas: Reconciling Methodological Individualism and Group Selection." *Cambridge Journal of Economics* online (November 21): 209.

Shapin, Steven, and Simon Schaffer. 1985. *Leviathan and the Air-Pump: Hobbes, Boyle, and the Experimental Life*. Princeton: Princeton University Press.

Shaw, Geoffrey. 2014. "H. L. A. Hart's Lost Essay." *Harvard Law Review*, vol. 127: 674.

Shook, John R. 2010. "Pragmatism, Pluralism, and Public Democracy." *Revue Francais D'Etudes,* 2e TRIMESTRE 2010, no. 124, 11.

______. 2004. "Dewey's Empirical Naturalism and Pragmatic Metaphysics Author(s): John R." *Transactions of the Charles S. Peirce Society*, vol. 40, no. 4 (Fall): 731–742.

Sidgwick, Henry. 1981 [1874]. *The Methods of Ethics*. Indianapolis: Hackett Pub. Co.

Singer, Marcus G. 1951. "Formal Logic and Dewey's Logic." *The Philosophical Review*, vol. 60, no. 3 (July): 375–385.

Singer, Peter-, and Katarzyna de Lazari-Radek. 2014. *The Point of View of the Universe: Sidgwick and Contemporary Ethics*. Oxford: Oxford University Press.

Sleeper, Ralph. 1993. "The Pragmatics of Deconstruction and the End of Metaphysics." In *Philosophy and the Reconstruction of Culture*, edited by John J. Stuhr. Albany: SUNY Press.

______. 1986. *The Necessity of Pragmatism: John Dewey's Conception of Philosophy*. New Haven: Yale University Press.

Solum, Lawrence B. 1987. "On the Indeterminacy Crisis: Critiquing Critical Dogma." *University of Chicago Law Review*, vol. 54: 462.

Spann, Girardeau A. 1985. "Simple Justice." *Georgetown Law Journal*, vol. 73: 1041, 1060.

Stikkers, Kenneth W. 2009. "Dialogue Between Pragmatism and Constructivism in Historical Perspective." In *John Dewey Between Pragmatism and Constructivism*, edited by L. Hickman, S. Neubert, and K. Reich. New York: Fordham University Press.

Stone, Julius. 1985. *Precedent and Law: Dynamics of Common Law Growth*. Sydney: Butterworths.

______. 1966. *Social Dimensions of Law and Justice*. Stanford: Stanford University Press.

———. 1950. *The Province and Function of Law: Law as Logic, Justice and Social Control, a Study in Jurisprudence*. Cambridge: Harvard University Press.

Strauss, David A. 1996, "Common Law Constitutional Interpretation." *University of Chicago Law Review*, vol. 63: 877–935.

Sullivan, Kathleen M. 1993. "Categorization, Balancing, and Government Interests." In *Public Values in Constitutional Law*, edited by Stephen E. Gottlieb. Ann Arbor: University of Michigan Press.

Summers, Robert S. 1984. *Lon L. Fuller*. Stanford: Stanford University Press.

______. 1982. *Instrumentalism and American Legal Theory*. Ithaca: Cornell University Press.

Sunstein, Cass R. 1999. *One Case at a Time: Judicial Minimalism on the Supreme Court*. Cambridge and London: Harvard University Press.

Talisse, Robert. 2007. *A Pragmatist Philosophy of Democracy*. New York: Routledge.

Tamanaha, Brian. 2009. *Beyond the Formalist-Realist Divide: The Role of Politics in Judging*. Princeton and Oxford: Princeton University Press.

Tate, C. Neal, and Torbjorn Vallinder. 1995. *The Global Expansion of Judicial Power*. New York and London: NYU Press.

Thayer, James B. 1893. "The Origin and Scope of the American Doctrine of Constitutional Law." 7 *Harvard Law Review*, vol. 129: 155–156.

______, ed. 1878. *Letters of Chauncey Wright, with Some Account of His Life*. Cambridge: John Wilson and Son.

Thompson, Dennis F. 2008. "Deliberative Democratic Theory and Empirical Political Science." *Annual Review of Political Science*, vol. 11: 497–520.

Tobia, Kevin. 2013. "Rule Consequentialism and the Problem of Partial Acceptance." *Ethical Theory and Moral Practice*, vol. 16, no. 3 (June): 643–652.

Tushnet, Mark V. 1998. "Defending the Indeterminacy Thesis." In *Analyzing Law*, edited by Brian Bix. Oxford: Clarendon Press.

______. 1984a. "Anti-Formalism in Recent Constitutional Theory." *Michigan Law Review*, vol. 83: 1502.

______. 1984b. "Critical Legal Studies and Constitutional Law: An Essay in Deconstruction." *Stanford Law Review*, vol. 26: 625.

Twining, William. 1973. *Karl Llewellyn and the Realist Movement*. Norman: University of Oklahoma Press.

Unger, Roberto M. 1987a. *Social Theory: Its Situation and Its Task*. Cambridge: Cambridge University Press.

______. 1987b. *False Necessity: Anti-Necessitarian Social Theory in the Service of Radical Democracy*. Cambridge: Cambridge University Press.

______. 1983. *The Critical Legal Studies Movement*. Cambridge: Harvard University Press.

______. 1976. *Law in Modern Society: Toward a Criticism of Social Theory*. New York: The Free Press.

______. 1975. *Knowledge and Politics*. New York: Macmillan.

Vahabi, Mehrdad. 2010. "Integrating Social Conflict Into Economic Theory." *Cambridge Journal of Economics*, vol. 34, no. 4 (July): 687–708.

Valverde, Mariana. 2003. *Law's Dream of a Common Knowledge*. Princeton: Princeton University Press.

Vanberg, Viktor. 2010. "On the Complementarity of Liberalism and Democracy: A Reading of F. A. Hayek and J. M. Buchanan." In *Ökonomische Analyse Politischer Institutionen*, edited by Herbert Brücker, Klaus Heine, Roland Kirstein, Jörn Kruse, Helmut Leipold, Theresia Theurl, Viktor J. Vanberg, and Uwe Vollmer. Berlin: Duncker & Humblot.

______. 1986. "Spontaneous Market Order and Social Rules: A Critical Examination of F. A. Hayek's Theory of Cultural Evolution." *Economics & Philosophy*, vol. 2, no. 1: 75–100.

Voparil, Christopher. 2011. "Rorty and Brandom: Pragmatism and the Ontological Priority of the Social." *Pragmatism Today*, vol. 2, no. 1: 133.

Wagner-Pacifici, Robin, and Meredith Hall. 2012. "Resolution of Social Conflict." *Annual Review of Sociology*, vol. 38: 181–199.

Waismann, Frederick. 1965. *The Principles of Linguistic Philosophy*. London: Macmillan.

______. 1945. "Verifiability." In *Logic and Language*, edited by Antony Flew. First Series. Oxford: Basil Blackwell.

Waldron, Jeremy. 2009. "Did Dworkin Ever Answer the Crits?" In *Exploring Law's Empire: The Jurisprudence of Ronald Dworkin*, edited by Scott Hershovitz. Oxford: Oxford Scholarship Online.

———. 1999. *Law and Disagreement*. Oxford: Oxford University Press.

———. 1992. "The Irrelevance of Moral Objectivity." In *Natural Law Theory*, edited by Robert P. George. Oxford: Oxford University Press.

Waluchow, W. J. 1994. *Inclusive Legal Positivism*. Oxford: Clarendon Press.

Wechsler, Herbert. 1959. "Toward Neutral Principles of Constitutional Law." *Harvard Law Review*, vol. 73: 1.

Weingart, Peter. 1969. "Beyond Parsons? A Critique of Ralf Dahrendorf's Conflict Theory." *Social Forces*, vol. 48, no. 2 (December): 151.

Weir, Robert F., ed. 1997. *Physician Assisted Suicide*. Bloomington and Indianapolis: Indiana University Press.

Westbrook, Robert B. 1991. *John Dewey and American Democracy*. Ithaca: Cornell University Press.

Whewell, William. 1837. *The History of the Inductive Sciences, from the Earliest to the Present Time*. 3 vols. London: John W. Parker.

White, G. Edward. 1993. *Justice Oliver Wendell Holmes: Law and the Inner Self*. New York and Oxford: Oxford University Press.

______. 1986. "From Realism to Critical Legal Studies: A Truncated Intellectual History." *Southwestern Law Journal*, vol. 40: 819–843.

______. 1972. "From Sociological Jurisprudence to Realism: Jurisprudence and Social Change in Early Twentieth-Century America." *Virginia Law Review*, vol. 58: 999–1028.

Williams, Bernard. 2005. *In the Beginning Was the Deed*. Princeton and Oxford: Princeton University Press.

______. 1985. *Ethics and the Limits of Philosophy*. Cambridge: Harvard University Press.

Winston, Kenneth, ed. 2001. *The Principles of Social Order: Selected Essays of Lon L. Fuller*. Oxford and Portland: Hart Publishing.

Wong, Stanley, and Philip Mirowski. 2006. *The Foundations of Paul Samuelson's Revealed Preference Theory: A Study by the Method of Rational Reconstruction*. London: Routledge.

Woodiwiss, Anthony. 1990. *Rights v. Conspiracy: A Sociological Essay on the History of Labour Law in the United States*. New York and Oxford: Berg.

Wright, Chauncey. 1865. "The Origins of Modern Science." In *The Philosophical Writings of Chauncey Wright: Representative Selections,* edited by Edward H. Madden. New York: The Liberal Arts Press.

Young, Robert. 2007. *Medically Assisted Death*. Cambridge: Cambridge University Press.

Index

abortion rights, 62, 71, 108–9
Abrams v. United, 26n29, 85n5, 100
acceptance, utilitarianism and, 54–56
action, theory of, 130–31
Addams, Jane, 22
Adler, Mortimer, 83, 97
affirmative action, Supreme Court rulings on, 91–92
The Ages of American Law (Gilmore), 69–70
agonistic pragmatism: balanced legal decisions and, 95–98; deliberative democracy and, 57–70; Dewey on conflict and, 13–28, 129, 136–37; Dewey's empirical naturalism and, 120; legal theory and, 66–70; Mouffe and Laclau on, 27–28; philosophy and, 120–25; uncertainty and, 71–82; utilitarianism and, 34–42
Aikin, Scott, 24
Alexy, Robert, 92–96
Alschuler, Albert, 104, 112
Altman, Andrew, 78n15
American Bar Association Journal, 85
American Philosophical Association, 23
antinomy: contemporary democracy and, 136–37; reason and fiat and, 87–88
Arrow, Kenneth J.: on authoritarianism, xiii; Dewey's conflict theory and, 137; General Possibility Theorem of, vii–xi, 127–29; on individual preferences, 118; on ordering of preferences, 14; pragmatism and, xv–xvi; on rationality, 10–12; on social preference, 7–9, 34; synchronicity in model of, 34n15; utilitarianism and work of, 43–44
Austin, John, 106
authoritarianism: Arrow on inevitability of, vii–xi; election failure and, 19–20; Holmes and, 85
Ayer, A. J., 98

Bacon, Francis, 77, 96–97, 106–7, 110–12
balanced decisions, legal principles and, 93–98
Beadel v. Perry, 79n16
behavior, preference revelation through, 8
Bentham, Jeremy, 106
Bergson, Abram, xv
Berlin, Isaiah, 16, 121, 124
Bickel, Alexander, x, 76; on empirical naturalism, 98; on judicial process, 88–92; on legal principles, 84, 112, 114
Bill of Rights: judicial review and, 84; legal principles and, 86

binary choice, conflict and, 24
Bloom, Allan, 104
Bobbitt, Philip, 106
Boyle, Robert, 58, 105–6, 113
Buchanan, James, 10–11, 34
Burke, Thomas, 31
Butler, Brian E., vii–xi

capitalism, Dewey's conflict theory and, 132
Cardozo, Benjamin, 87–88
Cardozo, Nathan, 60–61
Carnegie, Andrew, 103
changing preferences, Arrow's General Possibility Theorem and, 5–6
civil rights, utilitarianism and, 39
class conflict, 130n4
climate change, 137n26
Cohen, Morris, 105
Collective Choice and Social Welfare (Sen), 8–9
collective choice theory: majority voting and, 11n22; preference formation and, 8–9, 129; social states and, 6–7
Commentaries on American Law (Kent), 108–10
common law: Holmes on, 103; legal theory and, 79–82
The Common Law (Holmes), 107–8, 110
Communications Decency Act of 1996, 61
community: Dewey on democracy and, 18–19; of principle, Dworkin's concept of, 75; Rorty's idea of, 122
competing practices, principled adjudication and, 73–79
"Competition as a Discovery Procedure" (Hayek), 25–26
competitive equilibrium, Arrow's work and, xvn6
compliance, utilitarianism and, 54–56
The Concept of Law (Hart), 69–70
Condorcet, 127
conflict theory: deliberation and, 25–26; democracy and, 18–19, 127–29, 136–37; developmental logic of, 57n2; Dewey and, 30–34, 129–32; economic competition as, 26; empirical naturalism and, 99–100; feedback loop in, 27; Holmes on, 99–100, 107–9; legal theory and, 50–56; moral progress and, 19–24; normative development and, 48–56; pragmatism and, xiii–xv, 20–28; preferences *versus*, 40–42; selective emphasis fallacy and, 123–24; transformation and, 29–42; uncertainty and, 71–82; utilitarianism and, 38–42
constitutional law: Holmes's comments on, 84–86; legal principles and, 86–98
constructivism, Hayek on, 135
consumption, preferences and, 9
consumption-leisure-saving model, General Possibility Theorem and, 11–12
contemporary law, Holmes on ancient practices and, 110
contract, Holmes's theory of, 113–14
controlling norms, absence of, 94–95
convergence of interests, utilitarianism and, 49–56
Cox, Christopher, 61n9
Critical Legal Studies (CLS), 70, 75–79, 78n15, 81–82, 86
critical theory, legal theory and, 69–70
culture: moral values and, 83; preference aggregation and, 131
customs, utilitarianism and, 51–52

Dahrendorf, Ralf, 130
Darwin, Charles, 133
datum: hypothesis and, 32n10; legal theory and, 77
Debreu, Gérard, 8n15
decisiveness, Arrow's General Possibility Theorem and, 2–3

deductive reasoning, legal theory and, 105–6
deliberative democracy: agonistic deliberation and, 57–70; principles of, viii, 25
democracy: authoritarianism and, vii–xi; Dewey's thesis on, 13, 127–29; libertarianism and, 132–37; utilitarianism and, 55–56
democratic contractualism, eleven steps of, 20–22
descriptive optimism, Dworkin's concept of, 70n26
Dewey, John: agonistic pragmatism of, xiv, 13–28; conflict theory of, 20–21, 97, 129–32; disequilibrium and preference adjustment, 8n15; empirical naturalism of, 58–59, 97, 99–115, 120–25; on experience as resource, 59, 81–82; Holmes and, 99–100, 109, 112, 114–15; on legal process, 64–72, 90–91; legal realism and, 119; libertarianism and democratic theory of, 134–37; on logic of inquiry, 61; multiple problematic situations model, 5–6; naturalized objectivity of, 118–25; organic democracy theory of, vii–xi, 13, 15, 127–29; pluralism in work of, 15–17; pragmatism of, 2–6; on problematic preferences, 29–34; Rorty and, 117–18, 120–25; situation defined by, 30–34; on successive judgments, 47; on transformation through preference, xiii, xvi, 23–24; on uncertainty, 71–72; utilitarianism and work of, 36–42, 53–56
discourse model, real-world naturalism and, 20
"Discovery View," critique of, 20
Dixon v. Bell, 60
due process, 85
Dworkin, Ronald, x; on moral principles and legal theory, 72–79, 81–82, 84, 86, 97, 113–14; on rights and legal theory, 69–70, 80; "third conception" of law, 77n13

economic equilibrium theory, preferences and, ix, 128–29
empirical naturalism, x–xi; legal theory and, 99–115; sciences and, 58–59, 97–98
empiricism, Holmes and, 106
"Empiricism and the Philosophy of Mind" (Sellars), 118–19
Epstein, Richard, 112–13
equilibrium theory, preference stabilization and, 8n15, 128–29
ethical inquiry, Holmes on law and, 106–7
ethical noncognitivism, 83
The Ethical Project (Kitcher), 19
Ethics and Language (Stevenson), 98
European Court of Human Rights, 137n26
euthanasia, 22–24, 33–34, 40–42; legal theory and, 66–67
evolution, Hayek's model of, 133
experience, Dewey's concept of, 59, 81–82
Experience and Nature (Dewey), 74, 88, 98, 100, 115
extensional equivalence, utilitarianism and, 46–48, 53–56

false information, conflict and, 27
Feldman, Alan, 1, 8
fiat, reason and, 87–88
"The Fixation of Belief" (Peirce), xiv
foreseeability test, 60–61
formalism; legal realism and, 88; liability and, 62, 64–70
Forster, E. M., 37
Foucault, Michel, 18
Fourteenth Amendment, 22, 85
Freedom Rides, 39
free expression, Holmes's belief in, 100

Fuller, Lon, 84–85, 87–92, 102, 104, 112

Garfield, James A., 103
General Possibility Theorem (Arrow): analysis of, xvi; conflict and democracy and, 127–29; Kellogg's critique of, vii–xi, 1–6; preference formation and, 7–9; rational social choice and, 10–11; Sen's analysis of, 3–6; social states and, xv
gestalt switch, 64–65, 119, 122
Gilmore, Grant, 69–70, 104
Good Samaritan protections, 61n9
Gouinlock, James, 15, 31
Gray, John Chipman, 111
"Great Books" curriculum, 83

Habermas, Juergen, 20, 58
Hand, Learned, 84–86
Hart, Herbert L. A., x; Dworkin and work of, 72–75, 84; Holmes and, 106, 112–13; judicial process and work of, 88; legal theory and, 77n13; on preferences, 62–64; on realism and formalism, 69, 119, 122
Harvard Law Review, 87–88
Hayek, Friedrich, 25–26, 51, 129, 132–37
Haymarket bombing, 103
Hegel, G. F. W., 104, 111
Heidegger, Martin, 120
Henningsen v. Bloomfield Motors, Inc., 72, 73n4
Herzen, Alexander, 16n8
Heyek, Friedrich, xvii
Hobbes, Thomas, 105–6
Holmes, Oliver Wendell Jr., x; Civil War and, 103–4, 112; contract theory of, 113–14; criticism of, 104–6; Dewey's pragmatism and, 99–100; diaries and letters of, 108–9; early life and career, 103–4; on Massachusetts Supreme Judicial Court, 102–3; normative development and, 48; opposing poles principle of, 106–9; speeches on legal theory by, 102–3; on Supreme Court, 84–86, 90–92, 97–98; utilitarianism and, 52
"Holmes, Hobbes, and Hitler," 85
Honneth, Axel, 57n2
Hooker, Brad, 46–47, 52–54
Hutchins, Robert, 74
hypothesis, datum and, 32n10

ideal theory (ideal conversation): moral progress and, xiv, 20, 25; utilitarianism and, 54–56
ideology, legal theory and influence of, 71–72
immunity, inherently dangerous rule and, 60–70
independent alternatives, Arrow's General Possibility Theorem and, 2–3
indeterminacy: legal theory and, 74–82; natural language and, 74–75
inductive reasoning: legal theory and, 95–98, 105–15; preferences and, 41–42
inherently dangerous rule, history of, 60–70
inner morality of law, 84
inquiry, logic of: Dworkin's continuum of inquiry and, 75–79; Holmes and, 99–100, 105–15; inherently dangerous rule and, 60–70; pragmatic conflict and, 20–28; scientific method and, 131–32; situationism and, 32–33
integrity, Dworkin's concept of, 77–79
intelligence, logic and, 30–34

James, William, 99, 103–4, 111
judicial restraint: minimalist ideology and, 81–82, 86–92; moral principles and, 77–79; uncertainty and, 71–72
judicial review: Bickel's discussion of, 88–92; Hand's analysis of, 84

Kant, Immanuel, 104, 111, 119–20
Kennedy, Duncan, 69–70
Kent, James, 108–10
Kevorkian, Jack, 22–24, 39, 73
Kitcher, Philip, xiv, 19–23, 25–27, 57–59, 67, 122

labor law: Holmes and, 110–13; Supreme Court rulings on, 100–104
Laclau, Ernest, 20, 27
landownership, legal theory and, 79–82
Langridge v. Levy, 60
language: legal indeterminacy and, 74–75; of moral principles, 84; open area theory of legal principles and, 94–95
Language, Truth, and Logic (Ayer), 98
Laski, Harold, 100
Law, Legislation and Liberty (Hayek), 133
"Law in Science and Science in Law." (Holmes speech), 102–3, 107–9
Law's Empire (Dworkin), 75, 77n13
Law Without Values (Alschuler), 104, 112
Lazari-Radek, Katarzyna de, 35–36
legal principles: abuse of, 90–92; judiciary view of, 83–98; neutrality of, 88–92; open area theory and, 92–95
legal realism, 78n15, 88; Holmes and, 104
legal theory: empirical naturalism and, 99–115; history of, xvii; inherently dangerous rule in, 60–70; inner morality of law, 84; logic and, 103–15; moral principles and, 72–79; naturalism and legal principles, 83–98; naturalized utilitarianism and, xvii, 50–56; realism and, 67–69; situationism and, 69–70; uncertainty and, 71–82
Leipold, Helmut, 136–37
Levi, Edward, 52; dangerous instrumentalities theory of, 78–79; Holmes and, 104–5, 109, 114; on legal principles, 83; on legal theory, x, 60–61, 73–74, 76, 77n13, 81–82; legal theory and, 80; utilitarianism and, 65–68
liability: Holmes on, 112–13; inherently dangerous rule and, 60–70
Liberalism and Social Action (Dewey), 129
libertarianism, democracy and, 132–37
Lincolnian tension, Bickel's concept of, 89, 112–13
Llewellyn, Karl, x, 67–69, 76, 114
Lochner v. New York, 85n5, 100
logic: classical principles of, 105; Holmes on law and, 103–15; intelligence and, 31–32; situationism and, 30–34
Logic: The Theory of Inquiry (Dewey), 19, 61, 71–72, 109
logical positivism, 97–98
Longmeid v. Holliday, 60
Lyons, David, 45–47, 51–53

MacPherson v. Buick Motor Co., 60–61, 72–73
Macron, Emmanuel, 26, 40
markets, collective choice and, 11n22
Marxism: conflict theory and, 130; power-oriented class/group conflict model of, xiv–xv; preference and power conflict and, 18–20
Massachusetts Supreme Judicial Court, Holmes as judge on, 102–3
McDowell, John, 118–30
Mead, G. H., 130
Methods of Ethics (Sidgwick), 35
MeToo movement, 32, 66–67
Mill, John Stuart, xiv, 32n10, 35, 38, 77, 96–97; Holmes and, 103, 106–7, 110, 112
Mind and World (McDowell), 118–19
Minor, Virginia Louise, 22
monism doctrine, 16n8

moral principles: authoritarianism and, 19–20; constitutional law and, 86; Holmes on law and, 102–4, 106–7; language of, 84–85; legal theory and, 71–79, 84–86
Moral Progress (Kitcher), xiv, 19
Mouffe, Chantal, 20, 27
multiple problematic situations, preferences and, 5–6
Murphy, Arthur E., 122
mutually exclusive preferences, 4–6

National Council for Reconstruction, 26
naturalism: agonistic deliberation and, 59–70; Dewey's concept of, 23–24, 83; legal principles and, 83–98; objectivity and, 117–25; opposing versions of, 20–22; pragmatism and, 41–42; problematic preferences and, 29
naturalized utilitarianism, ix, xvi, 43–56
natural language, legal indeterminacy and, 74
Naziism, 123–24
neutrality, of legal principles, 88–92
The New Republic, 100
Nightmare/Noble Dream dichotomy, preferences and, 62–64
Nineteenth Amendment, 22
nondictatorship, Arrow's General Possibility Theorem and, 2–3
norm conflicts, legal principles and, 94–95
Novum Organum (Bacon), 111–12

objectivism, legal theory and, 64–70
objectivity: naturalization of, 117–18; relativism and, 122–25
Objectivity, Relativism and Truth (Rorty), 117
O'Connor, Sandra Day, 111
One Case at a Time: Judicial Minimalism on the Supreme Court (Sunstein), 72
online services, liability of, 61–62
open area, legal principles and, 92–95
optimum welfare, utilitarianism and, 36–42
originalism, Supreme Court and, 92

Pareto optimality, Arrow's General Possibility Theorem and, 2–3
Parfit, Derek, 35n17, 47
Parsons, Talcott, 130
"The Path of the Law" (Holmes), 84, 102–3
Pegler, Westbrook, 85
Peirce, Charles, ix, xiv, 23, 29, 41–42, 97, 99; Holmes and, 103–4, 110–11
Pennsylvania Coal Company v. Mahon, 112–13
philosophy: Dewey's contributions to, 119–25; Holmes's interest in, 104, 111–12
Philosophy and the Mirror of Nature *(Rorty)*, 23
Philosophy and the Mirror of Nature (Rorty), 120–25
Plant v. Woods, 101
Pluralism: Dewey's democratic theory and, 15–16, 31; incommensurability of values and, 16; legal theory and, 69–70; selective emphasis fallacy and, 124
Point, Christophe, 28n32
point of view of the universe, utilitarianism and, 35–42
political preferences, General Possibility Theorem and, 8–9
Popper, Karl, 29n1, 131
positivism: empirical naturalism and, 97–98; legal theory and, 69–70, 72–73, 77n13, 84–86, 106
power models: preference and, 18; real-world naturalism and, 20
practice view of utilitarianism, 44–46, 51–56; resolution and, 57
pragmatist philosophy: agonistic pragmatism, xvi–xvii, 13–28;

Arrow's General Possibility Theorem and, 2; conflict and, xiii–xv, 13–28; Dewey and, 2–6, 118–25; ethics and, 41–42; inductive reasoning and, 95–98; legal principles and, 89–92; naturalism and, 21–24; revival of, 23–24; Rorty and, 120–25; utilitarianism and, 47–49, 53–56; welfare economics and, x–xi
precedent, legal theory and, 74–75, 80–82
preferences: Arrow's General Possibility Theorem and, 2–6, 34; conflict theory and, xiii–xiv, 26–28, 131–32; Dewey's model of, 13–28, 118–25; economic theory and, viii–ix; equilibrium and stabilization of, 8n15; formation of, 7–9, 13; liability and, 62–64; pragmatism and, 41–42; Sen's analysis of, 3–6; social states and, 6–7; utilitarianism and, 38–42
principled adjudication, Dworkin's concept of, 74–79
problematic preferences, Dewey's focus on, xv, 29–34
product liability, legal theory and, 60–61, 72–73
The Proud Tower (Tuchman), 103
The Public and its Problems (Dewey), xiii, 13, 128
Putnam, Hilary, xvii, 64, 119, 122–24

The Quest for Certainty (Dewey), 97

rationality: agonistic deliberation and, 57–58; Arrow on, 10–12; problematic preferences and, 29n1
Rawls, John, 20, 44–46, 51, 57
realism: legal theory and, 78n15, 86; liability and, 62, 64–70; relativism and, 67–69
reason: fiat *versus*, 87–92; judicial reason, 78–79; transformation in, 23–24, 41–42
Reason, Truth and History (Putnam), 123
"Reason and Fiat in Case Law" (Fuller), 87
referendums, Arrow's General Possibility Theorem and, 4n6
relativism: legal theory and, 64–70; objectivity and, 122–25; philosophy and, 121–25
resolution, Dewey on, 58n4
Ridge, Michael, 47
right to die, legal theory and, 22–24, 39, 73, 82
Robbins, Lionel, xv
Roe v. Wade, 19–20, 63
Roosevelt, Theodore, 103
Rorty, Richard, xvii, 23, 57, 117–18, 120–25
rule-consequentialism: extensional equivalence and, 46–47; Hayek and, 134–35; history of, 60; normative development and, 48–50; summary and practice views of, 44–46; utilitarianism and, 44–56, 127–29
Russell, Bertrand, 30–34
Ryder, John, 18–19

Samuelson, Paul, xv
Scalia, Antonin (Justice), 92
Schick, Frederic, 37
sciences and scientific method: Dewey on inquiry and, 131–32; Dewey's naturalism and, 58–59; Holmes on law and, 105–9
selective emphasis, Dewey on fallacy of, 16, 88, 122–25
Sellars, Wilfrid, 118–19
Sen, Amartya: analysis of Arrows General Possibility Theorem, viii, xv–xvi, 3–6; on preference formation, 8–9, 14; on social choice, 14–15; on social states, 6–7; utilitarianism and, 37, 43–44
sex discrimination, Supreme Court rulings on, 91–92

Sidgwick, Henry, 35–38, 42, 49, 118, 127, 136
Singer, Peter, 35–36, 42
situationism: Llewellyn's concept of, 67–69, 76–77; logic and, 30–34; uncertainty and, 69–70
social choice: Dewey's discussion of, 16–17; Hayek and, 135; rationality and, 10–11, 27–28; Sen's discussion of, 14–15
Social Choice and Individual Values (Arrow), xiii, 1–6, 35
social intelligence: agonistic deliberation and, 57–58; Dewey's concept of, xvi, 31–32; utilitarianism and, 51–56
social state: Arrow's theorem and, xv, 6–7, 127–29; Hayek's social order and, 132–37; market and, 11n22
social welfare: Dewey on preferences and, 15–18, 43, 128–29; General Possibility Theorem and, viii–ix, 127–29; pragmatist philosophy and, x–xi; preference ordering and, 14–15, 39–42; utilitarianism and, 35–42
"Solidarity or Objectivity?" (Rorty), 117
Spann, Girardeau, 93–94
state law, Supreme Court interference in, 100–102
Stevenson, Charles L., 98
Studies in Logical Theory (Dewey), 32, 47, 65–66
subjectivity, legal theory and influence of, 71–72
successive approximation, Holmes on, 108
successive judgments, conflicts and, 47
suffragist movement, 21–22
summary view of utilitarianism, 44–46
Sunstein, Cass, 72, 81–82, 91–92
Supreme Court: abortion rights and, 62, 71, 108–9; fiat *versus* reason in rulings of, 88–92; Hand's analysis of, 84–85; Hart's criticism of, 62–63; Holmes's dissenting opinions on, 26n29, 85n5, 100–103; judicial reason and, 78–79; judicial review and, 84; minimalism in, 81–82, 91–92; Nightmare/Noble Dream dichotomy and, 62–64; property rights rulings, 79–82; suffragist movement and, 22
Supreme Neglect (Epstein), 112
A System of Logic (Mill), 103, 110
System of Logic (Mill), 107

Taking Rights Seriously (Dworkin), 69, 73n4
Tallisse, Robert, 24
textualism, legal theory and, 114
"Three Independent Factors in Morals" (Dewey), 31
Torricelli, Evangelista, 105n10
"Toward Neutral Principles of Constitutional Law" (Wechsler), 84
transformation: conflict and, 29–42; unification and, 33–34, 37–42
Tuchman, Barbara, 103
Tushnet, Mark, 69–70
"Two Concepts of Rules" (Rawls), 44–46

uncertainty: belief and, xvi–xvii; diachronic model of, 74–79; open area theory of legal principles and, 94–95; situationism and, 69–70
"Under Which Description?" (Schick), 37
Unger, Robert, 69–70
unification: induction and, 97; stability and, 37–42; transformation and, 33–34
unions: expansion of, 103; Supreme Court rulings on, 100–104
utilitarianism: agnostic pragmatism and, 34–42, 59–70; Arrow's General Possibility Theorem and, 2–6, 127–29; extensional equivalence and, 46–56; naturalization of, 43–56, 81–82, 122–25, 129; normative

development and, 49–56; problems with, 43–56; Rawls on, 44–46; successive judgments and, 47–56; *Utlitarianism and Beyond* (Sen and Williams), 37. *See also* rule-consequentialism

values: Dewey on preferences and, 14–15, 112; Holmes on law and, 102–4, 112; incommensurability of, 16; naturalism and, 74
Vanberg, Viktor, 136
Vegelahn v. Guntner, 100–101
violence, Dewey's conflict theory and, 132
Virginia Military Institute, 91–92
voting: Dewey on democracy and, xiii, 137; General Possibility Theorem and, vii–xi, 1–6, 127

Waismann, Frederick, 74
Waldron, Jeremy, 75, 78, 80
Weber, Max, 19–20, 130
Wechsler, Herbert, 84–92, 96, 114
Whewell, William, 96–97, 106
Whitehead, Alfred North, 122
Williams, Bernard, viii, 37, 43–44
Winterbottom v. Wright, 60
Wittgenstein, Ludwig, 120
women's rights movement, 21–22
Wright, Chauncy, 96–97, 103, 111
Wyden, Ron, 61n9

About the Author

Frederic R. Kellogg attended Harvard College and Harvard Law School and studied sociological theory under Talcott Parsons at Harvard. He earned the LL.M. and J.S.D. in Philosophy of Law at the George Washington University. Kellogg served in the U.S. Department of Justice as Assistant U.S. Attorney 1971–1973, and later as advisor to Attorney General Elliot L. Richardson, resigning with Richardson in the Saturday Night Massacre. He was Legal Counsel at the National Endowment for the Arts in 1986–1989. Kellogg published *The Formative Essays of Justice Holmes: The Making of an American Legal Philosophy* (1984), *Oliver Wendell Holmes Jr., Legal Theory, and Judicial Restraint* (2007), *Oliver Wendell Holmes Jr. and Legal Logic* (2018), and *Pragmatism, Logic, and Law* (2021). He is currently a research scholar at The George Washington University in Brazil.

www.ingramcontent.com/pod-product-compliance
Ingram Content Group UK Ltd.
Pitfield, Milton Keynes, MK11 3LW, UK
UKHW041838031026
15587UKWH00002B/860